THE FEARLESS COMPANION

Mohammad Latif Raja

Inquiries and Book Orders should be addressed to:

Leavitt Peak Press
Email: info@leavittpeakpress.com
Phone: 1-888-549-0988

ISBN: 978-1-965679-51-7 (sc)
ISBN: 978-1-965679-52-4 (ebk)

Abu Bakar Siddique, ALLAH be pleased with him. This will cover Abu Bakar's family, his embracing of Islam, the early deeds and his Hijra, or migration he had with the messenger of ALLAH, life in Mad_na, Abu Bakar as the Khalifa of the messenger of ALLAH, his inaugural address, Abu Bakar and the community, his appointed governors, the army of Usama, the war against the apostates, compilation of the Quran, the conquered of Iraq, war against the Romans, the appointment of Umar—ALLAH be pleased with him—and finally, Abu Bakar's death. Next Umar, ALLAH be pleased with him.

We ask ALLAH to bless this gathering. We ask ALLAH to make this beneficial for all of us.

We all know Abu Bakar is the greatest after the Umbia of ALLAH. Somehow we have special love for Hazrat Umar. Everybody is impressed with him with the personality of Umar bin Khitab and the strength of Al-Farooq. Sometimes we do not do proper studies on Siddique. Now I had the chance to be exposed to his personalities. His personality is amazing, surprising because whenever you pull out a list of good deeds, one will find the name of Abu Bakar on top. Whichever list you pull out, his name is on top and is the first name. He was a first Muslim. He was the first Khalifa. He was the first and only person with the messenger of ALLAH on Hijra. His Iman was the first.

Rasool ALLAH said, "His Iman was the greater than all of the Ummah," even on issues we regard as normal deeds.

Rasool ALLAH was sitting in the mosque and asked the Sahaba, "Who is fasting this day?"

Abu Bakar Siddique said, "I am, who has visited an ill person." Abu Bakar Siddique said, "I did, who has followed the funeral." Abu

Bakar Siddique said, "I did, who has given Sadqa on this day." Abu Bakar Siddique said, "I did."

Everybody else was looking around, and the only hand that was going up was the hand of Abu Bakar. In another narration, this happened after prayer of Fajar.

Rasool ALLAH used to meet Sahaba in the mosque and would talk with them. For example, they would talk about dreams. They would talk about other things. Rasool ALLAH would have conversation with sahaba. It says when Rasool ALLAH asked, "Who has followed funeral?" Hazrat Umar said, "We have just started our day."

"Then who has given sadqa?"

Umar bin Khitab said, "We have just started our day."

Abu Bakar said, "When I was coming, I saw a poor man, and I gave him sadqa."

When asked "Who has visited a sick person?" Abu Bakar said, "I heard that Abdul Rehman was not well. I paid him a visit before I came to the mosque." So whenever Rasool ALLAH would ask a question, Abu Bakar would say, "I did it."

Rasool ALLAH said, "If all these deeds are combined in one person, that person is going to heaven." So whatever list one looks at, Abu Bakar is on the top of the list.

Ali bin Abu Talib said, "He was the first, and whenever we would compete with him on any deed, he would come ahead of us." And that is the statement made by Ali bin Abu Talib. When Hazrat Umar wanted to compete with Hazrat Abu Bakar, keep in mind a competition in good is good. Competition in good deeds is a good deed. In Islam, we are not supposed to compete in the world.

For the world, Rasool ALLAH said, "Have taqwa, and take it easy." Rasool ALLAH said, "The holy spirit Jibrael has inspired to me that no one will die until they reach the end of their life and until they receive all of their provisions." So take it easy in the world, but look at the terminology used in akhrat, the words used when it comes to akhrat. Compete and think about it as a race. The places in jannat are in darjaat, and this is a hadees "that human beings, one person will go to jannat out of a thousand." This is very fearful and frightening. Hadees is in sahi Muslims.

ALLAH would tell Hazrat Adam, "Send out a portion of your children who are going to hellfire."

Hazrat Adam would say, "What portion of my children are going to hellfire?"

ALLAH would tell Adam, "Out of one thousand, 999 will go to hellfire."

Abu Bakar was a head, and that was throughout his life. He would always come out the first. The amazing thing is that it would not be seen that Abu Bakar was competing with anyone. It was natural when others try to compete with him. Umar bin Khitab tried to compete with Abu Bakar. Ali bin Abu Talib tried to compete with Abu Bakar, but Abu Bakar would do something as if he was all alone, and he would still do the same thing. That was his natural way. Poet said, "How could I compete with you when you are walking calmly and with confidence and you still come the first? It doesn't appear that you are rushing but still come the first."

The best way to start with the life of Abu Bakar is the statement of Hazrat Ali that he was the first. The question is how did he do it? How did he make it? As humans, there are things against you— for example, your age, your mental abilities, body strength—but somehow Abu Bakar was able to defy all the odds. In terms of body strength, Abu Bakar was described. It is a good place to tell you about his appearance so you can understand and visualize him. We want to dig deep in the personality of Abu Bakar. We shall try to live with him in these lectures. We shall try to see how Abu Bakar was from inside. Just imagine and ponder upon this; think with these people, the S of Rasool ALLAH. The more we learn about them, we shall love them more. It is not like some personalities in the history who have a bright side and a dark side with sahaba. No matter how deep one goes, all that we find is good. Hazrat Abbas said about Abu Bakar, "All of him was good. Everything about him is good. We try to live with Abu Bakar. Sahaba, every one of them, was different."

Abu Bakar was very soft and compassionate, very social. Umar bin Khitab was stern and firm. Subhanallah. When we are talking about Abu Bakar, we shall end up with talking about Umar; and whenever we are talking about Umar, we shall end up talking about

3

Abu Bakar. One of them brings the other as if they were two wings of Islam.

Whenever Rasool ALLAH was seen, people would see Abu Bakar on one side and Umar on the other side. Hazrat Ali said, "Rasool ALLAH would go out with Abu Bakar, and Umar and Rasool Allah would come back with Abu Bakar and Umar."

Abu Bakar represents the soft, compassionate, and merciful side while Umar bin Khitab represents punishment of ALLAH on evil. Umar bin Khitab was the worst thing that happened to Satan. Whenever Shaitaan would see Umar bin Khitab, he would have a bad day. Therefore, whenever Umar bin Khitab was following a path, Rasool ALLAH said, "Shaitaan would take another path. Shaitaan will try to avoid him." Because whenever Shaitaan saw Umar bin Khitab, that brought bad memories to him. Usman bin Afghan represents shyness. Ali bin Abu Talib represents the warrior. The wife's of Rasool ALLAH, Hazrat Ayesha, represents an inquisitive person. She was always asking questions, a young person eager for knowledge, while Hazrat Khadija represents a mature person, psychological support. Whenever Rasool ALLAH wanted to lean on someone, he would find Hazrat Khadija. Every sahabi has a personality.

Abuzar Ghafari is alone. There is a saying, "He accepted Islam alone, he died alone, and on the Day of Judgment, he will be raised alone." Because Abuzar Ghafari was brought up in Ghafar, now Ghafar people were not the business people like the people of Mecca nor were they farmers or agricultural like the people of Madina. The people of Ghafar used to raid caravans; that was their business—raiding the caravans of others. Because of this, Abuzar Ghafari left his people, and he lived in the desert alone and became a Muslim alone. Then Rasool ALLAH sent him back to give the message to his people. He was successful and brought all his people, and they became Muslims.

Rasool ALLAH knew the personality of Abuzar Ghafari and also the other side of his personality. Rasool ALLAH told him, "Never assume the responsibility even over two people, and never take care of the financial affairs of orphans." He was good in some things, but in others, Rasool ALLAH told him to avoid.

Abuzar was a zahid. Abdul Rehman bin was very rich. It is said that "Abdul Rehman passed away when he made hijra from Mecca to Madina." He became broke, poor, had no money. Rasool ALLAH made him brother of Saad bin Abida. He was a very wealthy leader of Ansaar. Saad bin Abida told Abdul Rehman, "If you want, I shall split my wealth in two, and I have two wives. I shall divorce one of them, and you choose who you want." This was brotherhood level and sacrifice of Ansaar. Just remember, they were new Muslims, but they had that spirit.

Abdul Rehman could have picked up this opportunity—half of the wealth of Saad bin Abida offered voluntarily—but he said, "No, may ALLAH give you blessing in your family and your wealth." He said, "I want you to point out to me the market of Madina."

He showed him the market of Madina, and after a short while, Rasool ALLAH saw Abdul Rehman with some yellow powder on his face—the yellow powder women used for makeup. Rasool ALLAH asked him about that powder.

He said, "I got married."

Rasool ALLAH asked him, "What did you pay her for mehar? You came from Mecca broke."

Abdul Rehman said, "I gave her gold."

He had already earned enough to buy gold and give to his wife as mehar. One day, people in Madina felt some shaking. When people inquired, they were told the caravan of Abdul Rehman had arrived from Syria—meaning now Abdul Rehman was a rich man. There were so many rumbles in the caravan one can feel the earth shaking. That is how wealthy he became. ALLAH blessed his wealth—that was Abdul Rehman.

When he (Abdul Rehman) passed away, he split up his wealth and gave it to his family, but there was so much of it he split it up and wrote in his will that this should be given to all the people who fought in Badar: "Everyone who fought in Badar and was alive, give him part of my inheritance."

Usman bin Unaan fought in the battle of Badar, and he was a Khalifa, but he accepted his share because he said the wealth of Abdul Rehman is pure. "And how can I turn it down—such a gift from ALLAH? This is a wealth that has barkat in it. It is all pure. So how can I turn it down?" although Usman bin Unaan was a very wealthy man himself and he was the Khalifa.

All the sahaba were different, but it is too important to learn about them because we cannot be the same. We have different abilities, have different skills. Nobody will be like Umar bin Khitab nor will there be anybody who has the personality of Abu Bakar Siddique, but one could be like Maaz bin Jabal. He was a sailor. One could be mujahid like Khalid bin Waleed. There are different miles, so it is important to study about sahaba so you could look up to one and try to be like them. One can follow the one who resembles closely to oneself, and the same could be said about the sisters by looking at the Ummal-Momineen and looking at the Sahabiyaat. Try to find for yourself a role model to follow.

Our lives could be normal usually on a daily basis. Nothing much is happening, not many events going on, but there will be a day in your life when you will be faced with a situation that will change the course of your future. These are marks that mean standing points. It is one moment in life, but it will change the direction of your life. These incidents are critical and bring out who you really are. These are the tests one will be faced; maybe in normal life things are normal and there is no difference, but perhaps one day, in a year or in a month, life is testing you through that. Where would you stand? Which position would you take?

Now we are looking at the life of Abu Bakar Siddique. We do not have the entire record of his life with us. We do not have 365 days of every year of his life in front of us, but we do have few stations of his life that tell us who he was, and some of the stations are a matter of seconds; some of them are long. Sometimes hours, days, and months will pass without anything happening but in one second would make a difference. Rasool ALLAH said if you could speak one word, because of that word, one may be able to enter jannat with the mercy of ALLAH; and at the other hand, one word may anger ALLAH's soul, and that person will be thrown in hellfire for seventy years. Just one word, and that is a standing point—a pivotal point in life.

In the life of Abu Bakar Siddique, there are some standing points, but five points are special.

1. His coming into Islam with everyone else. There is a saying in Arabic that

    For every horse there is a stumble. Every horse is one moment of time will make a slip or trip and will fell down no matter how perfect the horse is it will happen one day.

Now with every person who became a Muslim, there was such a moment of hesitation, giving it a second thought, sitting and thinking over it a day, with the exception of Abu Bakar. As soon as the message was presented to him, he said, "Kalma-shahadat." He did not give it a second thought—not because Abu Bakar was an easy person to convince, not because Abu Bakar will change his mind easily. In fact, Abu Bakar was very decisive in his decisions, and that is very apparent when he became Khalifa. Abu Bakar has the ability to stand up firmly against all the sahaba, and at the end, it turned out that he was right. Abu Bakar was not a person who when he became a Muslim, he knew exactly what was he getting into, but we shall talk about that in his Islam. Why did Abu Bakar accept Islam immediately? Why didn't he give a second thought? Why was it so immediate? This is the first incident.

2. The second standing point was a very special point in the life of Abu Bakar. That isra-wal-mirage—we shall talk about this briefly—there will be space given to all these topics. Now when this amazing journey happened to Rasool ALLAH, the people of Mecca were non-Muslim, secular people, and they were materialistic people. They would only believe whatever they can see or they can hear and whatever their hands can touch. They made a joke of isra-wal-mirage. They thought it was fun for them and this was their chance to embarrass Muslims and Islam and

7

Muslims will give up their religion. The Muslims will think that their prophet is insane. Abu Jahil was very happy. Abu Bakar Siddique was not there. They met him and told him what Rasool ALLAH said about the night journey. Abu Bakar had not met Rasool ALLAH as yet.

One of the non-Muslims went to him and said, "Do you know what your friend is claiming? The prophet is saying that he went to Jurshalam and came back in the same night." Now what was the response of Abu Bakar? If he was a weak man, he would say, "That is not true." If he was a person who could easily deceive, he would say, "Yes, that has happened." But Abu Bakar would not reject something Rasool ALLAH may have said. He said to the person who was speaking to him who was not a Muslim, therefore, cannot take him on the face value, "If Rasool ALLAH said so, then it is true." There are two parts of this statement: "If Rasool ALLAH said so—meaning I shall have to verify—if he said so, then it is true. We have to verify it first. Do not just accept it. We have to study if it is correct, then I shall not reject it."

3. The third standing point is during the death of Rasool ALLAH. The historian described it: when Rasool ALLAH died, Usman bin Unaan was hiding in his house. Umar bin Khitaab was carrying his sword and claiming Mohammad did not die but went to meet ALLAH, as Moses did for forty days, and he will be back and whoever claims that Mohammad is dead, he shall cut off his head, and some of the sahaba were crying in the mosque. This is the description given when Rasool ALLAH passed away. It was such a catastrophe; they were not able to handle it even though Abu Bakar Siddique had a close relationship with the messenger of ALLAH of all the sahaba; he was the one who brought them back. It shows the steadfastness of Abu Bakar Siddique and the faith and belief Abu Bakar had. The death of Rasool ALLAH is the greatest loss for Muslims,

and it is one of the big signs of the Day of Judgment that has happened.

4. Pivotal point in the life of Abu Bakar was before Rasool ALLAH passed away. Rasool ALLAH appointed Usama bin Zaid to lead an army and gave the following instructions, but before there was some background information, Rasool ALLAH appointed Zaid bin Haris, his former adopted son, a former slave, to lead an army that had the ability. There were sahaba in the army. He ordered the army to go and fight with Romans. That was the first confrontation with the Roman Empire. Rasool ALLAH appointed Zaid bin Haris to be the leader of the army. Subhanallah. For that battle, Rasool ALLAH had given the instructions that if the leader of the army is killed, then Hazrat Jaffar bin Abu Talib is the leader. If he dies, then Abdullah bin Rooh is the leader. That was a very risky operation, and Rasool ALLAH had nominated those three names as leaders. Now the Muslim army would be facing the Roman Empire. The army received the orders and went up north to face the Roman Empire. The message had to go to the whole world—the first battle ever between Muslims and Romans. The army was two thousand soldiers strong, and they were facing Romans—with an army that was two hundred thousand strong. Three appointed leaders were killed, and then Muslims appointed their leader, Khalid bin Waleed. Khalid bin Waleed made a successful retreat check to Madina. Usama bin Zaid was the son of Zaid bin Haris. Some days before his death, Rasool ALLAH appointed Usama bin Zaid, a leader of the Muslim army, and gave them directions: "I want you to lead this army and step over with your horses where your father was killed. Take this army to the same place where you father was killed." But Rasool ALLAH passed away before the army left.

Now Abu Bakar Siddique became Khalifa, and the tribes surrounding Madina apostated and left Islam. Sahaba were coming to Abu Bakar Siddique and telling him, "This army led by Usama is going to fight the Romans. Keep this army in Madina to protect Madina because this is our priority. This is where sahaba are and also the family of Rasool ALLAH and we have to protect Madina. This is where the army should stay."

Abu Bakar Siddique said, "Do you want me to reverse the order given by Rasool ALLAH? Since Rasool ALLAH sent this army out, this army will go out. And even if everybody in Madina is killed and I am the only person alive, I shall still send this army out." We shall talk about the implications of this order later on.

5. The final point was to deal with the apostates. One can ask why we have to talk about history and why it is important. Muslim youngsters have an identity problem. They need to know the history of Islam, the life of the prophets and sahabas. Now we are talking about Abu Bakar Siddique—not only his life but the time of Abu Bakar Siddique. We are talking about his Khilafat and what happened during his Khilafah. By studying his Khilafah, we shall know about Abu Bakar and his times. One of the classical sources used for Abu Bakar and his time is Tabree. There are many writers, and Tabree is one of them, also Ibne-K. The research is by reading different books and drawing the information.

His real name is not Abu Bakar. That was given by the people. It was a nickname. His original name was Abdullah. Some people also say Attiq, but majority agree on Abdullah because Attiq is a description. Siddique was the name given by Rasool ALLAH. His father nicknamed the names we know—they were not their original names. For example, Abdul Mutlib, the grandfather of Rasool ALLAH—that was not his original name. His original name was Shoaib. He was given that name *Shoaib*, which means "old," because when he was born, he had gray hairs. He was called Abdul Mutlib because one day his uncle brought him to Mecca, people thought he was a slave. Because his uncle's name was Mutlib, therefore, he was called Abdul Mutlib (slave of Mutlib). Later on, he became famous with the name Abdul Mutlib bin Hashim—Hashim was not the original name. His name was Aamir. *Hashim* means "crushing"—because he crushed bread with soup. That was the food he used to provide to pilguins. He was the first one who did that; therefore, he was called Hashim. In Arabia, parents would give a name, but people would pick another name. The real name of the father of Abu Bakar was Usman, but he was called Abu. The name of Abu Bakar was Abdullah bin Usman. He was named Abu Bakar—"one of Bakar" or "father of Bakar"; *Bakar* means "a young lively camel." It is a young camel.

With the war's apostates, they said, "We are not going to pay our money. Who is he? We used to pay our money to Mohammad (PBUH), the messenger of ALLAH—that was to purify us from our sins. Now we are not going to pay Abu Bakar."

They started to call him Abu Al-Faisal. *Al-Faisal* means "the infant camel." They indicated that Abu Bakar was a weak man. "We will not pay him." Ade bin Hatim told them that he was one of the stallions. Ade bin Hatim's words turned out to be true. Abu Bakar subdivided them, and they came to realize who Abu Bakar Siddique really was. The title given to him—the most famous is Siddique, which comes from "truth"—this title was given to him because of some incidents that happened in his life. The one that Hazrat Ayesha said, she mentioned the story of Asra. Abu Bakar said that was the truth, so Hazrat Ayesha said, "He was called Siddique, the believer," and this was narrated in Abu Al-Hakim. Rasool ALLAH also called him Siddique.

One day, Rasool ALLAH was standing on Audh Mountain with Abu Bakar, Umar, and Usman. There was a kind of earthquake. Rasool ALLAH put his hand on Audh and said to Audh, "Stay firm because on top of you is a prophet, a Siddique, and two martyrs," and the mountain stopped moving. Rasool ALLAH called Abu Bakar Siddique, Umar, and Usman martyrs. He was also called Siddique because he was very fast in accepting Islam. This is a very famous name. The other name given to Abu Bakar Siddique was "The Companion." All of the Sahaba were companions, but the companionship of Abu Bakar was unique. Rasool ALLAH had a special rela- tionship with Abu Bakar Siddique. They were very close even before Islam. They were also close in age—Abu Bakar Siddique was only two years younger than Rasool ALLAH while other sahaba were very young. Hazrat Ali bin Abu Talib was a child. Umar bin Khitab was considered to be a senior sahabi, but he was only twenty-eight years old when he became a Muslim. However, Abu Bakar Siddique was thirty-eight years old when he became a Muslim. They were close friends, and Islam strengthened it further. Abu Bakar Siddique was so close to Rasool ALLAH as if he was created for him. Abu Bakar Siddique was not only a friend; he was a companion and advisor, a financial supporter, a bodyguard, a confidant; he was all there for Rasool ALLAH, and this name was given to Abu Bakar Siddique in Quran.

ALLAH says about the journey of Hijra, "If you do not aid him, ALLAH has already aided him." When the unbelievers had driven him out as one of two, they were in the cave, and he said to his com- panion—it is in the Quran—"Do not grieve. Indeed, ALLAH is with us." ALLAH sent down tranquility on him and supported him with soldiers he didn't see and made the word of these who disbelieve the lowest while the word of ALLAH, that is, the highest. ALLAH is exalted in might and wise. Ibn-e-Hijar comments on this and says, "The companion in this Ayaa is Abu Bakar." According to the consenses of the scholars, there are many Hadees, and there is no one who shared this unique journey with Rasool ALLAH.

Another name is *Attiq*. *Attiq* means "emancipated," the one who was freed from slavery, the one who is liberated, but Abu Bakar was not a slave. So what is the meaning of Attiq? Hazrat Ayesha said, "Abu Bakar came to Rasool ALLAH. Rasool ALLAH said, 'O Abu Bakar! Receive the glad tidings and rejoice. You are the freed slave of ALLAH from hellfire.'" He was also called *Al-Attaqa*. It means "the most pious," and he was given this name in Quran in Surah Layal. The reason behind this is that Abu Bakar Siddique used to free slaves, the Muslim slaves who were under persecution. He would buy them and free them, but the slaves he would free were weak women. The tradition in Arabia was that when you free a slave, that slave will remain loyal to you because whoever freed a slave, the slave would have a special loyalty to that person when they are freed. It was not a relationship of slavery but a relationship of strong loyalty.

The father of Abu Bakar asked him, "My son! Why are you freeing their weak slaves, women, and children? Why don't you free some strong men that one day they will support you?"

Abu Bakar Siddique said, "The reason I am doing this is to please ALLAH. I am not looking for any worldly benefit."

ALLAH revealed in last Ayyat of Surah Layal, "But ALLAH will forgive him he who gives from his wealth to purify him." And he is not paying back, meaning those people have done him no favor and he is not paying back. He is not doing it for a reward for himself but only seeking countenance of his Lord most high and he is going to be satisfied. ALLAH says, "He is going to be satisfied." ALLAH will make Abu Bakar happy.

Abu Bakar Siddique was born two years after the year of the elephant. As Arabs didn't have a calendar system and, therefore, if an important event happened, they would call the year after this event. When ALLAH destroyed the army of Abra, ALLAH called it the year of the elephant. There is a special name for this year.

Later on, Umar bin Khitab developed a calendar when he became Khalifa. There were few cases taken to court. For example, someone gave a loan and said, "Pay me back in Shaban." Umar bin Khitab said the problem was it didn't say Shaban which year; they did not have a calendar. Umar bin Khitab wanted to sort this confusion out. They had to have a calendar, and now Islam was a Khilafa. Now it was not a small group where everybody knew each other. They had to have a system and started from Hijra, but before that, it was the year of the elephant. Abu Bakar Siddique was born two years of the year of the elephant, and Rasool ALLAH was born a few weeks after the event.

The physical description of Abu Bakar—there is not much that exist, but we may be able to develop a mental picture. Sometimes we have an image of a person. It may be wrong, but an image helps to understand a person when you look at a person especially if one has a Frasa. Frasa is the art of reading the face. One can tell a lot about a person, and Arabs used to use Frasa. It is a kind of science—art of reading the face. There is a saying that Umar bin Khitab was good at it. He saw someone and asked him his name.

He said, "My name is Flame."

"The family name?"

He said, "Spark."

"What is your tribe name?"

He said, "My tribe name is Fire."

Umar bin Khitab told him, "Go back home because your house is on fire."

It turned out to be true.

Umar bin Khitab saw another man and said, "This man is a magician, or he was a magician."

They called the man, and the man said, "Yes. I used to be a soreer in Jahilia."

Umar bin Khitab only saw his face. Then Umar bin Khitab asked, "What is the latest you heard from a Jin?"

He said some poetry that was talking about the coming of the prophet Mohammad (PBUH) that he heard from Jin.

We want to develop a mental picture you can contrast between Abu Bakar and Umar. Abu Bakar was medium to short in height. He was very slim. Once Rasool ALLAH said, "You should have the shawl above the ankle," but Azaar is open like a towel for the bottom half and, if they had money, then another piece to cover the top. Otherwise, they would not cover the shoulders. People had different types of clothes. Whenever Abu Bakar heard that Azaar should be above the ankle, he asked Rasool ALLAH, "My Azaar is not holding on to my waist." He was slim, and Azaar would fall and go under the ankle. "Is there anything wrong?"

Rasool ALLAH said, "No, not with you." He had slim legs. All his body didn't have any fat; even his face, one could see his cheekbones. His eyes were deep in the socket. He was fair-skinned relative to the people in the desert; normally they were dark-skinned. European were pink or red-skinned people. Abu Bakar Siddique was very a social person. He was very approachable and likable.

Umar bin Khitab was very tall, well built. He was anything but slim. He was tall and muscular. This was the description given to Khalid bin Waleed. Both Umar and Khalid bin Waleed were very tall, well built, and muscular. Both would jump on the horse. Umar bin Khitab gave this advice to sahaba: "Jump on a horse while the horse is running. Do not stop the horse and ride." This was the amazing advice. He said, "Walk barefoot. Run between the targets." In archery, they had two targets. They would stand near one target and throw their arrows that was in practice, obviously walk between the targets, pick up the arrow and shoot at the other target and also to lead a rough life and stay away from the habits of non-Muslims. That was to train them for a difficult lifestyle.

Abu Bakar was approachable and kind, but Umar bin Khitab, if one wanted to visit him, his knees would start shaking. He had a very strong presence when he was the Khalifa. He was walking with sahaba in Madina. He turned around to look behind. There was a pregnant woman behind. She had a miscarriage. Some of the sahaba said Umar should pay the blood money—that happened because of him. The others said he just turned around; it was not his fault. Ali bin Abu Talib gave the right order. He said that blood money had to be paid to the poor woman, but it should be paid from the treasury. That was not Umar's fault. That was the personality of Umar bin Khitaab.

Once Abu Musa Al Ashari knocked on his door three times, but Umar didn't respond. Abu Musa Al Ashari left. Umar bin Khitab called him back and said, "Why did you leave?"

Abu Musa Al Ashari said, "I heard Rasool ALLAH say, 'Seek permission three times. If permission is not given, then leave.'"

Hazrat Umar said, "You have to bring a witness that Rasool ALLAH said that."

Abu Musa Al Ashari went where some sahaba had gathered. When he came in, sahaba saw his face yellow. He was terrified. They asked him, "What happened?" After a brief conversation, the color of his face changed. That was the natural posture of Umar bin Khitaab. He was not doing this intentionally. His presence projected that impression among people.

Abu Bakar was a seasoned traveler. He was a successful businessman. He had been around, knew a lot of people, knew leaders of the tribe, and he was very famous. In fact, people were more familiar with the face of Abu Bakar than Mohammad (PBUH). During Hijra, people used to come and give him Salam, and they would ask him who the man with him was.

Abu Bakar would say, "This man is guiding me to my way" because that trip was top secret, and he had concealed the identity of Rasool ALLAH. He would say, "This man is guiding me." The person asking the question would understand it as "guiding through the desert," but what Abu Bakar meant was that "This man is guiding me through to paradise."

Abu Bakar was a specialist in genealogy. He knew the names of the tribes, their origins, where they were from and their ancestry. He was an expert in that field.

Hazrat Ayesha said, "He is the best man who knows the genealogy of Quresh," and this is in Sahi-Muslims. This was not just historical study, but this was an asset for Rasool ALLAH. Therefore, whenever Rasool ALLAH was meeting with different tribes during Hajj, Rasool ALLAH would take Abu Bakar with him always because Abu Bakar would tell Rasool ALLAH who they were, what were their qualities before Rasool ALLAH would meet them. The pros and cons of these people—where they came from, the location of the area—all that information was in his mind. Even Abu Bakar would do most of the talking. This was the most important asset for Rasool ALLAH.

One important quality of Abu Bakar was that he was a man with great aspiration to please ALLAH; it was not for the world but for the end. He was doing this for the sake of ALLAH. However, he had a slight hot temper.

Umar bin Khitab said, "Try to avoid the temper of Abu Bakar."

Hazrat Abbas said, "Everything about Abu Bakar is good, but he had hot temper." But he would come back very fast and seek forgiveness. He had a compassionate and kind nature, which made it acceptable to people. People appreciated his kindness. People understood his personality. Abu Bakar gave Kutba when he became Khalifa. "Sometimes I become angry, and therefore, avoid me when you see that happening because I don't want to harm any one of you." This temper was not out of pride but a natural makeup of his personality.

When talking about the sahaba, I shall try to give you the whole picture. We have to be realistic—messengers were guided by ALLAH faultless (Sahaba). They protect perfect humans with shortcomings. If we try to make them angels, that will be depressing for us because we shall never be like angels; but if we see sahaba, who they were, that gives us hope, and we shall try to be like them. But we have to admit that we shall never be like them.

The lifestyle of sahaba was very difficult, and ALLAH put them through tough tests. There are reasons why sahaba fought with each other, and they had their disputes. Sahaba had very active lives.

End of CD 1.

During the advances of the Muslim army under the leadership of Khalid bin Waleed, we talk about the defeat of Tala. Asidy Shuja was a woman from the tribe of Taghlib. They were Christians, and she came to be a prophet, came down from Iraq. A good number of followers were following her. She came and joined hands with Tala Al-Yazeedi and with Muslimsa Qazab, among the people who made a deal with her. These were political alliances than religious connections. That was Malik bin Naywara. He was a Muslim, but he refused to pay Zakat. When Shuja came, he joined her in a coalition.

When Tala Al-Yazeedi was defeated, Shuja withdrew to protect herself. Malik bin Naywara now was regretting what he did. He had made a deal with a false prophet and he was left alone and Khalid bin Waleed was around. Khalid bin Waleed decided to attack Malik bin Naywara. At first, Ansaar didn't want to join him, but because he was the Khalifa, they joined him. Khalid bin Waleed thought, *If I write for permission from the Khalifa Abu Bakar Siddique, I shall miss this opportunity*, so he had to attack now. Otherwise, it will be too late. They attacked Malik bin Naywara. There are two versions of what happened. One version is that Khalid bin Waleed captured Malik bin Naywara, discussed with him. Malik said, "I shall pray, but I shall not pay Zakat." Khalid bin Waleed ordered his execution.

The second version is that they were captured, and Khalid bin Waleed said, "Give them warmth" because it was a very cold night, but Arabs had different dialogue and meaning to the Arabic word which was spoken by Khalid bin Waleed. Arabs understood to kill them, and they killed them. After that, Khalid bin Waleed married the wife of Malik bin Naywara. There were a lot of rumors about this marriage and the execution of Malik bin Naywara. It was reported to Abu Bakar, but the man said, "I witness Malik making Azaan and praying and Khalid took over his wife." This incident is mentioned in the history and Tabree books. Umar bin Khitaab was very angry at this and told Abu Bakar that Khalid must be fired. Again, there are two versions whether Abu Bakar called Khalid or just sent him a letter. One version is mentioned in Ibn-e-Keer and Tabree that Abu Bakar called Khalid to come to Madina so that the matter could be investigated. Khalid bin Waleed came into Masjid-e-Nabvi in his chain mail. That was rusty because blood had accumulated on it, and he was wearing a turban and was decorated with arrows, which were sticking out. He walked into Masjid-e-Nabvi. When Umar bin Khitaab saw him, he jumped out and took out the arrows from the turban and said, "You have committed a hypocrisy by killing Malik and took over his wife."

Khalid bin Waleed did not answer back. He was silent, didn't say anything. Khalid thought perhaps this was also the view of Khalifa Abu Bakar, so he just stayed quite. However, when Abu Bakar investigated, he decided and said Khalid bin Waleed was so innocent and he should carry on as commander of the army.

Abu Bakar Siddique told Hazrat Umar, "I am not going to shed the sword that was drowned out by Rasool ALLAH." Therefore, we conclude, as the historians of Ahl-e-Sunnat Jammat, that there was some misunderstanding that happened. However, after investigating the matter, Abu Bakar came to conclude whatever happened, Khalid bin Waleed was not to be blamed and he should continue at his position as leader that Malik bin Naywara was playing going back and forth and he paid the price for his indecisiveness in and out of Islam according to the wind of change. If it appears that Muslims were riding the tide, he became a Muslim; but whenever Muslims went away, he joined hands with apostates and he ended up paying the price with his life—so Malik bin Naywara will be considered apostate as the marriage of Khalid bin Waleed carried on. That will only happen if he is considered apostate. It explained because this is one of the controversies that happened around the personality of Khalid bin Waleed, Ibn-e-Tania considered this between Abu Bakar, Umar, Khalid bin Waleed, and Abu Abida. He says Abu Bakar carried on sending Khalid bin Waleed in important battles even though it was reported to Abu Bakar Siddique that Khalid bin Waleed had committed some flaws and mistakes, but Abu Bakar did not fire him or change him because the benefit for keeping him was greater than harm; also there was no one who could fulfill his role as leader. Also he said if the Khalifa had a soft personality, then he should appoint a strong person to be his deputy; but if the Khalifa was firm, then a soft deputy will balance it. Since Abu Bakar was a soft-hearted person, he appointed Umar as his deputy and Khalid as his army leader; but when Umar bin Khitab became Khalifa, because of his strong personality, he replaced Khalid bin Waleed with Abida bin Jarah, who was a soft-hearted man, to lead his armies. Then Ibn-e-Tania said that made to fulfill the role of Khalifa Til Rasool ALLAH because the messenger of ALLAH himself represent the middle way. Because Rasool ALLAH had the middle way, he had two deputies, Abu Bakar and Umar—one represents one side; the other represents the opposite side. But now Abu Bakar and Umar had different characters, had put somebody who represents opposites so that they will be similar to Rasool ALLAH, the middle way. Rasool ALLAH himself represents both sides because Rasool ALLAH said, "I am the prophet of mercy and prophet of war." In the Redha of Bahrains, at the time of Rasool ALLAH, Bahrain used to include the island and other islands of Persian sea alongside the eastern coast of Saudi Arabia, UAE, Qatar. All of that was called Bahrain. Al-Hazri, head of the armies, fought the apostates in the area of Bahrain.

A few important events happened to Al-Hazri. When they had the base and chose a camp, something happened, and camels ran away with the luggage of the soldiers. Camels were aggressive and untamed at times. Now camels ran away, and soldiers were left without any transport and luggage in the desert, in the middle of nowhere. There was no water around. Late at night, they were worried what to do.

Al-Hazri said, "Are you not Muslims? Are you not fighting for the sake of ALLAH? Get together, and let us pray, make Duaa." They gathered and made Duaa and kept on and on. Now the time of Fajar, he said, "We saw clouds coming towards us then came rain over us, and water started to gather in pools. We drank water, and then all the camels came back to drink from that water. We got our camels back, our luggage, and we had water to drink." This was a blessing which happened with Al-Hazri.

There was a second blessing, but before that, they attacked the enemy and pursued them and camped next to the enemy at night. Al-Hazri heard some noise from the enemy camp. He told some of his soldiers to go and find out, get some information (spying). They went to find out that the enemy soldiers were drinking, singing, dancing, didn't know what they were saying. They were drunk. Al-Hazri said, "Get ready, and let us attack them in the middle of the night."

The Muslim army attacked them and killed some of them, but the enemy didn't know what was going on; they were drunk. One of their leaders, Al-Hatim, was sleeping. He woke up and realized that they were under attack. He jumped on his horse and didn't get his foot right and fell down and hurt his leg. He asked who will fix his leg.

One Muslim said, "I will just lift your leg." The Muslim soldier chopped off his leg and walked away.

Al-Hatim fell down and asked the soldier to finish him.

The Muslim soldier said, "I would not."

Al-Hatim was lying down with his leg amputated. Whenever Muslims passed by, he would ask them to kill him. He was bleeding; he would die anyway, but the soldiers said not to kill him. Later on, Qais bin Sabbit, an Ansaar, passed by. Al-Hatim asked to finish him off. Qais bin Sabbit, realizing he was a leader, killed him; but when he saw his leg—he was bleeding—he wished that he didn't kill him. There was cruelty in some of the ways Muslims were treating apostates, but we know Rasool ALLAH said, "Even if you kill, do it in a compassionate way." But sahaba saw that Redha was a great sin.

Now the Muslim army went to an island, and they regrouped. Now Al-Hazri had to cross a sea. God, how long but a boat would take a day to cross it. Now Muslims need to cross, but they had no boats at all. Also some of the sahaba had never been in the boat. They had to pursue the enemy. This was another blessing mentioned by Ibn-e-Keer and Tabree.

Al-Hazri said, "Let us pray to ALLAH, ask ALLAH to give us protection because we are Mujaheedin." And he said, "Bismillah," and they started to walk over the water. The narrator of this event said that water would get only up to the ankles of their horses. They were on horses and camels. Some were walking, and they said, "Only our feet get wet." They marched on water until they reached the enemy and defeated them and then came back, and the whole event happened in one day.

One of the soldiers said a line of poetry. He said, "Didn't you see how ALLAH humbled his sea for us and ALLAH brought His wrath on the enemy. We prayed to ALLAH to split the sea for us, but ALLAH gave us the miracle that didn't happen to the ones before us. We prayed to ALLAH to split the sea, and the sea even didn't have to split—we just walked over it."

We can see during the time of Abu Bakar we talked about two blessings that happened to Ambiya before. We talked about Kirnee that was burned in the fire, and that didn't affect him, similar to the miracle that happened to Ibrahim, and now Al-Hazri had a blessing happened to his army that only happened to Musa in Bani Israel. So ALLAH had given blessings to the followers of Mohammad similar to these given to Ambiya before.

The difference between a miracle and blessing—they are the same supernatural event; however, when it happens to prophet, it is called miracle, and when it happens to a Walli ALLAH, it is called a blessing. There had been a lot of blessings, and a lot had been written about blessing, but there is a lot of exception in it. But we do believe that ALLAH can support his friends Olia ALLAH with supernatural occurrence. That is part of our Imaan—ALLAH does that? But we have to be careful.

For example, someone searched his skin. When asked why, he said. "One of my students was drowning and he mentioned my name and my searching the skin saved him." Well, we only invoke the name of ALLAH. There is a rule, and that is key rule or general rule that applies to the end. If someone claims that a blessing happened in the contact out of Jihaad, then take it with a grain of salt. We know most of the blessings happened in that context or in the context of persecution like what happened to Abu Muslims Khulani. He was persecuted—that is a form of Jihaad or in the battles of Jihaad at that time of Jihaad—in that those people are close to ALLAH and attachment is stronger.

When Rasool ALLAH was asked about martyrs, Rasool ALLAH said, "It is enough that he went through with swords shining above his head—that is enough. When these people are going through that, that is the time when ALLAH gives them the special divine assistance."

We know the angels came down for Rasool ALLAH in the battle of Badar, and many of the blessings that happened to Sahaba were in that context. Remember when the water came out of the finger of Rasool ALLAH? That was in the context of the battle of Tabooq. Also when Jabbir invited Rasool ALLAH into his house and told Rasool ALLAH, "I have some food for you," all that Jabbir had was a small goat and some grain, wheat, or barley.

He told Rasool ALLAH, "I am inviting you," or, in fact, whispered in his ear, "Rasool ALLAH, I am inviting you with some of your close sahaba," and then Rasool ALLAH announced to everyone.

Then Jabbir went home and told his wife, "Rasool ALLAH has invited the whole community to our house."

She asked him, "Didn't you tell the prophet privately?"

Jabbir said, "I whispered in his ear."

Almost eight hundred people showed up. They all ate and had their fill, and there was still food coming out of the pot. It was a miracle that happened with Rasool ALLAH—that happened during the battle of Trench. We can go on and on. This is a general rule.

There was one priest from Bahrain who became a Muslim.

People asked him, "Why did you change to Islam?"

He said, "I was frightened if I didn't become a Muslim, ALLAH will transform me into something else to destroy me—to punish me because of all the sins that I have seen with my own eyes." This was the army supported by ALLAH. He said, "I heard voices of angels above the army of Al-Hazri." He said, "People who are supported with all these Ayyat and miracles must be on the true path, and if I didn't become a Muslim, ALLAH will punish me." And that is the reason he became a Muslim. This was the Redha of Bahrain.

The greatest Redha was of Bahrain. His description is that he was a short figure, fair-skinned, with flat nose, and he started out very early, studying the field of sorcery and having connections with and even just plain tricks of magic like cutting the wings of a bird and he would catch it again and the thing was just a trick—optical illusion—and he would travel around studying arts of deception. He started to claim that he was a prophet during the life of the prophet Mohammad (PBUH). His situation was becoming dangerous even during the time of the prophet Mohammad (PBUH).

He belonged to a strong tribe who had vast lands, powerful fighters. It was a very dangerous movement. He sent a letter to the prophet Mohammad (PBUH) with two of his followers. He told the messenger of ALLAH that the earth was to split into two halves—"one-half belongs to you, and one-half belongs to me." Quresh were people who were transgressing. He said, "You have to give me half of the territory because I was given partnership with you from ALLAH. I am your partner in prophethood."

Rasool ALLAH asked these two men, "What do you say about this?"

They said, "We say what our people say—he is a messenger of ALLAH."

Rasool ALLAH said, "If it was not the fact that messengers are not killed, I would have killed you, but there is a standard norm that carriers of messages are not killed." Then Rasool ALLAH sent back a letter.

> Bismillah. From Mohammad the messenger of ALLAH to the impostor, the liar. The earth belongs to ALLAH and he will inherit to whomever he wills and the end belongs to the righteous. The earth ALLAH can make it to rotate from one party to another it belongs to ALLAH but the end, the last round belongs to believers.

He sent the Sahabi Ansaar Zahid. He carried the letter and is upset with the response he received since he was called Muslimsa Qazab.

Muslimsa asked, "What would you say about Mohammad (PBUH)?"

Sahabi read Kalma-e-Shahadat.

"And what do you say about me?"

The sahabi said, "I can't hear you."

Muslimsa cut off parts of his body. He asked him again, received the same answer again. He cut off another part of the body. He kept on cutting his body until he fell down, dead. He was an evil man, but Habib was Shaheed in the court of Muslimsa Qazab, and other important figures in Redha Rijaal bin Hanfi was the part of delegation which came down to Banu Hanifa. Banu Hanifa said every other tribe had sent a delegation paying homage to the messenger of ALLAH and giving baith in Islam. Muslimsa was a member of the delegation and did give baith to Rasool ALLAH. Another narration is that he did not attend the meeting because he was guarding their belongings, but Banu Hanifa were followers of Rasool ALLAH. So Rijaal bin Hanfi stayed behind and was attending teachings of Rasool ALLAH. He memorized a significant portion of Quran. He had some knowledge, then Rasool ALLAH sent him back to convince his people that what Muslimsa was doing was false. Rijaal went back and turned around 180 degrees and became an apostle. His Fitna was worse than the Fitna of Muslimsa Qazab.

Abu Hurrairah said, "He was in a gathering with Rasool ALLAH, and Rasool ALLAH said, 'There is a man among you. He will go to hellfire, and his mold is bigger than the mountain of Audh.'" Abu Hurrairah said, "Everyone who was in that gathering died except myself and Rijaal bin Hanfi, and I was very frightened because of that until I saw Rijaal claim that Muslimsa is a messenger of ALLAH. I knew that Rasool ALLAH was talking about him." Abu Hurrairah said about him that "Rijaal was more significant among his people than Muslimsa." Question why? Because of his knowledge, the fitna of somebody or a scholar is greater than any other fitna. People know that a disbeliever is a disbeliever, but a munafiq who has knowledge is very dangerous.

There is a Hadees. Rasool ALLAH said, "The worst thing for Ummah is a munafiq who has very nice tongue—someone who knows how to play around with words." When a scholar deviates, entire people deviate with him.

Remember when Imam Ahmad bin Hamal was told by some of his contemporaries that "in your situation, you are excused to give into what persecutors want."

He said, "If I speak what they want me to say, that would mislead all of the people."

They wanted him to say that Quran was created.

He said, "If I say that, then people will go along with me," and he refused.

That is why Bani Israel of Isa bin Maryum when Isa gave them invitation. When the scholars turned it down, people didn't believe Isa (AS). They said, "Our scholars did not say so." That is the reason that people were deceived and the only people who followed were some fishermen and youth, but the majority remained behind their devious scholars. It is important to follow the scholars of Haq because it is not the knowledge the person possesses; it is a standard how close they are to ALLAH. Iblees was a big scholar, and we know many other stories where learned people refused to accept the truth.

In the time of Moses, when he left his people in the hands of Haroon because a summary was a crossmatic figure, he knew how to speak well. He deceived the people, and he pulled the rug from the feet of Haroon, who was a prophet of ALLAH. He took charge of people, and people left Haroon and followed him.

So Rijaal was a great and important figure. Now in the battle of Yamamah, Muslimsa appointed two men on his right and left flanks. Rijaal was one of them, and Mahokam was the other one. Muslimsa Qazab, although he was bright figure, when he tried to imitate Quran, he came up with funny things. People are not intelligent when they try to imitate Quran; they came up with foolish talk.

He would say, "O frog! Croak as you croak. The bottom of you isn't dirt, and the top of you isn't water."

He would describe a desert rat with big ears. He would say, "All you have is big ears."

He said, "Planting seeds and then the seeds grow and you harvest the grain and you crush it and you make bread out of it. You mix the bread with soup." Then he said, "Eat soup with bread." Somebody who was listening to so-called Surah, Harvest, said, "O Muslimsa! I am not sure whether your angel is descending on your heart or your stomach. It is all about food."

When he heard that ALLAH had given to Mohammad (PBUH) Al-Kousar a river in paradise, Surah Al-Kousar, Muslimsa would always try to imitate Rasool ALLAH. They told him, "Rasool ALLAH is giving Kousar. What are you giving?"

He said, "We have given you the key, so pray and rest." He has the key of paradise—that was what he would say. It is reported that Ammar bin Aas met him when Ammar bin Aas was a mushriq. Ammar bin Aas told him that ALLAH had revealed to Mohammad Surah-Asar.

Muslimsa said, "ALLAH has given me a Surah," which meant some rubbish.

Ammar bin Aas said, "I know that you are a liar."

Ibn-e-Keer comments and says that the words of Muslimsa were foolish that even a mushriq realized that. At the end, when Abu Bakar met the delegation of Abu Hanifa, came to give baith.

Abu Bakar said, "Please can you tell me about his Quran?"

They said, "O Khalifa! Excuse us," but Abu Bakar said, "I insist you to tell me some of his Quran."

He said, "How could any mind get into something like this?"

There was one man. He came and said, "I want to see Muslimsa."

His followers said, "Woe to you—say 'Muslimsa, messenger of ALLAH.'"

The man said, "I am not going to say 'prophet of ALLAH' until I meet him." He goes in to meet Muslimsa. He asked him "to narrate some of his Quran." Then the old man said, "I know that you are a liar, but a liar from my tribe is better than a true man from Quraish. You are from a tribe. I would rather follow you than the messenger of ALLAH—even though you are a liar and Mohammad is telling the truth." He was so foolish but deceived many people because of their ignorance. Everything which falls down, there will be somebody to pick it up.

But not all of Banu Hanifa followed Muslimsa. There were some steadfast among them.

One important person, Yamamah, told people, "There is no partnership in prophethood. Muslimsa is a liar and Mohammad is the true prophet and I am going to Khalid bin Waleed to ask him to give me peace."

He went to Khalid, who granted him and his people peace. and Yamamah was instrumental in fighting against apostates. The leader of the Muslim armies, Khalid bin Waleed, was ordered to attack Muslimsa Qazab. He was interested with this task in the time of Abu Bakar Siddique. Abu Bakar was so concerned about what was happening in Yamamah. He would go out and wait for the carrier to bring in the letters in the combat zone. It was a very dangerous event in the Khalafa of Islamiya. There was group of people, fifty to sixty followers of Muslimsa. They went out to raid another tribe because there was some problem. They were sleeping. They were close to the camp of the army of Khalid bin Waleed, but they didn't know this. Muslims captured all of them. Khalid thought they were spies.

They said, "We are not spies. We had an issue with another tribe. We raided them, and we didn't know you were around."

Khalid bin Waleed knew they were the followers of Muslimsa and ordered the execution of all. Their head was Monja. He was much respected among his people.

They said, "If you are going to execute all of us, spare this man (Monja)."

Khalid bin Waleed agreed. He saved him and had him hostage with him and Khalid left him tied up in his camp and his wife to take care of him. She was the ex-wife of Malik bin Naywara. Now she was the wife of Khalid bin Waleed.

This was a setback because he was a very prominent leader of Banu Hanifa. Now Banu Hanifa mobilized all their army. Khalid bin Waleed gathered his army, and they were meeting in the battlefield in Yamamah. Battle started. In the first wave of attack, the enemy was very strong. The enemy took the Muslims by surprise and pushed them back. The wave of attack was very strong from the enemy side that nomateds and now Muslims could not stand it and retreated.

Now the core group—Sahaba, Muhajeeren, and Ansaar—were surrounded. They had to retreat, and the enemy reached to the tent of Khalid, but he was not there. The tents were set behind the army. The army of Banu Hanifa came into camp and were about to kill Ummah Tameem but Monja, who was tied up in the tent.

He gave her protection, and he said, "She is a noblewoman. Do not kill her."

Muslims had to regroup. Muhajeeren and Ansaar went to Khalid and said, "Separate us. Every group should be under their own banners so we will know who is weak and where we are attacked from Muhajir, Ansaar."

Nomads knew Muslims. In the beginning new retreated an entire army had this set checked.

Now they were saying to Khalid, "Separate us."

Khalid said, "O people! Separate in your groups so we know the value or courage of each clan and we shall know where we are approached from the enemy."

There was blame going on. Each group was saying that others do not know how to fight. They had separate groups and banners to clear who was the weak link. The leadership of Muhajeeren was given to Abu Adifa. The banner of Ansaar was given to Sabit bin Qais. Now it would be a shame for the weak group. Sabit bin Qais made a hole in the ground that buried him knee high so that he could not retreat even if he wanted to. He held the banner and fought until he was killed. A servant held the banner of Muhajeeren. He was given the banner because he was Hafiz-e-Quran.

He said, "I know why you have given me the banner—because of Quran." He said, "I shall be a worse carrier of Quran if enemy approaches from my side." It is not appropriate for a carrier of Quran to do something against Quran. Quran is not only to be memorized in the heart; Quran is the way of life. That was the understanding of the sahaba. If Hafiz-e-Quran had to live up to a certain standard because one has Quran in the heart, they had to follow what they know—practice what you preach.

They fought. Muhajeeren were firm, and Ansaar were firm; but Banu Hanifa were putting up a stiff resistance, and attack was going on in waves. They would attack, go check, and another wave would come. Those waves were going both ways. Muslims were encouraging each other. There were speakers to give Qutba to encourage to fight. The brother of Umar bin Khitab, Zahid bin Khitab, told his followers to "grit your teeth"—meaning "press your nerves hard and attack and proceed straight ahead." They made a powerful and violent blow to the enemy, and Rijaal was killed. He was second in command after Muslimsa Qazab. Zahid bin Khitab killed him. Abdul Rehman bin Abu Bakar saw another leader of the enemy, Al-Mohakam. There were two flags of Muslimsa—Rijaal and Mohakam. He was speaking to his people, encouraging them. We know that Abdul Rehman bin Abu Bakar was a good anchor. He was able to strike Al-Mohakam right in his throat, and he dropped dead, but still Banu Hanifa were fighting.

End of CD 2.

Muslimsa was firm. He was in the heart of his army, and his people were surrounding him from each direction. It was like a hurricane with Muslimsa in the middle; they were revolving around him and fighting.

Khalid bin Waleed realized that there was no chance to stop this people from Banu Hanifa, and fighting was still going on. He realized that the only way to reach Muslimsa, who was the heart of his army. Tabree describes it and says Muslimsa was firm, and he was the eye of storm. Khalid bin Waleed took a group of fursan with him and said, "Let us charge straight through until we get through to Muslimsa and kill him."

Khalid bin Waleed, even though he was the leader of army, the head of the army, he would just strike through the ranks of the army, cut it like a knife through butter. Khalid bin Waleed and his group of fursan on their horses just broke through the rank of the enemy until they could see Muslimsa in front of their eyes. When that happened, Muslimsa and his army retreated, and Muslims followed them, killing left and right in their retreat until they cornered them into a garden from a ranch. That was fortified. Muslimsa and his army went in and locked the gates. Now Muslims was locked outside and unable to get in.

Albar-Ibn-e-Malik, the brother of Anees bin Aaqib, said, "Just throw me in."

Either Umar bin Khitab or Abu Bakar—one of them ordered Alber to join the army but sent a letter with him to the leader of army, saying, "Do not appoint Alber in a position of leader of any army because he will perish with everybody with him. Anybody with

Alber will just die. Do not appoint him as a leader. Let him do what he wants himself."

Alber said, "Just throw me on top of the enemy," but the leadership said no. But he insisted and said, "Just throw me in" in one narration. They just threw him over, another narration with the ladder.

In another narration, they lifted him up; and when he now has the army of Muslimsa right under him, he hesitated and was pulled back. He just saw a flood of people with their swords pointing, but when he took a breath, he said, "Throw me." They threw him, and people of Muslimsa saw him falling on them as a bird from the sky. He succeeded fighting with them until he got to the gates. He picked up the keys and opened the gate and allowed the Muslim army to come in. He had eighty injuries to his body. Muslims came in, and now there was nowhere to go. Now both armies were there—Khalid's and Muslimsa's—there was nothing to do but to fight to death.

Now the Jin of Muslimsa was coming to him. The story is that when his Jin would come to him, some foam would come out of his mouth, and he would obsess with his Jin. He had to throw itself to a wall. His eyes were just roaming around.

At that moment, Wehshi, the killer of Hamza in the battle of Audh, who killed Hazrat Hamza but later on became a Muslim, said, "Just as I have killed the most beloved servant of ALLAH. I am going to compensate by killing the enemy of ALLAH." He made his target that was going to use his skill to kill Muslimsa Qazab. He was very skilled in throwing the spear. He got him in his sight. He was able to strike Muslimsa Qazab, but at the same time, Abu Rajana, an Ansaari, the one who had the red hand on in the battle of Badar, took a hit at Muslimsa. Therefore, it is not clear who killed Muslimsa Qazab.

Later on, Wehshi would say, "Our Lord really knows who killed Muslimsa." Both of them took a hit on Muslimsa—the sword of Abu Rajana and spear of Wehshi. With the death of Muslimsa, the whole battle was over. That was the end. Muslimsa was the center, and mill was revolving around. The garden was called the garden of death. The Muslims' slogan on that day was "Ya Mohammada." They were calling the name of Mohammad (PBUH). It was only a slogan, supendialic. They were not asking Mohammad (PBUH) for help because help is from ALLAH only. We Muslims only ask ALLAH for help, but Muslims have slogans during wars. One of the Saraya slogan was "Ahmit Kill Kill." In this battle, the slogan was "Ya Mohammada." Ten thousand enemies were killed inside the garden. Muslims were killed in the garden of death, numbered six hundred. The total number of Muslims killed were 1,200.

There were some heroic acts we shall talk about.

(1) Abu Aqeel of Ansaar—he was one of the first injured in the battle. He was stuck by an arrow between his shoulder and heart. It didn't kill him but left his left side weak. He had to take rest in the tent prepared for the injured.

He heard a call: "O Ansaar, O Ansaar, attack the enemy of ALLAH."

Abu Aqeel tried to stand up and picked up his sword.

Sahaba asked him, "What are you doing?"

He said, "A man has called my name."

They told him, "He didn't called your name. He is calling the Ansaar."

Abu Aqeel said, "I am one of the Ansaar."

They told him, "You are injured. There is no fighting for you."

Abu Aqeel said, "I am an Ansaar and my name was called and I am going to respond to the call even if I have to crawl."

He went to fight and used his left hand for protection, but now no protection, he was injured and fell down. Before he died, Abdullah bin Umar approached him.

Abu Aqeel asked, "Who did this day belong to?"

Abdullah bin Umar said, "Rejoice because the enemy of ALLAH was killed."

Abu Aqeel said, "Alhamdulillah! Prays be to ALLAH," and he passed away.

All that he wanted to know was which side won. The day belonged to Muslims or to Muslimsa.

(2) Mushaba bin Qaib made an oath that she was not going to lay down her sword unless Muslimsa was killed. She participated in actual fighting. Mushaba bin Qaib was left with twelve injuries.

She had to be attended to in a tent, and she said, "Khalid bin Waleed took so much care for me that he sent a doctor for me who attended my injuries, and they used boiling oil to heal my injuries." She said, "I would rather have my limbs amputated than go through that pain." To heal the injury and to clean it, they would pour boiling oil to burn the entire injury—that was the medical treatment of the day.

God is great. Think about a woman fighting and being injured. Now we do not want to suffer any pain for the religion of ALLAH. For sahaba, Islam was not just lip service. It was a struggle, and they went through a lot of pain. We ask ALLAH to spare us on the Day of Judgment from hellfire. Women did participate. The wife of Khalid bin Waleed was given the responsibility of guarding a prisoner of war. Other duties were nursing and security guard role.

(3) The martyrs of the battle of Al-Yamamah Sabit bin Qais. He held the banner of Ansaar. He sat his feet on the ground so that he would not retreat. He was killed.

One Muslim soldier saw a dream after Sabit was killed. This is mentioned by Ibn-e-Qaseer.

In this dream, Sabit came to him and told him, "When I was killed, a Muslim came to me and took away a valuable shield that I had, and this person is in such a place. You will find his horse next to him. Then you will find my shield under a rock, and on top of it is a saddle. Go and take my shield, give it to Khalid bin Waleed, and tell him to send it to Abu Bakar to have him sell it to pay my debts that belong to so and so."

And then Sabit told him in the dream, "And beware to say it as a dream and neglect it. This is serious."

The man woke up and went and, as it was described in the dream, found the shield, took it to Khalid bin Waleed. He sent it to Abu Bakar. He sold it and paid off the debts of Sabit. His will was given after his death. It was a blessing of Sabit bin Qais because one cannot enter into paradise until he paid his debts.

Zahid bin Khitab was the brother of Umar bin Khitab. When the news reached Umar bin Khitab, he said, "May ALLAH have mercy on Zahid. He came first before me and received two greatest things:

one, becoming a Muslim and two, becoming Shaheed. He became a Muslim before me and became a martyr before me."

It was obvious that Umar bin Khitab was happy that his brother died as a martyr, but when Abdullah bin Umar came back, as soon as he came in and met his father, Umar bin Khitab told him, "Abdullah! How dare you show me your face? Why didn't you die as a martyr as your uncle?"

This tells us a lot about Umar bin Khitab and tarbeyat of sahaba. Instead of saying, "Alhamdulillah, he came back saved," he said, "How dare you show me your face?"

Abdullah bin Umar said, "O Father! I asked for it, but ALLAH decided for my uncle to be martyr and decided for me to live for another day."

Umar bin Khitab was happy that his brother had died as a martyr, but still it left a scar on the heart of Umar. He would always remember his brother.

In fact, whenever the wind would blow from the north, because a battle happened in Al-Yamamah, which is north, Umar bin Khitab said, "When the wind will blow from north, it would remind me of my brother Zahid."

Mohtamim bin Zahra, the brother of Malik, who was killed by Khalid bin Waleed, made some lines of poetry talking about his brother. When Umar bin Khitab heard those lines, he said, "I wish I had that ability to say poetry, and if I did, I would say similar words in the obituary of my brother."

Mohtamim told Umar, "If my brother died the same the way for the same cause your brother died, I wouldn't have any sadness. I wouldn't have regretted his death."

Umar bin Khitab said, "No one has ever given me counsel like you did. This is the best thing I have ever heard."

Mann bin Uddey was the appointed brother of Zaid during the brotherhood of Ansaar and Muhajeeren. That brotherhood was when Muhajeeren came to Madina. Later on, it was abrogated. That brotherhood was put ahead of blood brothers even in terms of inheritance. However, this special relationship was continued afterward, and this was the case between Zahid and Mann. They continued to have this very special friendship till the last day. They respected ALLAH. They both died on the same day. Mann bin Uddey also was a martyr in the battle.

Mann bin Uddey made an amazing statement.

When Rasool ALLAH died, some of the sahaba said<, "We wish we had died before Rasool ALLAH."

Mann bin Uddey said, "I would not desire that because I want Mohammad (PBUH). I want to believe in Mohammad (PBUH) even after this death as I believed in him when he was alive. I want to believe in Mohammad (PBUH) just as I believed in him in his life. Another sahabi, Abdullah bin Sohail, was also martyred.

Sohail bin Amar was the one who signed the contract with Rasool ALLAH in Suleh-Audebiya. His son Abdullah was handed over to mushirkeen according to the agreement. The terms of the agreement of Audebiya stated, "If a Muslim comes from Mecca to Madina, he should be returned. But if an apostate goes to Mecca from Madina, they are not returned."

Abdullah was a Muslim. He came from Mecca to Madina. According to the agreement, he had to be returned, so he stayed in Mecca and was persecuted. He came out with mushirkeen in the battle of Badar. He came with the Quraish army, but as soon as they reached the battlefield, he ran away and joined the Muslims. He died as a martyr in this battle.

Abu Dujana was marching in front of the army with the red head hand with pride. As a Muslim, one shouldn't be arrogant, but he was walking very arrogantly. Rasool ALLAH said, "ALLAH dislikes this way of walking except in this situation—because he was doing it to terrify the enemies of ALLAH." Abu Dujana was the partner with Wehshi in killing Muslimsa Qazab. He also died in this battle.

Tufail bin Amardosy was the chief of his people of Dosy. He was with his son Amar. He told his son, "I saw in a dream—I saw my head was shaven and a bird came out of my mouth and a womb of a woman swallowed me." He told his son, "Interpret it to mean that to me it is Shaldah. My head shaven is my killing and a bird coming out of my mouth is my soul and the woman swallowing me through her womb is Earth. I shall be buried."

His dream was fulfilled in the battle of Yamamah.

Ubaid bin Bushan was one of the notable among the Ansaar. He was part of a special operations team that assassinated Kab bin Ashraf. One night, Rasool ALLAH was praying Tahajjud late at night, and the room of Ayesha was adjacent to the mosque.

Rasool ALLAH said, "O Ayesha! Is it the voice of Abid?"

Ayesha said, "Yes!" and Rasool ALLAH said, "May ALLAH has mercy on him." This was in Bukhari.

Usually when Rasool ALLAH prayed for someone, may ALLAH have mercy on him, he would die as a martyr as the mercy of ALLAH is Shahadat.

Once an Ansaar was making singing for the army. Rasool ALLAH said, "May ALLAH have mercy on him."

Umar bin Khitab said, "Ya, Rasool ALLAH, we want to enjoy him," meaning his life will be taken away soon. Therefore, Duaa of Rutba means the person would die as a martyr.

He also saw a dream (blessing and dreams) happened a lot to Muhajereen because of Sadiq. The more truthful of you in words are most true in their dreams. Their dreams are not deceptive; their dreams are true. A person who is on the path of ALLAH, fighting for the sake of ALLAH, represents truth because they are giving up their lives for ALLAH.

He saw a dream. He told one of his companions. He saw the sky was opened, the heavens opened. He said he went through, and then it closed. He interpreted it to mean Shahadat. He saw after the battle with Talal his dream was fulfilled.

During the battle, Ubaid bin Bushan went on top of a hill and called Ansaar. Now you mobilize your own people—that was motivation as it was competition between Ansaar and Muhajereen. Nobody wanted to be the cause of defeat of Muslims. Therefore, they would call on their own people. Now Ubaid bin Bushan was motivating Ansaar. He stood on top of a hill so they could all see him and called them. A big group came to him. He took the sheath off a sword and broke it on his knees. When Ansaar saw that they broke theirs, that meant that this sword was not going back, and he said "Go ahead and they attacked and many of them were killed in that attack. He was killed at the age of forty-five.

Ubaid bin Bushan, with his group, played an important role in pashting Muslimsa in to the foam and them they went in and fought with them with closed gates. Ubaid bin Bushan did so much on that day, fighting, that he became an example for Banu Hanifa. Whenever they would see anybody injured, they would say, "You are injured by the Mujrib experienced man Ubaid bin Bushan." His fighting on that day became an example for other people.

When the battle was over, now Khalid bin Waleed wanted to see this man who was the root of this whole problem, Muslimsa. He took with him his Monja, his captain, the hostage who was in the tent under the care of his wife. He was holding Monja and walking through the dead bodies. Khalid bin Waleed wanted to know who was Muslimsa. They passed next to Rijaal. They carried on and entered into the garden of death, and then Monja pointed to Muslimsa Qazab. When Khalid took a look at it and said, "Is this the one who did to you what he did?" the way he looked didn't influence what he had caused, so Monja said, "Yes, this is the one."

Monja told Khalid, "I want to strike a deal with you for my people."

Banu Hanifa are different clause. Monja wanted to make truce with Khalid bin Waleed for his people. "I pay you this amount of gold, silver, and armory."

Khalid bin Waleed sensed he could continue fighting and could pick up many other fortresses and take all the women, children, and wealth, but Monja told Khalid, "There are many fighters in my fortresses, so let us strike a deal. This is how much I shall."

Khalid bin Waleed told him, "Go and discuss with your people."

Monja went inside his fortress. There were no men, only elderly and weak women and children. Monja told them all to dress up in armory and told the women to take the hair on their chest. In those days, men used to grow their hair long. He told woman to put on turbans, helmets, and carry weapons, put on armors, and to stand on the top of the roof and on the guarding points of the forts.

Khalid bin Waleed was at a distance, and the Muslims cannot see the faces.

Monja came back and informed Khalid, "My people has refused." He reduced the amount and said, "Let me try again with the people because they are ready to fight and take a look."

Khalid bin Waleed had a look, and he saw a blanket of black turbans as every woman and child was dressed in fighting uniform. That was all he saw covering the roofs with army although that was a trick but a successful trick. Khalid bin Waleed and the Muslim army were exhausted, tired. The army was weak because of the battle of Al-Yamamah. It had been very vicious but a hard battle that the Muslims had been fighting. One thousand and two hundred Muslims had been killed. That was the biggest single-day loss ever for the Muslims. Three hundred Muhajereen and Ansaar, sixty to seventy Hafiz of Quran had been killed that day.

Even though the news of victory reached to Madina, the news of the dead subdued the tone of happiness. This was the greatest loss Muslims suffered. The enemy suffered worst. Ten thousand were killed in the garden of death, but the Muslims were tired and needed rest. When Khalid saw the roofs covered with people, he accepted the deal.

"Okay, fine, agreed."

Monja wanted to have it written down. They wrote it, and then he opens the gates.

Muslims went in, and now they were only women and children.

Khalid said to Monja, "You have tricked me."

Monja said, "I did what I had to do to save my people."

Khalid bin Waleed asked Monja, "Marry me your daughter."

Monja said, "That will ruin my reputation and yours," but Khalid told him to marry his daughter with him.

Monja said, "Okay."

The news reached to Abu Bakar Siddique that Khalid bin Waleed had married again. Abu Bakar sent a letter to Khalid bin Waleed:

O son of the mother of Khalid, you find yourself free to marry a woman, when in your courtyard there is blood of 1200 Muslims and that blood has not dried yet. And then you allow Monja to trick you when ALLAH has handed them over to you.

Abu Bakar Siddique was very upset, and this was a very stunned letter.

When Khalid bin Waleed read the letter, he said, "This is the work of a left-handed man," meaning Umar bin Khitab.

Khalid wrote the letter and said, "Aan baad, I didn't marry until the victory was achieved," meaning "We are celebrating victory. I married after the fighting was over." He also said, "I married the daughter of a man. If I was in Madina, it would be worth travelling all the way to marry his daughter, but I was there next to him. Monja is a person among his people. If you had religious or worldly reasons, then could he be excused for blaming me? There is no reason to get angry for what I did."

And then he said, "In terms of my sadness for the loss of Muslims, if sadness will bring them back, then my sadness should be enough to bring them back to life." Khalid was saying, "I am in pain for the loss of my army, and I would throw myself among their ranks until I am certain that I shall die and I would give up living." Khalid was saying, "I have put myself in a situation where I would give up hope for living and see death as certainty."

Tabree said,

When Khalid bin Waleed throw himself amongst the enemy, he would eat everything around him. Everything around will fall down dead. Khalid was looking for death but no one could kill him. Khalid says he is not tangled with world. He marrying twice may he interpreted otherwise. Khalid bin Waleed, in his own statement, said, "If a beautiful woman whom I love is married to me or I am given the news of a new born male child, that is less dear to my heart than sleeping in a tent in a cold windy night planning to ambush the enemy the next day. Next day he may be killed. Also he is a leader of an army, the loss to army. That is how much they loved Jihaad."

Hazrat Abu Bakar Siddique also said, "You were tricked by Monja."

Khalid bin Waleed said, "Saying Monja tricked me, my opinion was not wrong on that day and I do not know the unseen and ALLAH has done well for Muslims. They have won, and the end belongs to Mutaqeen. Monja tricked, but his people became Muslims."

Abu Bakar Siddique in Tabree said,

Abu Bakar sent a letter saying, "Whoever lands in your hands from Abu Hanifa execute them" but Khalid received the letter after he had executed the truce between himself and Monja. Abu Bakar Siddique wanted to punish the apostates. It is the respect of ALLAH that Monja and his people became Muslims.

When Abu Bakar Siddique received this letter, that softened his heart, but then some people from Quraish and other tribes came to argue on behalf of Khalid.

Abuzar Aslami said, "O Khalifa! Khalid cannot be considered as lacking courage or betraying his trust to Muslims. Khalid has searched, has put himself in situations in search of martyrdom. He did his best, but he won, and the truce he concluded with people—that was pleasing truce to him. One cannot say his view or opinion was wrong because he saw women covering the roof and he thought they were men."

Abu Bakar Siddique said, "I believe what you have said, and you have given me a more valid reason than his letter." Abu Bakar Siddique agreed, and the issue was over with. Khalid was forgiven.

Next topic to deal with, Al-Yamamah, may be the last. So many Hafiz of Quran were killed.

Umar bin Khitab came to Abu Bakar Siddique and said, "So many people who memorized Quran have died and Quran is in the hearts of men and if men have gone, then Quran may be lost. Therefore, why not compile the Quran?"

Abu Bakar Siddique said, "How can you ask me to do something that Rasool ALLAH did not do?"

Umar bin Khitab argued with him. Abu Bakar Siddique thought about this and came to adopt the opinion of Umar bin Khitab. Zahid bin Sabit, an Ansaari, a twenty-one-year-old man from Ansaar, received the message that "the Khalifa wants to meet you."

Now Zahid bin Sabit was telling the story.

He said he went to meet the Khalifa and Umar bin Khitab was sitting next to him and Abu Bakar Siddique told Zahid bin Sabit, "Umar bin Khitab came to me and told me that so many Hafiz of Quran are killed and, therefore, why don't you compile Quran and protect it? But Abu Bakar said this is something Rasool ALLAH did not do and thought over it and agreed with Umar bin Khitab. Now I am giving you responsibility of compiling the Quran."

Zahid bin Sabit said, 'If Abu Bakar Siddique would load a mountain on my shoulder, I would be lighter in weight than the mission he gave to me."

But Abu Bakar Siddique said, "The reason I am appointing you to compile the Quran—you are a young man, you are mature and wise and we trust you for this mission and you used to write the revelations for the messenger of ALLAH."

Even at that young age, Zahid bin Sabit was a scholar of Quran. He said, "I shall have to go around to people, collecting Quran from the hearts of men and collect all the manuscripts of Quran that existed."

He picked up palm leaves; they used to write on palm leaves and on flat curved rock, also used to write on the shoulder bone of camels that is a flat plate; therefore, they would write on that. They also used to write on leather. Zahid bin Sabit collected all that material, and then he compiled the Quran. The original copy was with Abu Bakar Siddique until he passed away. It was handed down to Umar bin Khitab. When he passed away, it was given to Imaan Hafsa, the daughter of Umar bin Khitab. That is the story of compiling the Quran.

End of CD 3.

Some lessons from the wars of Redha.

(1) Abu Bakar Siddique made this land separate from others, and Islam did not contaminate with Shirk. The early stage of religion was very susceptible to change. It was very critical for Abu Bakar Siddique to ensure that Islam, during that critical stage, do not change and was kept as Rasool ALLAH left it. Hazrat Abu Bakar Siddique said that "revelation has stopped with the death of Rasool ALLAH, Jibraeel will not bring any messages from ALLAH, and our mistakes will not be fixed. Jibraeel would not descend, and religion is complete, so I am not going to allow it to diminish while I am alive." Abu Bakar Siddique did not want to change a saddle of a horse or a string of a camel. He wanted Muslim people to practice the same religion as in the time of the prophet. By the end of Redha wars, the whole Arabia came to conclusion that Islam is the same as what it used to be during the time of the prophet.

(2) Abu Bakar Siddique purified the Arabian Peninsula and prepared it as a launchpad for the conquest which will come later on and cannot expand without a strong base.

(3) Time to know people during fighting helped him in the choice of future leaders.

(4) Practical victory of Redha. During the time of the prophet, there was no practical Redha. That was Abu Bakar Siddique who explained practically what Redha is. Now the base was strong to send out the armies of ALLAH next to the conquests.

The conquest of Abu Bakar Siddique was the first the conquest of Iraq. With the opening of Iraq, Sheikh Raksa bin Shabaan came to Khalifa. He proposed an idea to the Khalifa, which was under consideration even before. He asked to be appointed as authority over his people in his area to wage war against the enemy of ALLAH. Iraq was a part of the Persian Empire. Abu Bakar Siddique approved his proposal. Musneya bin Harisa wanted legitimacy, and Abu Bakar Siddique did not have to send an army. He was a chief of his tribe. He had the army to fight against non-Muslims. Abu Bakar Siddique agreed. Musneya bin Harisa started guerilla attacks (cur and fur)— the attack and retreat against Persian armies. He had a small force so could not go and march straight.

There was another leader who approached Abu Bakar Siddique and asked if he could be appointed the leader of Muslims in that area instead of Musneya bin Harisa. Musneya bin Harisa also wrote a letter informing Abu Bakar about the man who was competing for the same position against Musneya bin Harisa.

Abu Bakar Siddique, to solve this issue, sent a letter to the new person, saying, "I accept what you have said about yourself and I want you to join hands with Khalid bin Waleed, who was on his way to Iraq, and follow Khalid bin Waleed."

Al-Mazoor and Musneya bin Harisa all agreed with the abilities of Khalid bin Waleed. Abu Bakar Siddique wanted to send two armies to Iraq—one army to attack from southeast and the other army to attack from northwest. The army which will attack from southeast will be the army of Khalid bin Waleed.

Abu Bakar sent a letter, saying, "Go on to Iraq because Khalid was in Al-Yamamah. Begin with the gateway to India." The area around Bara was called gateway to India. "Enter into Iraq from gateway to India. Render those nations in that area, then send an army from northwest under the leadership of a sahabi. Tell him to attack from northwest. Both had to attack in Iraq and head to Heera, and whoever gets to Heera first is the leader over the others."

Heera was the midway. It was a very strategic position. It was near the Persian capital. Abu Bakar wanted Heera to be the base.

The army base of Heera was toward the south—Ayaz bin Ghanam and Khalid bin Waleed. Khalid bin Waleed knew that he would not sleep and would not allow anybody to sleep. He asked for reinforcement. Who can Abu Bakar send? He sent him one man— Al-Kaka bin Umar—reinforcement by one man.

Abu Bakar said, "If Al-Kaka is part of the army, those armies cannot be defeated."

Khalid bin Waleed arrived first and appointed the leader over all the force's armies totaling 18,000 troops. Khalid bin Waleed sent a letter to Herzaman, one of the kings of the Persian Empire. The letter said,

> I call you to ALLAH and Islam. If you accept you are Muslims, if refuse pay Jazeya. If not then I bring people who love death as you love life. We shall fight until ALLAH decides between us and you.

Herzaman refused and decided to fight. They went to the battlefield that is called the battle of chains because the enemy was weak and had to chain them with one another to fight to stop them from fleeing while Muslims were so eager to die you have to chain them to bring them back.

It was a big defeat for the enemy. Khalid bin Waleed moved to Al-Mizaar, another defeat to the enemy. Muslims reached the heart of Iraq, a beautiful land with plenty of produce. Khalid bin Waleed gave Khutba before the battle.

Khalid said, "Can you see all the produce of this land by ALLAH? If we struggle for the sake of ALLAH but the opinion is that we strike this countryside until we win this land and we leave, hungry, behind whoever did not join you."

Khalid bin Waleed was looking at this blessed land. He said, "If Jihaad was not our duty, just the beauty of this land and its wealth is sufficient to invite us to come here" and also said, "Leave the hunger for those who stayed behind although Jihaad is not done for the sake of wealth, but ALLAH gives rewards in longer life."

Again Khalid bin Waleed, with the Muslim army, conquered, and a great many died in this battle. The news was coming to Abu Bakar Siddique, victory after victory.

Abu Bakar Siddique said, "O people of Quraish! Your lion has overcome the enemy lion, taking away the pieces of his prey." Then

Abu Bakar said, "Women will never give birth to the like of Khalid. Women cannot give birth to a man like this."

Now they reached Heera. Khalid bin Waleed was also good at diplomacy along with fighting, convincing people to surrender, giving up without a fight. The major parts in Heera belong to Christian Arabs. Khalid bin Waleed would give them three options: (1) to accept Islam, become Muslims, (2) to pay Jazeya, and (3) fighting. The Christian Arabs agreed to pay Jazeya.

Khalid said to them, "May you perish. Woe to you." This belief is the desert that makes them lose the way. It is only the foolish one among the Arabs who will follow it. That also shows that the intentions of Jihaad was not Jazeya or money. Financially, it was better for the government that people didn't become Muslims, but they insisted and didn't become Muslims. Khalid knew if ALLAH guides one man to become a Muslim, that is better than a flock of camels. Hadees in Bukhari Shareef contract was written in the name of ALLAH, the merciful.

This is the government made by Khalid bin Waleed between himself and the other party for 190,000 dharams payable annually for Jazeya working in this world including their monks and priests except for those who have no work, cut off from worldly life, and those who are travelling. In return, Khalid promises them protection. If Muslims cannot protect them, they have to pay the money back. If they are breached, then Muslims' conscience is free from any obligation to them. This was the agreement between Khalid and the people of Heera, and now Heera is the new base for Muslim forces in Iraq.

Now Khalid bin Waleed was sending the letters to the kings of Persia, to all prominent leaders. One letter was send to the kings and another to the governors.

The letters sent to the kings, in the name of ALLAH, the all-compassionate and merciful from Khalid bin Waleed:

> To the kings of Persia, praise be to ALLAH,
> who has discovered your order, major plotting
> weak, divided you among yourselves, therefore
> enter into our faith. We shall leave you and your

land alone and pass on to others different than you. If not, that will happen anyway, meaning become Muslims, so we can go behind you to other people. If you do not become Muslims, that will happen. We shall cross over you and reach others. If not, that will happen by force by people who love death as you love life.

This letter took kings by surprise. They couldn't believe this. "These people came out of nowhere. They have established base in our land. Now they are telling us to become Muslims or otherwise." There were direct and stern terms that drove them crazy, and they became very angry.

Remember when Rasool ALLAH sent the letter to the king of Persia—what did he do? This was an empire that was very proud and arrogant. He tore the letter of Prophet (PBUH). When Rasool ALLAH found out, he smiled and said, "ALLAH will tear apart his kingdom."

Khalid bin Waleed sent letters to the governors of the states:

In the name of ALLAH, compassionate and merciful, from Khalid bin Waleed to governors of Persia. Embrace Islam so you may be safe. If not, make a covenant of protection with me and pay Jazeya. Otherwise, I have brought people who love death just as you drink wine.

A blessing happened to Khalid bin Waleed in Heera. One of the leaders of Heera who had a contract with Khalid bin Waleed was carrying something in his belt. Khalid bin Waleed grabbed it. He poured it on his hand and asked, "What this is?"

The man said, "This is poison that kills within an hour."

Khalid bin Waleed asked him, "Why are you carrying it?"

The man said, "I wanted to see whether you are truthful or not. If you are not, then I shall try to kill you."

Khalid bin Waleed said, "Bismillah, in the name of ALLAH, in his name nothing can harm you in heaven and on earth."

Khalid wanted to swallow the poison, but everybody around jumped at him, tried to prevent him. "What are you doing?" But he was faster than them and swallowed the whole poison.

The man was shocked to see that and said, "If it is true, then your people will rule over the world."

No harm happened to Khalid bin Waleed. This is the amazing blessing. It is in all the books; therefore, it is an authentic story.

Khalid bin Waleed wouldn't had done it if he had any doubt because it would be considered suicide. When Khalid bin Waleed did that, he was at the level of faith ALLAH inspired him: "Nothing will harm you." Also, prayer is like a sword which will destroy the enemy. When we pray, we say weightily that ALLAH will accept it; in fact, problem is not with the prayers but with the person who is making the prayer. Prayer is like a sword, very sharp. The problem is with the one who is carrying the sword. If people are strong, they can use it, and some weak people cannot use it. Khalid bin Waleed believed in ALLAH and made a prayer that solved the whole thing.

He moved onto Alanbar, destroyed the enemy. He conquered Iraq. Now between the Roman Empire and the Persian Empire is a place called Jandal. It was a very critical place. Dhooma Tal Jandal, the prophet of ALLAH, had interest in Dhooma Tal Jandal during his lifetime. Therefore, Muslim armies were sent to Dhooma Tal Jandal. This is a triangle where the Arabian Peninsula meets with the Persian and Roman Empires.

Khalid bin Waleed was now moving toward Dhooma Tal Jandal. He was moving very swiftly. The news reached the leaders of Dhooma Tal Jandal. There were two leaders; one of them, O'Kadeer, had made a peace agreement with Rasool ALLAH and then he broke the agreement. Khalid bin Waleed had captured O'Kadeer and took him to Madina. O'Kadeer met Rasool ALLAH, and he promised to Rasool ALLAH that he will not be against Rasool ALLAH anymore. Rasool ALLAH granted him peace, and he left, but then O'Kadeer betrayed his promise to Rasool ALLAH and turned against Muslims. This is the background of O'Kadeer.

O'Kadeer received the news that Khalid was on his way toward them. He knew Khalid because Khalid captured him. He knew

Khalid was a good Oh Man Sign; there was nobody who was equal to Khalid in war. Enemies, whether in a large group or small group, when they saw the face of Khalid, they flea. Therefore, O'Kadeer told his people to obey him and make peace with Khalid bin Waleed, but his people refused. O'Kadeer left his people. Khalid received the news and was successful against those people and captured O'Kadeer again and executed him because of his betrayal. Khalid bin Waleed opened Dhooma Tal Jandal, and Khalid bin Waleed won all the other battles as well against enemies.

But two stories: (1) A man was surrounded in his house with his wife, his daughter, and his sons. He had a big pot of wine in front of him. It was late at night. He was telling his family to drink. They said, "It is late," but he said, "Drink it. You will never be able to drink after this because Khalid and his troops will never leave us alone." They started to drink, and he said a few lines of poetry. He was sure that death was around the corner. Ahdey bin Hatim said, "We landed in his camp, we cut off his head that landed in his pot of wine, then we executed his sons and took his wife and daughters."

(2) Another incident happened. There were two Muslims. They had peace agreement with the Prophet (PBUH). They were killed. The families complained to Abu Bakar Siddique that these two Muslims were killed. Abu Bakar Siddique paid the blood money but said, "This happens to people who live in the land of Herbunder, living in the land of Herb." And this is what happens to people who do that, saying it is their own fault.

Now Khalid bin Waleed was deep in the areas of Iraq and Shaam. He conquered Iraq, set base there. Now he was among the territories of Persian and Roman Empires. He reached Al-Feraat. This is not a famous battle, but it is a very important event because Khalid bin Waleed met the international coalition of two superpowers along with puppet Arab governments, Roman Empire, Persian Empire with the tribes of Taghab, Neymar, and Eyaad. Tabree narrates the Romans became hot and angry and sought help from the nearby Persian posts, who were also hot and angry, and sought reinforcements from Taghab, Eyaad, and Neymar. The archenemies were Romans and Persians. The Romans were furious Khalid bin Waleed was in their land. They were seeking help from Persians. They had an international coalition to fight against the Muslims. Also Christian Arabs of the area joined them. That was a huge army, but Khalid bin Waleed dealt with them. Khalid bin Waleed defeated their huge army.

What happened before the fight? They were separated by the river. The Muslim army was on one side of the river, and enemy armies were on the other bank of the river.

They said to Khalid bin Waleed, "Either you cross over to us, or we shall cross over to you."

Khalid said, "You come over to us."

They agreed and wanted Khalid to get back so that they can cross over.

Khalid bin Waleed told them, "We shall not move back. You have to find the way to cross over. We shall not move."

They went around and crossed, but Khalid bin Waleed defeated them. Romans and Persians sensed that this man was fighting on the basis of religion, so they warned each other to protect their kingdoms. They knew Khalid was intelligent and knowledgeable. They gave him the credit.

When these armies were defeated, Khalid was not satisfied and pursued them. Khalid did not want to give them a break and rest and continued as far as he could. This was his practice—whenever an enemy falls, Khalid would pursue them. He would carry on as far as he could go. This was Khalid's reputation. The enemy knew even if they were defeated, Khalid bin Waleed would follow them. Even before they were ready to fight, their knees were shaking because of the stories of the bravery of Khalid and, of course, the swallowing of poison. Enemy forces would feel fear in their hearts that whatever Khalid did, nothing could harm him, and also the rumors that he received the sword from heaven. The enemy misunderstood the meaning of Saif-Ullah (the sword of ALLAH). The enemy understood that he (Khalid) received the sword from ALLAH.

There is a story it is in many books, and it is true. In one of the battles, Romans asked Khalid to come forward. The leader of the Roman army wanted to investigate this matter.

He asked Khalid bin Waleed, "Is it true that you have been given the sword by the Prophet which came from God?"

Khalid bin Waleed said, "No! This is not true, but the Prophet said, 'I am the sword of ALLAH.'" He did not lie. He told them the truth.

This is another story. It is an amazing story. Khalid bin Waleed and his army were in Farahat, which is between Syria and Iraq, a far-away land. Khalid bin Waleed wanted to go back to Iraq, Al-Heera army base. This was a huge distance. Usually when travelling long distances, the army would be divided into small units, and the army at the area would protect the army in front. The army was marching in two groups, and there was some difference between them—could be hours or could be days. He sent a major army in front and a smaller unit behind to protect it especially when he had just defeated the Romans, Persians, and Christian Arabs. The armies travelling from Syria, west of Iraq to Heera, which is a central area of Iraq, closed to Karbala and Najaf. Khalid bin Waleed was with the small unit of the army.

Khalid went to his close friend. It was Hajj season, and he asked the friends, "How about the Hajj this year?" They drew nearer to Kabah. If one has visited Kabah, one would like to see it again and again. Khalid wanted to go to Hajj. It was already late.

His friends replied, "What are you talking about? We are hundreds of miles away."

Khalid said, "Just believe me, and let us go."

He chose his close friends. They decided to go for Hajj. This was a new territory and they had never travelled in that land before and there was no guide. They wanted to go for Hajj. This kind of ventures were for young men, and Khalid was a mature old man, but Khalid was an audacious person. He would take any risk. That was his makeup and personality.

"Let us try." He only told his very close group. They started but had no direction or idea where they were heading in the unknown territory. Tabree said,

They followed the path which was not used
by human before. In the desert there are some
paths and some sign posts for guidance.

Khalid bin Waleed took a new route. He did something, and
ALLAH had given him some blessing. Tabree said,

He was rushing recklessly going on a path,
he did not know, until he came up in Arafat.
They completed their Hajj. Shaved their heads
and came out without telling anybody.

Abu Bakar Siddique heard the news when he was back in
Madina. Abu Bakar Siddique was very angry. Khalid bin Waleed
made it back to his army before it arrived at Heera. The army was in
Iraq. Khalid went and performed Hajj and joined the army in time.
Abu Bakar Siddique was told that Khalid left his army without telling anybody, went for Hajj, and came back. The feeling of Abu Bakar
was anger and surprise. How could anybody do that?

Abu Bakar wrote a letter and asked Khalid bin Waleed to go to
the Muslim armies in Yarmook. Yarmook is in Jordan. "Go to the
Muslim armies in Yarmook. They are distressed. Muslims are having
a hard time against Romans. Go and help them. Do not return to
the likes what you have done. Do not do something like that again."

He gave him clear orders. It was a very sharp tone but said,
"After ALLAH, there is no one who can break the enemy like you,"
meaning "Do not put yourself at risk because after ALLAH, no one
can break the enemy like you, and no one can relieve the Muslims
from distress like you. The Muslim armies are distressed against the
Romans. No one can relieve them from distress like you. Take care
of yourself."

Then Abu Bakar said, "Congratulations for what you have
achieved. Therefore, complete your work. ALLAH will make it complete for you. Your role is not over yet. ALLAH will raise you further
up. Do not let self-admiration enter into you."

Abu Bakar Siddique was not only the leader; he was not only Khalifa. He was a fatherly figure for all the sahaba. He was a scholar, their sheikh. He was the closest to the Rasool ALLAH, and he was in his sixties. He was also most knowledgeable. The relationship was more than a government member. It was the kind of relationship with an older brother. He was giving them advice. He was sending out armies and telling the leader of the army to have Khashwa and Salah. Usually this kind of teaching is given by a teacher to his students. That was the relationship between Khalifa and his followers. Khalid bin Waleed has a high status. Abu Bakar wanted to make sure that his heart was clean and Shaitaan didn't get into it.

"Do not let self-admiration enter into you so you fail and fall. ALLAH controls everything, and ALLAH gives the rewards. Do not let anything into your heart, and do not depend on your deeds."

The letter was delivered to Khalid bin Waleed. He was told to leave Iraq and go to Yarmook, Jordan. Now Khalid was told to split the army between himself and Mosneya bin Harisa. Mosneya bin Harisa would lead the army in Iraq while Khalid went with the other half of the army to Shaam. Khalid split the army and put all of the companions of Rasool ALLAH in his half.

Mosneya told Khalid, "I did not accept this half that you gave me. I cannot allow all the companions of Rasool ALLAH to go with you."

The companions of Rasool ALLAH equaled to a hundred. They were trained in Madina. Persian and Roman empires didn't even know Madina, but what they didn't know was that the seeds of their destruction were planted in Madina. Khalid bin Waleed gave Mosneya one companion of Rasool ALLAH after another until he was pleased, then Khalid moved on toward Shaam. We shall talk about this adventure later on.

When Mosneya met Rasool ALLAH before Hijra, he offered Rasool ALLAH protection from Arabs but could not guarantee from the side of the Persians and Romans. But not at the time of Abu Bakar Siddique. He was a Muslim and a changed man. He told the story himself.

Mosneya said, "I have fought against the Arabs and non-Arabs in Jahileya and after Islam." He said, "It used to be a hundred non-Arabs. Non-Arabs were stronger than a thousand Arabs, but now a hundred Arabs are stronger than non-Arabs because of Islam." Then he said, "So do not allow their numbers to strike fear in your hearts, and do not let their tall lances, spears, and powerful bows intimidate you because once they lose their weapons, they turn into cattle, and you can chase them the way you want." He was saying that disbelievers, without their equipment, are just like cattle. Mosneya was giving a strong note to Muslims because of their equipment and training. They were very strong against Muslims.

Ibn-e-Kaim said,

> Romans and Persians had large armies and battle equipment and also well-built while Muslims were less in numbers and thin and slim.

Umar bin Khitab and Khalid bin Waleed were well built and large men, but in general, Muslims came from the desert. Therefore, the Roman armies were well-built people, but Ibn-e-Qaim said,

> But their hearts failed them when they needed the most. These big bodies don't have strong hearts. Therefore, Muslims should not fear them. ALLAH can put fear in the hearts of the armies even when they had got most fearful weapons in their hands. They can function because of fear. ALLAH controls the hearts.

Mosneya bin Harisa was a great leader and was given the authority over Muslim forces in Iraq. He was the one who started in Iraq and continued with the victories in Iraq, a great general after Khalid bin Waleed. He needed some reinforcements and requested this from Abu Bakar Siddique, but Abu Bakar Siddique was even busier with other priorities. That was the conquest of the Holy Land. Abu Bakar Siddique delayed his response to Mosneya, and when Mosneya did not get a response, he decided to go on by himself to meet the Khalifa, but the Khalifa did not have any force to give him. Abu Bakar Siddique had taken all the fighting men and sent them to the Holy Land, then Mosneya requested to be reinforced by ex-apostles. Abu Bakar Siddique was on his deathbed at that time. His entire period of Khalafat didn't allow ex-apostates to join Muslim armies. Now things were different. Apostles had stood firm on Islam. He tested them for two years. Abu Bakar considered and told Umar bin Khitab, the next Khalifah.

Abu Bakar said to Umar bin Khitab, "O Umar! Listen to what I say, and then act accordingly. I hope to die this day of mine. If I die, do not wait for evening to find the men to go with Mosneya. If I am delayed, summon the men by morning to go with Mosneya. Do not allow any catastrophe to keep you away from the matters of your religion and your Lord's council. You know what I did on the day when Rasool ALLAH passed away." Abu Bakar Siddique was telling Umar, "Even if I die, do not allow this to hold you back from mobilizing the force to go with Mosneya." Then he said, "You saw what I did on the day the messenger of ALLAH died. That was a much greater catastrophe. I want you to follow my way after my death." Then Abu Bakar Siddique said, 'If I had weakened, then ALLAH would have punished me, and Madina would have been destroyed by fire. If ALLAH gives victory in the Holy Land, then return the troops with Khalid to Iraq, for they are his people, meaning people of Iraq should go back to Iraq to control the enemy." So Mosneya bin Harisa was reinforced.

End of CD 4.

Shabbir bin Hasna, one of the companions who led armies against apostles, came to Khalifah Abu Bakar Siddique and said, "O Khalifa Til Rasool ALLAH! Are you thinking about conquering Shaam? Are you thinking about fighting Romans?"

Abu Bakar Siddique said, "Yes, I am, but I have not told anyone about my intentions. How do you know about this?" Abu Bakar was thinking attacking Shaam. He was considering it. Shaam had been in the Muslims' minds since the day Rasool ALLAH made the journey of Al-Asra. Rasool ALLAH went to Jurashalam and led the Ambiya in Salah. This was symbolic. Syria was the key to the Holy Land. ALLAH says, "This is the blessed land." It is mentioned in Quran.

When Rasool ALLAH went there and led the Ambiya, many of them lived in the Holy Land. The fact that Rasool ALLAH was leading them, therefore, Rasool ALLAH was the leader, inheritance of Haq, and carrier of the torch. Even though Muslims were not in charge of the Holy Land, very early on, they set their sights on Bait-Ullah. Rasool ALLAH, even before he finished opening Arabia, he was sending Muslim armies to Moteyeha, battle of Moteyeha, deep in the land of Shaam, led by Zahid bin Harisa; and before that, Rasool ALLAH had sent the letter to the king of Gayaan.

When the king received the letter, he became very angry and wanted to attack Madina, but the Roman emperor told him not to do so. His loyalty was to the emperor. Then in the ninth year of Hijra, Rasool ALLAH went there himself, the battle of Tabook, which never took place. This was the header line between Hajaz and Shaam. Then Rasool ALLAH sent Usama bin Zahid, but Rasool ALLAH died, and Abu Bakar sent him out. Muslims were thinking about Shaam a lot. This was the land of Ambiya. Muslims should inherit it.

Now Abu Bakar Siddique was thinking about all-out attack in Shaam on the Romans to take over the land. It was not sending an army in and out.

Habib Al-Husna came and asked Abu Bakar, "Are you thinking of attacking Romans in Shaam?"

Abu Bakar Siddique said, "Yes, but how did you know?"

Habib Al-Husna said, "I had a dream. The dream was I saw you walking among the people and then you climbed over a very rough terrain and you made your way up to a very high peak, then you, with your companions, took a look from that point to the people under you. Then you descended from that peak to very fertile plains, a plain which is lush with vegetations. It is full with towns and fortresses. Then you told to wage war against the enemies of ALLAH, and I guarantee you victory and booty, and you gave me a banner. I went ahead with it, and I came to a town. People offered me peace, so I opened it peacefully, and then I came back to you. I found you in a great fortress, sitting on a throne, and then a voice came to you and said, 'Rejoice with victory, so thank ALLAH,' then this voice recited to you. At that time, I wake up. That was the end of dream."

Abu Bakar Siddique, with tears welling in his eyes, said, "You have given me the glad tidings of opening and also my obituary." Abu Bakar Siddique used to interpret the dreams even in the presence of Rasool ALLAH. Once a dream was presented to Rasool ALLAH, Abu Bakar said, "Let me interpret, O messenger of ALLAH."

His interpretation of the dream was as follows: "When you saw me climbing a very rough terrain, this means myself, my army soldiers, and enemy will have a very rough time. It will be difficult, hard. First you saw me among the people."

Then Abu Bakar Siddique was climbing this rough train. "It means a rough conflict. When you saw me at the top of the mountain, that means at the end, we will prevail victorious. The next, we came down to a very fertile valley, many towns and fortresses. It means after that, we shall have a comfortable living. Muslims will have easy lifestyles. When you saw me sitting on a throne, this means ALLAH will make me rise and make the enemies of ALLAH low. It means ALLAH will prevail me over the enemies of ALLAH. Then you heard a voice telling me 'You will be victorious, so thank ALLAH and seek his forgiveness.' This means my death is approaching because that Surah-e-Nasr was given to Rasool ALLAH before he died."

Then with tears flowing down his cheeks, Abu Bakar Siddique said, "In the name of ALLAH, I am going to enjoin good and forbid evil. I am going to mobilize and prepare the soldiers to the east and west of the earth until they say ALLAH is one without any associates or until they pay me the Jazeya and they are humiliated. This is the command of ALLAH and sunnat of Rasool ALLAH. When ALLAH takes away my soul, ALLAH will not find me weak. ALLAH will find me searching for rewards of Muhajereen."

Abu Bakar Siddique had made up his mind that they would start against the Romans. He called Sahaba to an assembly gathering, and he would present to them his ideas.

Abu Bakar Siddique invited Usman bin Unnan, Umar bin Khitab, Ali bin Abu Talib, Abdul Rehman bin Audh, Mashad bin Waqas, Talha, Ubaid Ullah, Zubair bin Awam, along with the leaders of Muhajereen and Al-Ansaar.

Then Abu Bakar Siddique, after praising ALLAH, said, "I am thinking about conquering Shaam, fighting Rome. If some dies, they die as martyr, and if they live, they live with victory and booty. What do you think?" He asked for advice. "Give me your opinion."

Umar bin Khitab was first to speak. Umar bin Khitab, after praising ALLAH, said, "In my view, ALLAH gives his blessings to whomever he wishes. I have been thinking about this. I wanted to present the idea to you, and here you are doing it before me. Because whenever we raise something good, you always come first, and this is the favor of ALLAH. He gives to whomever he wishes." This showed that Sahaba were thinking seriously about the issue of Shaam, how to deal with it.

Umar bin Khitab said, "My view is you send army after army into their land. Send armies in groups. ALLAH will give honor and victory to his religion."

Abdul Rehman bin Audh said, "I disagree with what Umar said. This is Rome. Arabs would call them yellow. They have strong backs. This is not an issue which should be taken lightly. They have very vast lands and heavy reinforcements. Whenever we get into their land, they will have people behind that to support them in conflict with us. They have an entire continent, and in addition, they are ruling over North Africa, Egypt, and Shaam." Abdul Rehman was telling the Khalifa that "This is not a regular foe. This is Rome."

In his view, to deal with the issue should be as follows: "Send in bands of horsemen to raid their land and raid the remote areas of their empire. Rather than sending the conventional armies, send in raids, small hands, capture booty, and come back." (1) He was saying, "You will weaken them by doing that. Keep them on alert, hitting their defenses without giving them a chance to hit back." (2) He was thinking how to finance this campaign—"Through the booty, you can finance the campaign. The Muslims' treasury would not have to pay for it. Once you feel the right time to strike, then I suggest you send out messengers and recruit from Yamen and from every corner. Then you lead the army or appoint someone to lead. Inshallah, ALLAH will give you victory."

Umar bin Khitab wanted an all-out attack, different personalities, but Abdul Rehman wanted to test the waters first and mobilize huge armies and attack. "Do not jump in it at once."

Usman bin Unaan gave his opinion and said, "O Khalifa! Your opinion is blessed. Whatever you see befitting, go ahead with it, and we shall follow through," saying, "We trust your opinion, your view, and your wisdom. You make the decision, and we shall follow you."

Talha, Zubair, and other sahaba said the same thing, and Hazrat Ali bin Abu Talib was quiet.

Abu Bakar Siddique said, "We have not heard from you. Why you are quiet?"

Hazrat Ali bin Abu Talib said, "You are a blessed person, and you carry good, O man! If you lead the army yourself or appoint someone in your place, you will be victorious."

Abu Bakar Siddique said, "How wonderful these words are. How do you know? Why, have you given the judgment that I shall win?"

Hazrat Ali bin Abu Talib said, "I have heard Rasool ALLAH say that this religion will prevail against all the enemies until it stands up firm with Muslims prevailing. This is the saying of Rasool ALLAH—it will happen."

This was a positive point the sahaba had—even before a battle, they knew the outcome. "ALLAH will give us victory."

Abu Bakar Siddique was very happy to hear these words, and he made up his mind. It was a mixture of both opinions of Umar bin Khitab and Abdul Rehman bin Audh. Abu Bakar Siddique sent out four armies. That was the opinion of Umar bin Khitab, and then the second part of the opinion of Abdul Rehman—that was to mobilize people from every corner to bring them ahead to fight this war against the Romans. He was bringing people who were far away from the battlefield, bringing the people of Arabia from Iraq and people from Yamen, taking them all the way to Shaam. It was an additional effort, but since it was a confrontation with the superpower of the time and dispute over the Holy Land control, which they view as their heartland, it was not an easy affair, which needed some special recruitment effort.

Abu Bakar Siddique sent Anees bin Malik with the letter to Yamen. The letter stated:

In the name of ALLAH the all compassionate and merciful, from the successor of the messenger of ALLAH to whomever this message is read to from believers and Muslims people of Yamen. Asalaam'o'Alaikum, ALLAH has prescribed Jihaad on believers and commanded them to set out to heaven. ALLAH says to fight with your wealth and yourself, Jihaad is a mandate and its rewards from ALLAH is great. He has assembled Muslims for Jihaad against Romans. The armies have already set out so hasten towards what they hastened toward. Then you will get one of the best either martyrdom or victory and Booty. Allah is not pleased with words alone without deeds. So Jihaad must continue until they accept the truth and government of the book of ALLAH. May

ALLAH protect your religion, guide your hearts,
purify your deeds and grant you the rewards of
Mojaheedeen.

In this letter, Abu Bakar was telling the people the objectives of
fighting for the sake of ALLAH, which were two: (1) This is the part
of Ibadat regardless he said, "ALLAH does not accept words without
deeds." For your words to be true, they must be accompanied with
Jihaad Fee Sabeelillah. (2) People either become Muslims or give
Jazeya. By giving Jazeya, they have accepted the Hakim of ALLAH
and Quran. Jazeya is the command of Quran. These are the two
objectives of fighting. Anees bin Malik would go and read this letter
to people of every town. Anees bin Malik came back and gave good
news to Abu Bakar Siddique.

He said, "Rejoice, the people have come to you covered in dust
the brave men of Yamen and heroes among them and knights. They
came with their families and their wealth."

This was a campaign that demanded that people should move
out of their lands because of the long distance. They were moving
out Fee Sabeelillah. This was the level of sacrifice demanded that day.

One of the kings from Yamen, his name was Talgalal Hameeri,
came to Madina five days after Anees bin Malik arrived, an immediate response. He came with a few hundred of his followers. He came
in with his crown and all jewels in it and dressed in garments with
gold in it. Very extravagant he was, a king. He came into Madina and
met Abu Bakar Siddique. He (Abu Bakar) was wrapped in ordinary
clothes, without any bodyguards, living in a mudhouse, having seen
the Khalifa of Muslims like that, that affected him so much. He took
off all those expensive clothes, went to the market of Madina where
all one can find were rough fabrics. He bought some of those and
put them on.

His people told him, "You will embarrass us in front of
Mohajeereen and Ansaar."

He said, 'That is it. That way is over. Now we shall follow the
ordinary way of Muslims."

When people see a role model in front of them, it is more powerful than words. Also people usually follow the person who is in power. People also usually follow the powerful nations. The weak follows the strong. Talgalal Hameeri was a king now under the Khalifa. His role model was Abu Bakar Siddique. Therefore, Sahaba were setting new standards and giving new examples. Sahaba went to other lands, not requesting but with armies. Therefore, when they went to the mosque, people would follow them and learn from them. The method of sahaba was to present Islam in an honorable way.

Now Khalifa dispatched four armies. The first army, the leader was Yazeed bin Sufyan. He was appointed over seven thousand soldiers. His destination was Damascus. The second army, under the leadership of Shriqeeb bin Hasna, had an army of three thousand. His destination was Tabooq and to protect the areas of Muslims and to reinforce because Tabooq was close to Madina. The third army, led by Abu Abida bin Jarri, had three thousand men. The destination was Hans in Syria. The fourth army of seven thousand was led by Amar bin Aas. His destination was Palestine. He sent them out, and Khalifa would walk with every leader while they were riding their horses and Khalifa was walking and Khalifa would advise them.

The advice to Yazeed, the first army, was to march out.

Abu Bakar Siddique said, "I am appointing you to lead this army to test you and to try you. If you perform well, I shall give you more, and if you do not, I shall change you. I advise you to have faith on ALLAH because ALLAH can see your inside as you can see your outside. I am appointing you to the post of Khalid bin Saeed bin Aas. Stay away from tribalism of Jaheeliya. When you join your soldiers, be a good companion. If you speak to them, be brief. Otherwise, they will forget the message. Improve the state of yourself—the state of your soldiers will improve. Pray Salat at the appointed time, and complete your Rako and Sajda and have Kashoon Salat.

"When you receive envoys from your enemy, be kind with them and generous, but do not allow them extended stay. Otherwise, they will learn your weaknesses. Have them stay among your strongest forces, and allow no one but yourself to speak to them. When you seek counsel, be truthful and straightforward in order to receive the best advice. Spend time at night talking to your soldiers, then you will receive news, and veils will be lifted. Spread out guards and pay them unannounced visits and whenever you see carelessness in guarding your army, then punish them moderately. Do not spend time with people who waste their time, but spend time with people with truth and loyalty. Beware of financial abuse because it draws poverty close and victory further away. You will find people deviated in monasteries—leave them alone." This was a wonderful advice that Abu Bakar Siddique gave to Yazeed.

Lessons could be learned: (1) Being a leader, you will be held accountable for what you do. To test and try. If performing well, I will give you more. If not, I shall change you. This is not for life. (2) Faith of ALLAH is most important. Fear ALLAH. (3) Warning about nationalism and tribalism. Yazeed bin Sufyan came from a very prominent family in Quraish. His father, Abu Sufyan, was a leader of Quraish, and he was the one who fought the messenger of ALLAH for a greater part of his life, but Abu Sufyan became a Muslim when Mecca was opened. Abu Bakar Siddique was pointing his son Yazeed to lead the Muslim army. Abu Bakar Siddique was warning him from any remnants of Jaheeliya that would still be in the heart of new Muslims. Now it was a brotherhood of Islam. Abu Bakar Siddique told him to be brief with soldiers when speaking to them. "Do not give them long reminders." This is good for every speaker. Do not give long reminders because the latter part will make you forget the earlier part. Be brief especially when you are delivering to them instructions.

Then Abu Bakar Siddique said, "Take care of yourself first." As a Khalifa, he was teaching the leaders that "If you want your soldiers to improve, then you have to improve yourself first. If you have faith, they will have faith." (6) The importance of Salat. Abu Bakar Siddique was sending out an army to fight an enemy. Victory comes through Ibadat. (7) Kindness toward envoys of enemies. Keep them among strong forces. Do not allow anybody to speak to them and allow them to stay for short periods. (8) Shohra only works with honesty and truth. Tell them the whole story. (9) Intermingling with army. Nighttime is a good time to investigate. (10) Guarding the

Muslim army. (11) The importance of good company. (12) The handling of money.

When Khaleeb bin Hasna was setting out, he said, "Did you hear my instructions to Yazeed?"

He said, "Yes!"

Then Abu Bakar Siddique told them to follow that and a few more. Be patient when you meet your enemy. Patience is the key. ALLAH says, "Be patient and do your enemy in patience."

This is the story about Anthara. He is a legendary figure in courage and bravery.

Anthara was asked, "How are you always winning against your enemy?"

Anthara said, "I shall tell you the reason. You stick your finger in my mouth and I shall stick my finger in your mouth and then we shall both bite."

They agreed, and now both were biting each other's fingers. The man, after a while, screamed and gave up.

Anthara said, "If you had just waited for just one more moment, I would have given up. This is how I am always winning against my enemies. It is that one moment when you outdo your enemy that makes it or breaks it."

Second advice is to visit the injured and sick and attend funerals. The leaders should be part of the people. Finally, remember ALLAH a lot. Amar bin Aas was appointed to Oman. Amar bin Aas was appointed as the governor of Oman by Rasool ALLAH. When Redha apostacy happened, they moved out, but Abu Bakar sent him a letter:

> I have restored you to the office to which the
> messenger of ALLAH appointed you. But I would
> offer you the preferable life here and Akhrat. But
> the choice is yours. Saying I have something bet-
> ter for you.

Abu Bakar did not want to change the post of anyone who had been appointed by Rasool ALLAH unless there was something better. Abu Bakar Siddique did not fire anybody who was appointed by

Rasool ALLAH. What Abu Bakar Siddique had in mind was opening of Palestine. That was a better position for Amar bin Aas in Duneya and Akhrat.

Amar bin Aas replied and said, "I am one of the arrows of Islam, and after ALLAH, you shoot them and collect them. Look for the strongest target, and aim me at it. I shall die your soldier." Abu Bakar Siddique called him to Madina and appointed him the leader of the army which is going to Palestine. Now four armies took separate routes to Shaam, and Heracle, sensing the danger, set a base in Intakiya and also, in turn, arranged his armies. He also sent out four armies to descend on the four armies of sahaba. The first army led by his brother Theodour had ninety thousand soldiers, and they were to meet Amar bin Aas and his army of seven thousand—seven thousand against ninety thousand.

George, the son of Theodour, was to meet Yazeed. No numbers were given. Another army to meet Shirqeeb bin Hasna and another army, sixty thousand, to meet Amar bin Jarah Abu Abida. These were huge armies. When Sahaba, the leaders of Muslim armies, saw the enemy numbers, they started sending letters to Khalifa for help for reinforcements. They were all asking for help. Khalifa was receiving so many messages from the generals from the field.

Abu Abida sent a letter, saying,

> In the name of ALLAH compassionate and merciful, to servant of ALLAH. Abu Bakar the successor to the messenger of ALLAH. From Abu Abida Amar bin Jarah, Asalaam'o'Alaikum. I praise ALLAH and ask ALLAH to grant victory to Muslims. I received news that Heracle, the kings of Romans has set base in Shaam in a town called Intakiya. He has sent out his people and mobilized them. They responded to his call in great numbers. I want to inform you this to give us your opinion. Asalaam'o'Alaikum Wa Rehmatullah Wa Barakatu.

Two things were set out in this letter: (1) Heracle is in Intakiya, meaning Herculous was so serious about this that he has moved out of his capital, Constaple. He came out to Intakiya to be close to the field of operations, so Romans were taking this very seriously. (2) He sent out the people of his kingdom, calling them, and they had flooded from every direction in huge numbers. These were the two things in the letter.

Abu Bakar Siddique sent a letter back:

> In the name of ALLAH all compassionate and merciful. I have received your letter about the king of Romans, what he has done in regard to his setting base in Intakiya. It is his defeat and your victory.

Abu Bakar Siddique was a leader who had confidence of victory in ALLAH. He wanted to give the confidence in the hearts of the leaders who were leading this battle. Abu Bakar Siddique was in charge of a very difficult campaign. First of all, this was not the only thing he was doing. He was running two campaigns—one in Iraq against the Persian Empire and a second in Shaam against the Roman Empire. He had to deal with two fronts at the same time and also was running low in terms of resources. He did not have any more fighting forces, and in terms of finances, the treasury was empty.

The situation was very difficult, and only a very strong, competent leader could deal with the situation. Firstly, it was all voluntary; he did not have to send these armies. The Romans were not an imminent threat for Madina. He could have waited, but Abu Bakar Siddique didn't want to waste a second without spreading the message of ALLAH. As we know, he told Umar bin Khitab what he did on the day Rasool ALLAH passed away, meaning "Do not allow any catastrophe to stop you from what ALLAH has appointed you for. Even the messenger of ALLAH has died, and that is the greatest disaster to befall on us. I was still working on the issue of Khalafah. Three days later, I am sending out the army of Usama."

Abu Bakar Siddique wanted to give good hope to Abu Abida.

Heracle is in Intakiya. That is a good a news that he will be defeated and you will be victorious. If he has taken it seriously, it means that he is afraid and that is to our benefit. It shows the positiveness of sahaba. The fact that huge armies are assembling, that we already knew would happen. There is nothing new. We and you already knew and expected that it will happen. People would not leave their kingdom without a fight. Romans would not just walk out of Shaam. Romans will fight with their full strength—that is expected. You have not told me anything new. This is the price we have to pay for Jihaad. But you know that attacking them are men who love death just as they love life. They love Jihaad more than virgin women and wealth. One man is stronger than a thousand enemies. Face the enemy with these men and do not need Muslims who are not with you because ALLAH is with you. Do not ask for any reinforcement.

Abu Bakar Siddique was establishing Aqeeda in the heart of Abu Abida, but then he turned around and said, "Nevertheless, I shall still reinforce you until you are satisfied. Trust in ALLAH."

When Abu Abida read this letter to his army, this was good news for them that uplifted their spirits. Numbers was not a problem. One of them was equal to a thousand of the enemy. Herceles was in Intakiya—that was a good news. That was the end of his kingdom. Four armies were there, and enemy numbers were huge although Khalifa was giving the encouragement.

A letter which went to Yazeed:

All praises to ALLAH. During the time of Rasool ALLAH, ALLAH has given us victories through putting fear in the hearts of enemy and

ALLAH assisted Muslims with angels. And ALLAH is our Lord today and in future.

Abu Bakar Siddique was telling Yazeed the situations that he did not witness. Yazeed was a late Muslim. He did not attend Badar on the side of Muslims. Abu Bakar Siddique was telling him:

> At that time Muslims did not have numbers, but ALLAH still gave us victories. Also the ones who believes ALLAH is one are not the same who associate other gods with ALLAH. A small group can gain victory over a large group if they have Takwa of ALLAH.

And at the end, Abu Bakar Siddique, the Khalifa, told him that "I shall assist you with reinforcements."

Response to Amar bin Aas:

> You have told me that the Romans have assembled huge armies, but ALLAH during the time of Rasool ALLAH has given us victories not through numbers. We used to fight with only two horses at the time of Rasool ALLAH, and we used to take turns on riding our camels. In the battles of Audh, we had only one horse. Rasool ALLAH would ride and then, in turn, give it to us.

Then he told Amar bin Aas, "Yourself and your army should stay away from sins. These were the advices of Khalifa."

Now, what was the plan to deal with this situation? The Muslim armies were faced with very large enemy armies. Although Abu Bakar Siddique told his commanders in the field to seek assistance from no one but ALLAH, he felt that still there was need to reinforce these armies—but there were no other soldiers. He brought out people from all corners. Where else could he get up some soldiers?

The only option was to ask Khalid bin Waleed to split the army in Iraq and reinforce Muslims in Shaam against Romans. That was the only resource he had left. By doing that, the army in Iraq would lack in strength, but Abu Bakar Siddique felt that he could afford that sacrifice. Abu Bakar Siddique wanted to send this army of Khalid bin Waleed to Shaam and finish the job there and the army would go back to Iraq where it belonged.

We have talked about the army half and half between Khalid bin Waleed and Mosneya bin Harisa. Now we shall talk about how Khalid bin Waleed came to Shaam from Iraq. Khalid bin Waleed received this letter from Khalifa, telling him,

Immediately to go and rescue the Muslims of Shaam. Urgent.

And this was after the Hajj of Khalid bin Waleed, where Khalifa reprimanded him never to do that kind of venture again. Then Abu Bakar Siddique told Khalid bin Waleed that

No one will relieve the Muslims like you, and no one will crack the enemy and break the enemy like you.

Khalid bin Waleed received the letter and realized the urgency that he should reach into Shaam immediately. These four Roman armies were a formidable force. For Khalid bin Waleed, time was the asset. If he was delayed, it will be too late. The problem was that all routes from Iraq to Shaam were lined up by Roman garrisons, armies. If Khalid bin Waleed took the normal routes, he had to fight with Roman armies on the way, and that would hold him back. That would delay his assistance to Muslims in Shaam. He needed to get there immediately. Khalid bin Waleed all his desert guides because sahaba did not know this territory, but they had guides.

He told the guides, "I want to go to Shaam behind the enemy lines. I want to dig deep into Shaam without meeting the enemy."

The guides said, "There is no way. All the rational routes are manned by Roman armies. This all we can offer you," but Khalid bin Waleed asked them, "You have to find the way. It is urgent."

The only other route which was never, ever been crossed by any army—this was the path even a lone traveler taking would fear for his life. A lone traveler may take it, but it was difficult and very risky. For an entire army loaded with weapons and equipment, it was impossible, and nobody had ever done this. The Romans had been there for some time—centuries—they never did this. The Persians had been there, and they never did this. Nobody did this before.

Khalid bin Waleed said, "If that is the only way, tell me how to do this."

None of the guides were willing to take responsibility but one guide, Rafah bin Umair. He said, "I could help you with this."

The Muslims were discussing with Khalid bin Waleed. "It could be a disaster on the entire army. Half of the forces in Iraq will perish in the desert."

The guides had given their opinion to Khalid bin Waleed. They told him, "You cannot do it."

Khalid bin Waleed responded, "He, a Muslim, should not care about anything he does if he has assistance from ALLAH on his side."

Khalid bin Waleed was willing to take the risk. He was that kind of a person.

He said, "We should not care about anything if ALLAH is with us. Tell me what we should do, and we shall do it."

Rafah bin Umair said, "O Khalid, if you want us to do this, then give me the strong camels—twenty of them. Deprive them plenty of water to drink. Then cut off their lips, mask them and prevent them from urinating and make sure everybody has transportation. Ask them to load up five days of water, and start with the name of ALLAH."

They started from Crooker, and the destination was Sowa, five days' travel, without any source of water and without any settlements along the way.

"It is very rough terrain. If you can make it from Crooker to Sowa in five days, then there are settlements where you can survive."

They started the journey. Khalid bin Waleed would travel in the morning and at night, doubling the distance by this method. They went through this desert under the guidance of Rafah bin Umair. After five days, they ran out of water. They slaughtered the camels, and horses would drink the contents of camels inside. Then the soldiers would drink from their supplies of water. After five days, Rafah bin Umair told them that they will find water, but he could not see because he had disease in his eyes which temporarily blinded him. After five days, no more water.

"Tell us where the water is."

But the guide could not see, but he was the only one who could give some guidance.

Rafah said, "Look for a particular tree in that area."

They went looking for a tree but could not find it.

Rafah said, "Look again."

They found the tree, but it was chapped, cut. They found the trunk of that special tree.

Rafah said, "Dig next to the tree."

When they were digging, they came to a spring of water.

Rafah told them, "I have never been here except once with my father, thirty years ago." But he knew the tree and water, but now he was blind—maybe the reflection of the sun. There was some poetry:

> May ALLAH reward Rafah, how was he guided to travel all the way from Crooker to Sowa, five days an army marches, it would cry, no one marched there ever before you. This was the first this happened.

Khalid bin Waleed was now in the depth of Shaam. It was a surprise for the Romans. How could he make it with such speed? How could he make it unnoticed? What happened to all-over garrisons and military parts on the way? The Romans had been there for centuries. They knew the traditional routes were protected. Now they found Khalid bin Waleed with his army in their midst, and they already had heard the reputation of Khalid bin Waleed. For them, this was a miracle. They were hearing all their stories about Khalid bin Waleed. Now these stories were confirmed. "Khalid bin Waleed landed from out of nowhere in the middle of our land with such speed and unnoticed." That just struck fear in their hearts.

Khalid bin Waleed was in Shaam and ready to reinforce the Muslims. He had a plan—"That we should not fight them separately. Four armies are easier to take on than one."

Khalid bin Waleed was a born leader. He told all Muslim armies to join together.

He said, "When your numbers are small, do not fight the enemy separately." Three armies were told to withdraw from all the territory they occupied. "Leave all fronts, and come to Yarmook"—the Battle of Yarmook, present-day Jordan. They would meet Romans in Yarmook. Three armies withdrew successfully—Yazeed, Shriqeeb, and Abu Abida with their armies. Amar bin Aas got banged down in Palestine because the distance between the Muslim army and the Roman army was very short. He could not turn his back without being hit from the rear. He had to manpower slowly.

Khalid bin Waleed had two choices—either to tell Amar bin Aas and they give the Romans a shot, which was ninety thousand strong. Khalid went with the latter. He went in. He rushed into Palestine, joined hands with Amar bin Aas, and they fought the battle, which was a great victory for the Muslims and a disaster to the Romans.

The news reached Herceles. He said, "This is the beginning of the defeat."

Khalid bin Waleed and Amar bin Aas withdrew and moved to Yarmook.

Now Herceles was already sensing the danger. He knew his army would have a hard time standing against the Muslims.

Herceles told his generals, "Choose a battleground with open front but narrow from the back in order to refuse our soldiers the options of retreating. He saw this is the only way to deal with the Muslims. The Roman soldiers cannot stand in front of them. The Romans choose Yarmook; it was open front, and behind them was a cliff. Obviously they would not be able to run away.

Amar bin Aas, when he saw that, said, "Rejoice." Sahaba would find a positive point in anything. "Rejoice. Victory is on its way because they have cornered themselves, and rarely a cornered man ever survives. They have chosen that, and rarely, if someone has chosen a corner for himself, not a good choice for Romans."

The enemy, the Roman army, was 250,000 strong while Muslims, all together, were 40,000 strong. This was a battle of Yarmook. Armies were facing each other. Muslims assembled their army of 40,000 soldiers; the Romans were 250,000 soldiers. Herceles had chosen the battlefield by sending a letter to his brother Theodor, who was also the commander of his armies. He wanted plenty of ground for fighting but very narrow for retreat.

The Romans had some experience of fighting with Muslims. In addition to the narrow back, the infantry, the Romans had every ten soldiers chained together to stop them from running away. It would also make them difficult to move therefore—almost a fixed position. Not all, but a huge number were chained together in groups of ten. They had used that method before. This was the method to force their soldiers to fight.

The Romans chose that, and Amar bin Aas, when he saw it, said, "Rejoice for good news."

The Roman army was divided into squanders. That was their method in fighting. It was not a tradition in Arabia, but first time it was used in Yarmook. Khalid bin Waleed suggested to use this method. He divided the army into squanders. Each squad was made up of a thousand soldiers, about forty squadrons in the army. A leader was appointed over each group. The center, or heart, was made of eighteenth squadrons, about 18,000. This was headed by Abu Abida Amir bin Jarah. The night flank was tenth squadron, ten thousand. This was headed by Amir bin Aas, and Shibreeq bin Hasna was assisting him. The left flank, tenth squadron, was headed by Yazeed bin Sufyan.

In the middle, Khalid bin Waleed placed a small group of cavalry that was very fast in maneuvering, and they were not restricted in their movement. That group was placed in front, and finally, at the rear, he placed a group of five thousand under the leadership of

Sayed bin Zahid. The role of this group was to take care of Muslim families and Muslim property. All of these Mojaheedeen—they came with their families and property, wealth, everything. They could not be left unattended without protection. They were accompanying the army in order to be close. It was not an easy task. It was difficult and risky. It was not like go in the army for six months and then come back. It was a great sacrifice—especially the ones who came from far-away lands. Not everybody had their families with them. They would bring their families and would settle in that land. When Shaam was opened, many of them didn't go back to their original land. They settled there and stayed there. They would invite people to Islam. Their whole lives were given to ALLAH—that was how they lived life of a Mojahed.

This was the formation of the Muslim army. Abu Darja was appointed Qazi to judge for the army. The army had to have a judge to solve the disputes. Abdullah bin Masood was the pay master, dealing with finances of the army. Al Moqaddaro bin Umar was the Qari for the army. This was something started by Rasool ALLAH in the battle of the Badar. Rasool ALLAH appointed Al-Moqaddaro bin Umar to go around the army and recite Surah-Al-Anfaal. He would go around reciting Ayyat from Surah-Al-Anfaal. That tradition was carried on and was employed in the battle of Yarmook. Khalid bin Waleed appointed the same person to do that. Al-Moqaddaro bin Umar did that in the battle of Badar with Rasool ALLAH. There was a motivator for the army, Al-Daaod. He would go around encouraging the soldiers because Shaitaan was going to come. He would remind about the family and also would remind about the wealth. Shaitaan would throw Waswasa in the heart, and there should be someone who would give naseehat. In Surah-Al-Asar,

> ALLAH tells us about the solution to the state of loss that every man is in. The man is in state except those who believe and they do well and they support and advise each other in haq and sabar. In truth which is Islam and encourage each other to be patience. When you see me weak

you up lift me and if see you weak I shall do the
same. Encourage each other to be patience. The
one who would do that for the army was Abu
Sufyan. This is the power of Islam.

Abu Sufyan was the leader of Quraish and forefront against the
messenger of ALLAH all the way throughout his life until the messenger of ALLAH was closed to his death. He turned around and himself
became a Muslim, a very enthusiastic one. Now he was motivating
and mobilizing all the tribes to fight against the enemies of Islam, but
previously, he was encouraging and motivating all the tribes against
the Prophet (PBUH) and Islam. Abu Sufyan would go and speak to
each squadron and gave them a lecture and would go to the women
and gave the lecture as well because women had a very important role
to play. They were not just sitting and being defended by the men.
Women were responsible for the services of the army in addition to
their role in fighting. In the battle of Yarmook, women did participate in fighting. We shall come to it and explain why the women had
to fight.

The general commander was Khalid bin Waleed himself. Khalid
bin Waleed invented this method to divide the army because it was
a large army. This is the first time that the Muslim army was forty
thousand strong. Previously, the army was a small army, and there was
no need to split the army. In the battle of Badar, the Muslim army
was little, over 300 to 313. They did not have to split. With Rasool
ALLAH, the formation used was center, right, and left—that was that.
This carried on, and some of the battles were raids, attacking and
retreating. Now it was the large army that had to be organized.

Khalid bin Waleed gave Khutba before the battle. He said,
"This is a day from among the days of ALLAH. Every day belongs to
ALLAH, but this is a day—it means this is a special day." These battles
were decisive in the moments of history. Many of the battles took
only one day. The battle of Badar was only one day. Audh was one
day. Fatah-e-Mecca was one day, but these battles were life changing
and also changed the course of history.

Khalid bin Waleed was telling them before the battle, "This is the day from the days of ALLAH. There should be no pride in it nor wrongdoing." Now Khalid was dealing with different people from different tribes. Therefore, there was a lot of room for competition, pride, and showing off who was strong and who was brave.

Khalid bin Waleed was saying, "Leave this behind, and this is not the day for wrongdoing. We should stay away from sins every day, but there is a special day. There is also called emphasis. Be careful on this day. Be close to ALLAH than usual. Make your Iklaas. Death is near, seeking by your work." Then Abu Sufyan would go around encouraging the army. One of the leaders of the Romans wanted to meet with Khalid bin Waleed. He came and asked Khalid bin Waleed to meet him. They had a meeting.

Dehaan, the Roman leader, said, "We have heard that you were in search of booty because you are very hungry and destitude people. Therefore, I offer you ten dinar each soldier in addition to new set of clothes and food, and next year, we will give you the same again." (1) It is true that was the reputation of Arabian tribes—that their lives was based on raiding others. (2) Many people cannot understand the motivation behind Jihaad Fee Sabilillah. Until this day, they do not understand. They fail to see that a person is dying for the sake of ALLAH for something greater like Genna and also to please ALLAH. For some people, thinking is limited to this world and cannot go behind that. They do not understand this concept. Why are you killing yourself? How can you do that, take unnecessary risk?

He was saying, "If you are here for money, we shall give you money. Go back to your land."

Khalid bin Waleed responded by saying, "No, this is not why we came. We came because we are people who drink blood, and we have heard the best-tasting blood is the blood of Romans." Walla-Alam. How and why Khalid bin Waleed said that—perhaps because the Roman leader belittled Arabs and Muslims, but Dehaan, the Roman leader, did not like what he heard. Dehaan said, "Yes, we heard that about you—that you are very ruthless people."

That was the reputation of Khalid bin Waleed. The legend of Khalid bin Waleed was developing around him—some of it was true, and some of it was false.

Later on, when battle started, it was narrated in Tabree. A man named Gerga—maybe his name was George but in Arabic Gerga—he was one of the Roman generals. During the fight, he came to Khalid bin Waleed, wanted to meet Khalid bin Waleed. They met.

Gerga said, "I ask you in the name of God, and tell me the truth. Do not lie to me because a free man does not lie."

Khalid bin Waleed said, "I will tell you the truth."

He asked, "Is it true that your Prophet (PBUH) received a sword from God and then he gave it to you. Therefore, you do not lose any battle?"

Khalid bin Waleed could have said yes and built upon the reputation that already existed and carried the legend further and could have promoted it, but he did not. He said, "No, that is not true. What happened is that ALLAH has sent us a Prophet who invited us to the truth. Some of us believed him while some of us fought against him. I was among those who fought against him until ALLAH took us by our hearts, gripped our hearts and us brought towards Islam—and I became a Muslim." Khalid bin Waleed was saying, 'We were his enemies, then ALLAH gripped our hearts and brought us to Islam. It was something from the hearts. Nobody forced us. Mohammad (PBUH) did not force it through our throats. ALLAH brought our hearts to him."

Amar bin Aas, before his death, said, "At one time Mohammad (PBUH) was the most despised person on earth to me. At that time, my greatest desire was to lay my hands on him and kill him if I could, but then ALLAH put the love of Islam in my heart, and Mohammad (PBUH) became the most beloved person to me." He said, "I have so much love and respect for him. I could not look straight into his eyes. I would lower my gaze when I see him."

Khalid bin Waleed said, "ALLAH gripped my heart, and I became a Muslim and then the messenger of ALLAH. (Mohammad [PBUH]) told me that 'You are a sword among the swords of ALLAH, and ALLAH has drowned you out against the disbelievers.' Thus, I am called the sword of ALLAH, and I am the harshest Muslim against non-Muslims."

That was the harshness of Khalid bin Waleed. His ability and his intelligence, his speed, his willingness to take risks has made Khalid bin Waleed the man he was.

We know his adventure to go for Hajj and his decision to cross the desert that no one else has crossed before. That quality is last. Everything is by the attributes of ALLAH. At the end, ALLAH is the one who gives success.

As a Muslim, we cannot succeed in anything without the Tofeeq of ALLAH. We are not attributing anything to their skills. As with Karoon, he did not thank ALLAH for his wealth, which ALLAH has given him. When he was asked, "How did you make your wealth?" He said, "I made my fortunes because of my skills." He did not say that "ALLAH has given it to me"—that is being ungrateful, rejecting the attributes of ALLAH. We say, "Alhamdulillah! Praise be to ALLAH"—what ALLAH has asked us to do, but we have to improve ourselves and have to put the efforts in it. We ask ALLAH for help, and we thank ALLAH for allowing us to be successful. We Muslims have to change. Our Rizaq is going to come from ALLAH.

This Roman general, George, asked Khalid bin Waleed, "What does your religion teach you?"

Khalid bin Waleed said, "We invite you to Islam."

Gerga said, "If we do not accept Islam?"

Khalid bin Waleed said, "Then you must pay Jazeya (tax) and obey the rules of Jazeya."

Gerga said, "If we do not pay Jazeya?"

Khalid bin Waleed said, "Then you will have to fight with us."

Khalid bin Waleed told him the three levels. "If you accept Islam, you become one of us, then Jazeya, and finally, fighting."

Now Gerga asked, "If I accept Islam, what will be my status among you?"

Khalid bin Waleed said, "You will be one of us—equal."

Gerga asked, "Even a later comer is equal to all seniors?"

Khalid bin Waleed said, "Yes, but you become better."

Gerga asked, "How could that be possible then?"

Khalid bin Waleed said, "We have seen the miracles of the Prophet (PBUH). We witnessed with our own eyes—it was obvious for us—but you have not met the Prophet. You did not see him. You did not see his miracles. Nevertheless, you become a Muslim. That gives you a higher status."

Gerga asked, "What is it that one has to do to become a Muslim?"

Khalid bin Waleed told him, "You have to read *Kalma-e-Shahadat*."

Gerga read *Kalma-e-Shahadat* and turned around, changed sides, fought against the Romans and died, was killed in that battle as a martyr.

The Muslim scholars say,

> To die as a martyr does not need any good deeds before it. It is a good deed which is good enough deed of its owner. Martyrs receive a higher level of Guina even though he did not do any good deeds before. No Salat, no Zakat, no Hajj. Nothing but died as a Muslim martyr— that is good enough.

Subhanallah.

The battle started. Khalid bin Waleed told right and left flanks to move ahead. Muslims charged. The difference between then numbers of the Muslims and the Romans were overwhelming. In the beginning, when right and left Muslims armies attacked, the Romans responded. The multitudes of Roman numbers coming forward were difficult to handle; therefore, the right and left flanks retreated. The Muslims retreated so far that the Romans were able to reach the campgrounds of Muslim women, and that was when the Muslim women had to join and fight. The Romans pushed so far back that they reached the fixed campgrounds. Women came out and fought.

The daughter of Abu Sufyan, Wadreya, was fighting. Ami Hakeem was fighting.

The daughter of Amar bin Aas was running to Muslim men, saying, "Shame on you. Are you going to run and leave us?"

Muslim women played a double role. Some fought with swords in their hands, and others were throwing rocks on Muslim soldiers who were running away and encouraged them to go back and fight. This was the role Muslim women played in the battle of Yarmook.

Muaaz bin Jabeel was encouraging the ones around him. Abu Sufyan was going around.

One of the sahaba said, "There was a calmness during the fight, then I heard the voice over to you, 'O ALLAH, come close' time and time again, repeating the same. I wanted to find out who had that loud voice. I went and found Abu Sufyan going around his sons and encouraging every one and praying to ALLAH—that is how enthusiastic Abu Sufyan was in the battle of Yarmook."

There were some improvements, and Muslims started to push them back and, finally, pushed them back to the original lines and original position and now even further back. Now tables were turning. Khalid bin Waleed was heading a group of horsemen of about one hundred, which was very swift and maneuverable. He decided to attack on the left flank of the Roman army. Wallah-Alam. Why he decided that may be due to the location. Khalid bin Waleed made a very strong attack, and it was a heavy blow for the Romans. Six thousand Roman soldiers died in that single attack, so it was a heavy blow to the Roman left flank.

Then Khalid bin Waleed withdrew back and told his men, "In the name of ALLAH, the enemy has patience and strengths more than you have seen. In other words, we pushed them to the limits they cannot do any better. That means we have to push them further to the breaking point."

Khalid bin Waleed attacked again and encouraged the right flank. Amar bin Aas was to attack and push them back to besiege them. Just imagine—forty thousand beseiging two hundred thousand. The Muslim army besieged the enemy army. Wallah-Alam, how Khalid bin Waleed made that judgment—perhaps by looking at their faces.

Khalid bin Waleed said, "Just attack and surround them."

The Muslim army surrounded them from three sides, and the fourth side was a cliff. That was a large army under siege. Khalid bin

Waleed ordered to drive a wedge between cavalry and infantry of the Roman army. They succeed in doing that. Now the cavalry was separated from the infantry. The horsemen were separated from the foot soldiers.

Then Khalid bin Waleed gave his command to Amar bin Aas. He told him, "Open an exit door for the cavalry."

Khalid bin Waleed knew that their will to fight was over now. They just wanted to survive. They had been pushed to the limit, and that was the end of their resistance. Khalid bin Waleed told Amar bin Aas to open up and give them the way out. As soon as Amar bin Aas did that, the cavalry just ran out and went into the desert. Each one was trying to survive. Now foot soldiers had no cover. At the same time, the Muslim army started pushing the enemy further and further back.

Kabrees said that, "As soon as two men out of ten chained together were knocked away or killed, they would drag the entire group." Kabrees said, "Eighty thousand Roman soldiers were plunged from the cliff. The total losses for the Roman army were 120,000 soldiers, 80,000 in the cliff." By now, it was the right time, and soldiers were running away in all direction. Some of them were jumping off the cliff. Also, the men who were chained together, the chains ended up killing them.

That was the prophecy of Amar bin Aas, who said these people have cornered themselves. Cliff and chain—that is about all you need.

Khalid bin Waleed spent the night in the panillion of Theodoor. Theodoor himself was killed. Khalid bin Waleed stayed in the tents of the Roman general. The fight was going on at night. The Muslims were finishing off these soldiers, who were left behind and could not run away. It was a great victory for the Muslims, and that is the reason that day of Yarmook is such a memorable day and a great event in the history of Islam not only because of what happened on that day, but it was a turning point in the Koneeyat of Shaam. Because of what happened in Yarmook, the Romans resistance in Shaam was broken. After that, it was just one city falling after another. Syria Shaam was the gateway to Africa and Europe. That was how Muslims opened Egypt and North Africa. It was a very important event.

Three thousand Muslims died martyr among them. There was many sahaba. One of them was Akram bin Abu Jahil. The situation was fascinating. First, he was the son of Abu Jahil, the worst enemy of prophet Mohammad (PBUH). He was the Feroon of this Ummah. Secondly, Akram himself was not different than his father. Akram bin Abu Jahil was the second most important after Khalid bin Waleed in the battle of Audh. Khalid bin Waleed at that time was fighting against Muslims. That was Khalid bin Waleed and Akram bin Abu Jahil who routed the Muslims and caused the defeat for Muslims in the battle of Audh. Akram bin Abu Jahil was the worst enemy of Rasool ALLAH until Fatah-e-Mecca. One the day of Yarmook, just look at what Akram bin Abu Jahil did.

Akram bin Abu Jahil said, "I have fought against the Prophet Mohammad (PBUH) so many times. Now on this day, shall I retreat? I have fought against Rasool ALLAH so many times. I need to make up for that. On this day, when ALLAH is giving me this chance, shall I retreat?"

To ensure that he will fight till the last moment, he called upon his close associates. He was head of a squadron. He called upon his close associates, among them were his uncle Haris bin Shaam and Daaod bin Asoor, many of the other sahabas.

He said, "Let us give each other a pledge to die Fee Sabilillah. We shall plunge into the enemy army, and since we have made an oath not to live, we shall stay there until we get Shahadat. This is bea baith, pledge to die. We pledge allegiance to die. We are not going to come back alive."

This is one evidence that scholars use for the validity of martyrdom operations. Akram, Haris, and Daaod, they were sahaba, but the total number of group were four hundred. It was used as evidence because they promised to die and to do their best to get Shahadat. The entire group of four hundred were laying down on the battleground. They fulfilled their oath. Some of them were killed, and others were injured so severely that they could not move any further.

They did their best. The ones who survived because they could not move anymore—they fulfilled their oath.

Ladies and gentlemen, you must have heard the stories that in the battlefield some injured people asked for water and each one of them turned the offer down and asked the water should be given to the next person. This actually happened to this group in the battle of Yarmook. Water was given to one. He said, "Give it to my brother. He needs it more than I do." The water would be offered to other person. He would say, "Give it my next brother. He needs it." The water made a full round and came back to the same person, but by the time, most of them were dead. This is an example of no fear, willingness to die for the sake of ALLAH. This is sacrifice for your brother—"He needs water more than I do."

It was a great victory for the Muslims, but the tone of celebration was subdued because the news of Abu Bakar Siddique (RA) Khalifah was announced.

According to the story of Tabree, before the battle started, Khalid bin Waleed received a messenger from Madina. The messenger gave a letter to Khalid bin Waleed, stating that

> Abu Bakar Siddique Khalifa has passed away
> and the new Khalifah is Umar bin Khitab. Umar
> bin Khitab is giving command to Abu Abida bin
> Jarah of the Muslim army. Khalid bin Waleed
> was moved from his post as commander in chief.
> And he was replaced by Abu Abida bin Jarah.

According to Tabree, Khalid bin Waleed concealed this letter and told the messenger not to speak to anyone. In fact, held him in his tent to make sure that he will not leak out the news. Khalid bin Waleed made a judgment that if the news of the death of the Khalifa reached to the soldiers at this critical moment, it was not a good timing. Now the army should be thinking about what was facing them. The battle had not started yet. Khalid bin Waleed did not want to distract them with this catastrophic news—the death of the Khalifa Abu Bakar Siddique. He decided to hide the news until the battle was over. Victory was achieved, then he announced the news to the army. He stepped down and handed over the command of the Muslim army to Abu Abida bin Jarah. That was the last time Khalid bin Waleed had the leadership of the Muslim army.

Umar bin Khitab had decided that the sword of Khalid bin Waleed was too sharp and this was the time to change him. Ibn-e-Tasneya said the reason behind this is if the Khalifah is very strict, he should have somebody under him who is soft; but if the Khalifah is soft, he should have somebody under him who is strict. Therefore, Abu Bakar Siddique and Khalid bin Waleed went together very well. One was lenient, and other was strict. Umar bin Khitab and Abu Abida went together very well because Umar bin Khitab was strict and Abu Abida was soft and compassionate.

Abu Bakar Siddique had a bath shower in a very cold day. He caught fever. This fever was developing day by day, and his situation got worse every day. Abu Bakar Siddique felt that this was the end of his life. The concern was whom to appoint as Khalifah, as his successor. He made Shurah. He invited Abdul Rehman bin.

When he came in, Abu Bakar asked him, "What do you say about Umer?"

Abdul Rehman bin said, "Anything you ask me, you have better knowledge of that." What Abdul Rehman bin was saying was that "You are most knowledgeable amongst us."

Abu Bakar said, "I want to hear your opinion."

Abdul Rehman said, "In my view, Umar bin Khitab is better than what you think." Abdul Rehman knew why Abu Bakar Siddique was asking who was the best person to fit for Khalifah. Abdul Rehman was saying, "He is even better than what you think of him." In other words, "He is the right man for the job."

By the way, Abdul Rehman could be the contender for the job. He was one of the Hashra of Genna. The post of the Khalifah was not going out of the ten if there was someone among the ten living. These ten and the greatest, according to condensers of the Sahaba, are (1) Abu Bakar Siddique (2) Umar bin Khitab (3) Usman bin Unaan (4) Ali bin Abu Talib (5) Abdul Rehman bin (6) Talha bin Abdullah (7) Zubair bin Awam (8) Abu Abida Aamir bin Jarah (9) Saeed bin

Zahid (10) Saad bin Abu. These were the ten. Abdul Rehman bin was one of them.

He was saying, "He is better than you think."

Abu Bakar Siddique then said, "Conceal this matter, and do not tell anybody about this conversation."

Abdul Rehman said, "Of course," and left.

Abu Bakar Siddique invited Usman bin Unaan. Abu Bakar Siddique asked, "What is your view on Umar bin Khitab?"

Usman bin Unaan said, "In the name of ALLAH, I believe what Umar bin Khitab does in private is better than what he does openly," meaning "What we see of Umar bin Khitaab—the greatness— he is better inside, and there is none among us like him."

Abu Bakar Siddique told Usman bin Unaan, "If I bypass Umar bin Khitab, it is not going to get behind you," meaning "If I do not appoint Umar bin Khitab, the post is yours."

Then Abu Bakar Siddique invited Awais bin Khabeer. Abu Bakar Siddique sought his opinion on that.

Awais bin Khabeer said, "I think he is the best after you. He is happy with what pleases Muslims, and he dislikes what Muslims dislike—a man for the Ummah. He cares for the Ummah. His concern is for Ummah. If something pleases Ummah, it pleases him. If something harms the Ummah, he dislikes that. He is not a person who will look for this own benefit to the detriment to the Ummah. He is a person who will live for us."

Everyone whom Abu Bakar Siddique consulted give him the same answer with the exception of Talha bin Abdullah. He was the only who had a different view.

He told Abu Bakar Siddique, "What will be your answer to ALLAH on the day of judgment? When ALLAH will ask you about Umar bin Khitab ,to appoint him to lead us, when you know he is so harsh. Umar bin Khitab—that was his makeup, his personality. He is a very strong man, and he had a great presence that demands respect. His physical stature was huge that added to his presence."

He once knocked the door of Umar bin Khitab. When he did not answer back, Abu Moosay left.

Umar bin Khitab came out and asked Abu Moosay, "Why did you leave?"

Abu Moosay said, "I heard Rasool ALLAH said if you knock three times, ask permission three times, and if permission is not given, then leave."

Umar bin Khitab said, "You are going to bring me another witness that Rasool ALLAH said that."

Abu Moosay left and went to a meeting of Ansaar. Abu Sameed, who was narrating this story, said when Abu Moosay came in, his face was yellow. The color of his face changed.

Then Ansaar asked him, "What happened?"

Abu Moosay said, "Umar bin Khitab has asked me to bring a witness that Rasool ALLAH said that."

Abu Saeed Khadim said, "The youngest among us will go with you as a witness."

The Ansaar, their youngest, would study with Rasool ALLAH while other Sahaba were busy with work. They had stores, farms, and other jobs. They could not spend all their time with Rasool ALLAH, but the youth, because their families were taking care of them, they could afford to spend all their time with Rasool ALLAH or some of the other sahaba who made conscious decisions to do.

For example, Abu Hurairah—he paid the price for that. He said, "I would accompany Rasool ALLAH on an empty stomach." Later on, when Abu Hurairah knew more Hadees, people started asking questions. "How you know more Hadees than the rest? Sahaba who became Muslims before you do not know all the Hadees."

Abu Hurrairah said, "Because they had work to do. They had businesses. They had farms and I had nothing and I would accompany Rasool ALLAH on an empty stomach."

So one of the young Ansaar as witness for Abu Moosay—the point is that was the personality of Umar bin Khitab.

Talha bin Abdullah said to Abu Bakar Siddique, "What will be your response to ALLAH on judgment day?"

Abu Bakar Siddique said, "Are you threatening me by ALLAH? If ALLAH will ask me why did I appointed Umar bin Khitab as Khalifah, I would say, 'Because he was the best among us.' Every person has his personality. There are things you may dislike, but Umar bin Khitab is the best among you." Abu Bakar Siddique took this comment seriously because he was reminding him of ALLAH, what he will say.

In another narration, "If ALLAH asks me why did I appoint Umar bin Khitab? I shall say, 'Because he is strong and trustworthy.'"

These are the two words the daughter of Hazrat Shoaib in Madian used when she went to her father after Moses (AS) provided water for their flock. She told her father, "Why don't you hire that man because the best man to hire is strong and trustworthy?" That was how Hazrat Moses (AS) got a job in Madian. He lived there for ten years. This girl at the time was very young. She was very wise, and ALLAH mentions it in Quran:

> There are the two requirements if you want
> to hire someone.

This is what you should look for in an interview if you ask someone to work for you—strength— not physical but competence in the field of work. Umar bin Khitab was the perfect person for this role. He was very intelligent, very wise, very strong, and very determined. He had solid opinions, he could make decisions, and he demanded respect from people around him.

These are the reasons Abu Bakar Siddique said, "I am going to appoint Umar bin Khitab as Khalifah."

Abu Bakar called Abu Abida to write down the appointment of Umar bin Khitab. Once it was written down, then he had it announced in the mosque. Then he had asked people to give Bia to Umar bin Khitab. This did happen after the death of Abu Bakar Siddique. As soon as Abu Bakar Siddique died, Umar bin Khitab assumed his position as Khalifah. There was no Bia after the death of Abu Bakar. It was already complete. The illness of Abu Bakar Siddique carried on and worsened until the fifteenth day.

Abu Bakar Siddique asked his daughter Aisha, "On what day did Rasool ALLAH die?"

She said, "Rasool ALLAH died on Monday."

Abu Bakar said, "Today is Monday. I think this will be my last day." This was a very interesting statement. Abu Bakar Siddique was very keen on following Rasool ALLAH. His whole Khalafah is an example following Sunnah. He was following Sunnah on things which will cost him and the whole community their lives. The issue of sending the army of O'sama—that was a very serious risk—and then insisting appointing O'sama as a leader and not someone older because O'sama was only eighteen years of age and the fact that Abu Bakar never changed anybody from his post appointed by Rasool ALLAH, and making it clear, "I am a man who will follow Rasool ALLAH and will not call for biddah." He was very insistent and persistent to follow the Sunnah of Rasool ALLAH, and it seemed he even wanted to follow Rasool ALLAH in his death so he expected do die on the same day Rasool ALLAH died—and it happened. He died on Monday, and Rasool ALLAH died on Monday. Rasool ALLAH died at the age of 63. He was following Rasool ALLAH in his life and in his death. His last words in Duneya were "My Lord, take me as a Muslim, and join me with the righteous. Make me join my closet friend Mohammad (PBUH). Make me join the Sahaba who passed away before." These were his last words. He died on the 21st, the thirteen years of Hijra. His Khalafah was two years, three months, and ten days. All of these events, battles, Dowah were done in two years, three months, and ten days.

Umar bin Khitab had the honor of leading Salat of Janazah on Abu Bakar Siddique. The imam prays for the person who dies, makes Duaa, and everybody behind makes Duaa for the deceased. You can imagine Abu Bakar Siddique was wrapped in Kaffan, and Umar bin Khitab led Salat-e-Janazah. Umar was making Duaa for his close friend Abu Bakar Siddique, asking ALLAH to grant him the highest level in Genna, then Umar bin Khitab and Usman bin Unaan and Talha bin Abdullah and Abdul Rehman, him Abu Bakar Siddique. They were the ones who lowered the body of Abu Bakar Siddique in his grave. The grave of Abu Bakar Siddique would be in the room of his daughter Ayesha, right next to the grave of Mohammad (PBUH). Out of respect of the Prophet Mohammad (PBUH), the head of Abu

Bakar Siddique was placed as the level of the shoulders of Rasool ALLAH. He was not put next to him but a little behind.

Abdul Rehman came washing. He wanted to enter into the grave and wanted to lower the body, but he came when the body was already lowered, and his father told him that it was already done. The ones who did that were Umar bin Khitab, Usman bin Unaan, Talha bin Abdullah, and Abdul Rehman bin Abu Bakar. After two years, three months, and ten days, Abu Bakar Siddique succeeded in (1) establishing the rule of Khalifah in Islam, (2) starting the mission of carrying out daraha to the entire world. During the time of the Prophet (PBUH), the Dorah was still within the peninsula. The only exception to that was Gazwa Modiya and Jang-e-Tabooq. Even though Modiya and Tabooq were in the Roman territory, they were part of Shaam.

Abu Bakar Siddique started the mission of Dowah into different nations of the world, the Persians and the Roman people and beyond. He was the teacher and the guide of the Mojaheedeen and the Duaa. He never allowed himself the luxury of spare time. He never allowed himself relaxation. He never allowed himself to benefit from his post.

He had a family. What he was getting was not enough. He neglected them. He was very generous. Before his death, he had some wealth left from his business days before Khalifah. He had pieces of land.

He told his daughter Ayesha, "I want you to sell my property and pay back to Muslims' treasury all that money I took as salary during Khalifah. I have the money to give back to Muslim treasury."

When Umar bin Khitab heard that, he said, "May ALLAH have mercy on Abu Bakar Siddique. He is making it difficult for those who will come after him. He set a standard that is too high. It will be difficult on us. You return all that money even it was Halal for you. It was already less than what he deserved. He had to have money to support his family. Now that he has money left over, he will pay it back to treasury. On that day, all of what was taken by Abu Bakar was returned."

Some loose ends—to start with, Bilal Ibn-e-Zubair, when the Khalifah Abu Bakar was recruiting fighters, spreading to Iraq and Shaam to call the people to Islam and fight in the path of ALLAH, Bilal was watching all this, and his heart was aching.

He went to the Khalifah, then he said, "O' Successor of Rasool ALLAH, you have freed me so that I can be near to yourself, but this is preventing me from what I love to do. Then I shall stay beside you, but if the reason you have freed me was for the sake of ALLAH, and you are going to allow me to choose what is better for me in this life and life hereafter, then please allow me to go and fight Fee Sabilillah."

Abu Bakar Siddique freed Bilal for the sake of ALLAH.

Abu Bakar said, "If your heart is attached to Jihaad, if that is what you want to do, then I am not going to prevent you from doing that. But the reason I wanted you to stay is that you say Azaan and because I shall miss you. However, no doubt, one day we shall be separated. It will be permanent separation, and only we shall meet on the day of Judgment again. Then if we depart and go our different ways, then I advise you, O'Bilal, to do good deeds. It will be your food in this world, and ALLAH will record it for you."

Bilal said, "Jazakallah, may ALLAH reward you for your favors on me." Then he went out with Maseed bin Aamir to join the army.

Abu Bakar wanted Bilal to stay in Madina, but Bilal did not want to make Azaan after Rasool ALLAH. After Rasool ALLAH passed away, Bilal did not want to make Azaan for another Imaam. He was the mozzan of Rasool ALLAH, and he wanted to remain the mozzan of Rasool ALLAH and not be the mozzan of anyone after him.

He made his request to Abu Bakar Siddique, who said, "If this is what you want to do, then you are free to leave."

Bilal Ibn-e-Zubair left and did not come back to see Abu Bakar Siddique because he passed away shortly after that.

Next, the recruits for Jihaad from the south would come into Madina. They would gather there, and then he would appoint them to their specific armies and give them their banners. The meeting place was Madina (congregation). All these tribes' men coming into Madina were somewhat different than the people of Madina. The Sahaba who had spent time with Rasool ALLAH could see their manners, their conduct, their behavior were different. Rasool ALLAH had changed their lives. The longer the period the people would spend with Rasool ALLAH, the more different they became, but now these recruits were new Muslims. Some of them became Muslims during the time of Rasool ALLAH, but many of them had met Rasool ALLAH for a short period. There were a lot of misgivings in Islamic history like all early Futahat were done by sahaba, and that was not correct. If you look at the sahaba, who spent more time with Rasool ALLAH, they were Mohajeeren from Mecca. How many Mohajeeren embraced Islam in Mecca? That was the foundation of Islam. They were a little over a hundred—that was all—but each one of them was equal to an Ummah.

Al-Ansaar were more; they were a few hundreds. The sahaba who were with Rasool ALLAH in Bait-ul-Rizwan were 1,400. The ones who attended Hajj with Rasool ALLAH were 90,000 and the number of sahaba who prayed Janazah of Rasool ALLAH were 124,000.

Our scholars would consider a Sahabi who saw Rasool ALLAH as a Muslim. All that was required to be a sahabi was that person was Muslim and he saw Rasool ALLAH. The question was if a Mushrike saw Rasool ALLAH and later on became Muslim, even a child who saw Rasool ALLAH was a sahabi. At the time of Hajj-Tul-Widah, 90,000 people performed Hajj then left and went home, but people in Madina were most affected by Rasool ALLAH. These new recruits came to Madina. Some of them were rude and some were harsh. There were some problems in Madina, but sahaba were patient.

Abu Bakar Siddique sensed the discomfort of Sahaba. Abu Bakar gathered all of the Sahaba, stands on the pulpit, and said, "I ask you in the name of ALLAH to be patient with these people and if their tongues are sharp not to respond back to them and if they abuse anyone of you, be patient, and do not respond back as long as what they have done does not reach a level of crime that is punishable in Shirah. Overlook their mistakes." Then he said, "These are the men whom ALLAH will use to destroy Herceles and Romans, so it is appropriate for us to be patient and overlook their mistakes."

The Muslims said, "Yes."

Abu Bakar said, "These are your brothers in religion and they are your supporters against your enemies and you have some duties towards them, so be patient with them." Abu Bakar could see the wisdom behind this. These are the people who did not go through training yet, but they were going to be the foundation of Muslim armies. The number of Sahaba was very small. They will fill all the leadership positions, but the foot soldiers were going to be from these recruits. They will be fighting for Islam Fee Sabilillah. "Therefore, we should overlook their flaws and mistakes," and this advice holds true all the time. Fighting soldiers, after some time, develop attributes. Some become harsh. They could turn ruthless after some time—that is something which happens.

Many of these recruits were tribal warriors. They must have been fighting for all their lives. These were the people who responded first to the call of Jihaad. When Abu Bakar was asking recruits for Yamen, these people would come. The soft ones, who are better on the manner side, would stay behind. Therefore, these recruits had harsh attitudes which sahaba did not like. Sahaba represented perfection. They had seldom any weakness in all directions.

Abu Bakar Siddique was saying, "Treat these new recruits with care because we have a greater cause. Therefore, rules should be relaxed a little. Because of these, Islam will spread. Give them time, and they will change."

Next, Abu Bakar Siddique once went to visit a Jewish seminary, a Jewish shawl, where they taught Tora. He went there with invitation to Islam. These were some rabbi teachers. One of them was named Fanhas.

Abu Bakar Siddique walked in and said to Fanhas, "Fear ALLAH and become a Muslim because you know this—that Mohammad (PBUH) is messenger of ALLAH and he came with truth from ALLAH. You find it in Tora and Gospel."

Fanhas responded, "In the name of ALLAH, O'Abu Bakar, we do not need ALLAH but ALLAH needs us and we do not pray to ALLAH but he prays to us and we are rich and he is poor. If ALLAH was rich, ALLAH would not ask us to give charity as your Prophet (PBUH) claims. He tells us not to pay Rehba and then gives it to us. If ALLAH was rich, he would not give us Rehba."

Fanhas was being sarcastic. He was saying, "Mohammad (PBUH) is asking you to give charity, which was an indication that your God is poor."

Abu Bakar Siddique became angry and started beating the face of Fanhas until he injured him. Abu Bakar Siddique said, "In the name of ALLAH, if we did not have treaty with you, I would have to kill you."

Fanhas went to the Prophet (PBUH). This was during the life of the Prophet. Fanhas came to Rasool ALLAH and complained and said, "Look what your friend has done to me."

Rasool ALLAH asked Abu Bakar, "O'Abu Bakar, why did you do this?"

Abu Bakar said, "The enemy of ALLAH has said something great. He claims that ALLAH is poor and they are rich. When he said that, I became angry, and that is why I have beaten him."

Fanhas lied and said, "I did not make that statement."

Fanhas lied. The Quran Ayyat came down in Surah-Al-Imran. ALLAH says, verse 181,

> ALLAH has heard the statement of those Jews, where they said ALLAH is poor and we are rich. We will record what they said and of killing of the Prophet without right. And we say, "taste the punishment of burning fire."

Quran came to agree with what Abu Bakar has said of the man. It happened in Mecca and in Madina where sahaba would give invitation politely but would not accept abuse against ALLAH and the Prophet (PBUH).

Abu Bakar Siddique had fear of ALLAH in his heart. One of the Tajasiheen said, "There is no one who had more fear of ALLAH than Abu Bakar after Rasool ALLAH." By the way, fear of ALLAH is the fruit of knowledge. ALLAH says, "The one who fears ALLAH are the scholars." Therefore, knowledge should lead to having fear of ALLAH.

If a person has knowledge but do not fear ALLAH, then they have not benefited from their knowledge.

One of the Imaam, Ahmad bin Hamal, heard one of his contemporaries. They said, "He does not have knowledge. He is an ignorant man."

Ahmad bin Hamal said, "He has the fruit of knowledge," meaning "Yes, the man does not have knowledge but has fruit of knowledge, fear of ALLAH, so he has already the result of knowledge." Abu Bakar Siddique had so much fear of ALLAH. Sometimes he would say, "I wish I was a tree cut down and eaten, and that is the end and no recognition on the day of Judgment."

In the terms of Imaan, he had the greatest Imaan of Ummah.

One of the Sahaba saw a dream. He went to Rasool ALLAH and said—in fact, Rasool ALLAH asked, "Has anybody seen a dream?" and this man said, "Yes ya, Rasool ALLAH. I saw a dream. I saw a scale that came down from the sky. You were placed on one side and Abu Bakar on the other side of the scale. You are heavier than Abu Bakar, and then Abu Bakar was placed on one side and Umar on the other side. Abu Bakar Siddique was heavier than Umar, and then Umar was placed on one side and Usman on the other side, and Umar bin Khitab was heavier than Usman."

Rasool ALLAH did not like this and said, "It will be Khalafah on the path of prophethood, then it will be kingdom. Rasool ALLAH interpreted the dream the time of Khalafah after him will be short, and after that, it will turn into kingdom. First Rasool ALLAH then Abu Bakar then Umar bin Khitab and Usman, and at the time of Hazrat Ali, the Fitna would have started.

There was another Hadees; this was in Bukhari Shareef. The Imaan of Abu Bakar, Rasool ALLAH, after the salat of Fajar, would talk to sahaba. They would talk about dreams. They would discuss it in one narration. Sahaba would make jokes, and Rasool ALLAH would sit quietly and smile.

One day after the salat, Rasool ALLAH said, "One day a man was with his cow. He mounted his cow. Cow told him, 'I was not created for this. I was created for tilling the land.'"

Sahaba said, "Glory be to ALLAH, a cow is speaking." Sahaba was surprised. "How can a cow speak?"

Rasool ALLAH said, "I believe in this, and so does Abu Bakar and Umar." Then Rasool ALLAH said, "One day a wolf took away a goat from a shepherd. The shepherd pursued the wolf until he released his goat from the wolf. The wolf turns around and says, 'You were able to release your goat from me, but what you will do on the day of the beast when there will be no shepherd but me?' The wolf is saying, 'The time will come when goat and sheep will have no shepherd but us, the wolves.'"

Sahaba again said, "Glory be to ALLAH, a wolf is speaking."

Rasool ALLAH said, "I believe in this, and so does Abu Bakar and Umar."

Abu Huraira was narrating the hadees and said, "Abu Bakar and Umar were not even present. Nevertheless, Rasool ALLAH was saying, 'Myself and Abu Bakar and Umar believe in this.'"

Rasool ALLAH was telling sahaba that "Abu Bakar and Umar believe what I say—even they do not know this. Their Imaan is so high. They do not need evidence. This is a very important attribute of a Momin."

ALLAH describes in Surah-e-Bakra that Al-Motaqeen believe in the unseen. The element of belief is very important. Believe in what ALLAH says and what his messengers say or do. It does not need to be confirmed by other people around you. Abu Bakar Siddique had the greatest Imaan of this Ummah. Abu Bakar Siddique was the most beloved person to Rasool ALLAH.

Amar bin Aas asked Rasool ALLAH—this Hadees is in Bukhari Shareef—"Who is the most beloved person to you?"

Rasool ALLAH said, "Ayesha."

Amar bin Aas asked, "What about among the men?"

Rasool ALLAH said, "Her father out of the women, Ayesha, and out of the men, Abu Bakar Siddique."

It was another Hadees. This Hadees was in Bukhari Shareef.

Rasool ALLAH said, "Whoever will be called from the gate of Salat and whoever will be called from the gate of fasting and whoever will be called from the gate of Jihaad, whoever will be called from the gate of Sadqa."

What did Abu Bakar say? "Is there anybody who will be called from all these gates?" Abu Bakar was expecting invitation from eight gates of heaven.

Rasool ALLAH said, "Yes! And you are one of them."

Abu Bakar Siddique is one of the exclusive groups who will be invited from all the gates of heavens. The gatekeepers of heaven—who are they? The angels, and everyone will try to convince Abu Bakar to enter from his gate. They are competing with each other to have the honor of Abu Bakar entering heaven from his gate. God only knows which gate Abu Bakar will choose.

Ibn-e-Tima said,

> The knowledge of Abu Bakar. It is the con-sences of this Ummah that Abu Bakar is most knowledgeable. That is because he has spent long and exclusive time with Rasool ALLAH. Abu Bakar is the only one who can accompanied Rasool ALLAH in the journey of Hijra. That 11 days long Abu Bakar had the exclusive time with the messenger of ALLAH. Only two of them and only ALLAH knows what conversation took place between them. Also Abu Bakar Siddique was with the Prophet (PBUH) from first day in Mecca. He spent entire 13 years with him. Then Abu Bakar would spend time alone with Prophet (PBUH) because Ayesha says, "Rasool ALLAH used to visit us once or twice every day." He was meeting with Rasool ALLAH on daily basis. It is reported that in Madina Abu Bakar would go to the house of Rasool ALLAH at night. He would spend time with Rasool ALLAH alone throughout the proph-et-hood 23 years. Abu Bakar would get special time with the messenger of ALLAH. Therefore Abu Bakar Siddique have heard somethings

from Rasool ALLAH that no one else has heard. And that makes him most knowledgeable man in the Ummah. Sahaba used to go back to Abu Bakar Siddique. He was their Sheikh. He was the scholar of the Sahaba. At the time of death of Rasool ALLAH that Abu Bakar who brought back everybody to the right course. The place of burial of Rasool ALLAH, Abu Bakar Siddique told them that, "Rasool ALLAH should be buried in the place where he died." The rules of inheritance, even the daughter of Rasool ALLAH, Fatima did not know. That was Abu Bakar who told that Rasool ALLAH said that, "The Ambiya do not leave behind any inheritance" Abu Bakar Siddique had more knowledge than the direct family members of Rasool ALLAH. Fatima and Ali bin Abu Talib, Albas the uncle of Rasool ALLAH was also involved in that. In the case of Khalafah of Quraish. Abu Bakar went and told Ansaar that we were at present when Rasool ALLAH said that leadership is among the Quraish. In the issue of Zakaat, who did not pay Zakaat, the issue was not clear to sahaba whether we can fight them or not. That was Abu Bakar who gave the Fatwa on that issue. In the issue of sending the army of O'sama. Abu Bakar was their reference. Abu Bakar Siddique was also very knowledgeable in interpreting dreams. Sahaba used to give weight to dreams and Abu Bakar had the ability to interpret dreams.

Once a dream was presented to Rasool ALLAH. One of the sahaba said, "I have seen a dream and I saw a cloud and dropping from the cloud was honey and butter. People were taking it. Some were taking a lot, and some were not. Then rope came down from heavens, and you, O messenger of ALLAH, climbed that rope until you disappeared in the heavens, and then a man after you came and climbed. The rope was cut, but it was connected again."

Abu Bakar Siddique said, "O messenger of ALLAH, allow me to interpret it."

We know Abu Bakar would give Fatwa in the presence of Rasool ALLAH. Now we would interpret dreams in the presence of Rasool ALLAH.

The messenger of ALLAH said, "Go ahead."

Abu Bakar Siddique said, "The cloud represents Islam, and honey and butter that is coming down is Quran. Some people are taking a lot, and some are not—that is some people are taking a lot of benefit from Quran and some are not. Quran is honey and butter, the blessing. Then the rope, O messenger of ALLAH, you climbed means you will be elevated in status. Then somebody will come after you. They will be elevated in status and then someone will come and that will be elevated in status." That was the interpretation of Abu Bakar Siddique.

Abu Bakar Siddique asked Rasool ALLAH, "Did I interpret right?"

Rasool ALLAH said, "Part of it was right, and part of it was wrong."

Abu Bakar asked, "In the name of ALLAH, tell me what was wrong?"

Rasool ALLAH said, "Do not swear," and Rasool ALLAH refused to tell him what part was wrong.

Ayesha said she saw a dream where three moons fell down on her house. Three moons descended in her room. Every wife of Rasool ALLAH had one room.

She went to her father and asked, "What is the interpretation of this dream?"

Abu Bakar Siddique said, "If your dream is true, it means that the three greatest men on the face of the earth will be buried in your room."

When Rasool ALLAH passed away, Abu Bakar told Ayesha, "This is the best of your three moons."

To show the interest Abu Bakar had in dreams, Ayesha had told him the dream long time ago, but he remembered it; and when Rasool ALLAH passed away, Abu Bakar said, "This is the beginning of interpretation of your dream." In fact, Abu Bakar said, "For a Muslim man who has complete Wuzzu, seeing a dream is better to me than this and that," meaning "It is very valuable and worth more than a lot of things," meaning "It is a true dream." Also said, "If you see a good dream, then let us know about it."

Abu Bakar Siddique went to Rasool ALLAH and asked, "Teach me a prayer."

Rasool ALLAH said, "Pray O ALLAH, I have committed wrong against myself, and no one forgives sins but you. So forgive me and have mercy on me because you are forgiving and merciful." The admission of sin, the prayer of prophet Younas—it started with admitting the guilt.

"O ALLAH, there is no God but you. Glory be to you. I have committed wrong against myself." Admission of guilt ALLAH likes. Ask ALLAH to forgive—something that ALLAH loves.

Rasool ALLAH said, "If people stop sinning, ALLAH will create people who commit sins so they will ask ALLAH for forgiveness and ALLAH will forgive them."

Next, some general issues about invitation and Jihaad of Abu Bakar Siddique. Why did the Muslims win against their enemies? How did Abu Bakar Siddique and the Muslims defeat the two superpowers of the time, enemies of ALLAH? How were the Muslims able to turn around so swiftly with little over two years and destroy all opponents of Toheed, Arabia then spread the message to Persia, Iraq, and the Roman Empire? The Romans were sending spies to mix within the Muslims. They would send Arabs because they had within their territory Gusaan and other areas; there were Arabs living under Romans. They would send spies because they could go unnoticed as they could speak the language and knew the culture. They would go mix with Muslim armies and report back. Romans would study the reports. The orientals would translate the views of Muslims because it was a new phenomenon for them. They did not know anything like that before.

One of their spies went back and reported to them (Romans) after spending some time among the army of Khalid bin Waleed. He reported, "There are people who pray at night and fast during the day, and if the son of their leader steal, they would cut their hand. If any of them, high or low, would commit a crime, they would be punished. They worship ALLAH night and day and have established justice."

When the army came back from Yarmook, dragging their tales of defeat, they met their leader Herceles. Herceles had lost his brother Theodour in the battle.

He said, "Woe to you. These people—are they now men like you?"

The army said, "Yes."

"Are you more in numbers? Are they more than you?"

The Roman army said, "We are more in numbers."

Herceles asked, "How are you losing? And how are they winning?"

The following are the words and answer they gave to Herceles. One of their elders said, "The reason they are winning and we are losing—because they pray at night and they fast during the day and they fulfill their covenant. They enjoy good and prevent evil and they are just among themselves, but we drink alcohol and we commit adultery and fornication. We commit every sin. We betray our promises. We oppress. We commit wrong and transgression. We commit evil, and we prevent what pleases ALLAH and because we are corrupt in the land."

Herceles said, "You are telling me the truth. Unless the Muslims go back and do what sahaba were doing, the situation of our Ummah will not change."

Another narration, name given to sahaba was that they were fighters during the day and monks at night. There were some questions: What was the purpose of fighting at the time of Abu Bakar Siddique? How did they make invitation? What were the rules for accepting soldiers in their armies? The purpose, according to Abu Bakar Siddique, could be clear from the letters he sent to Yamen for recruitment. He said,

Jihaad should continue against the enemies
of ALLAH until they accept the rules of ALLAH
and follow the book of ALLAH.

Some would say it contradicts the Ayya, where it said, "There is no corruption in religion." When ALLAH is telling the messenger of ALLAH, "Are you going to compel people to become believers?" how can we combine the words of Abu Bakar Siddique and his actions? The way Abu Bakar Siddique attacked apostates and the way he attacked the Roman and Persian Empires. The Roman and Persian Empires did not attack Madina. Therefore, clearly an offensive Jihaad. Abu Bakar Siddique sending his army to Persia and Roman lands and writing letters to them either to become Muslims or pay Jazeya. In some cases, the war, which was initiated by Abu Bakar and later by Umar, were unprovoked.

Rasool ALLAH said, "I was commanded to fight people until they say there is no God but ALLAH and Mohammad (PBUH) is his messenger."

This Hadees Mutwatir, which is the highest level of strength in Hadees, was narrated by Bukhari, Muslims, Burani Al-Hakim, Mosesi, Abu Daaod, Tirmazi, and it was narrated by over twelve sahaba. When we say Mutwatir, it is the highest level. How to combine these two, Ibn-e-Hijar said a few different interpretations of Hadees.

He said, "Rasool ALLAH and who takes after him, Khalifah, should fight the people until they become Muslims or they accept the order of ALLAH, the rule of Quran, which in this case is Jazeya."

The purpose of fighting is to eliminate any opposition to the rule of ALLAH—either people accept Islam or the laws of ALLAH and then can follow whatever religion they want to follow. The laws of ALLAH are dominant, meaning of the Ayya is one cannot force an individual to adopt the religion. Only they have to accept that the earth belongs to ALLAH and the laws of ALLAH should be applied on earth. After that, people have freedom to choose whichever belief they want to choose. What Abu Bakar Siddique was doing—he was following these definitions of Jihaad. He was fighting to eliminate the government of Kufar. Well, many people in Shaam continued practicing Christian religion and Judaism. That is the reason there are all religions in the Middle East. Even after 1,400 years, these religions survive, but they accepted that fact that the law of ALLAH will apply on their land and they have to pay Jazeya to Muslims.

The method of invitation—Abu Bakar Siddique sent a letter to Herceles, asking for his permission for sahaba to go and distribute leaflets in Damascus and Jerusalem, but sahaba were not allowed; therefore, they fought with them. For the invitation, what Rasool ALLAH did, and sahaba followed, was to the leaders of the people—they would go down to Moses but straight to the leadership. Rasool ALLAH would go and speak to the leadership.

When Rasool ALLAH went to Taif, he spoke to the leaders. During the Hajj, Rasool ALLAH would go to tribe leaders directly or send them letters. The acceptance of the leader was taken as acceptance of everyone, and the rejection of the leader was taken as rejection of everyone. Therefore, the war was justified.

When Herceles turned down the invitation of Islam, Muslims had the right to fight all the people, and they were all targets for Jihaad of sahaba. When Qisra tore the letter of Rasool ALLAH, Abu Bakar Siddique sent armies to fight even though the general public did not hear the invitation of Islam.

Next, fighting was the last resort after a person had been through Jihaad-ul-Nafs. There was a lot of preparation before a person can fight Fee Sabilillah.

When Rasool ALLAH was in Madina, when someone came and accepted Islam, he would immediately send them out in the armies. Rasool ALLAH would not take them into the spiritual training session for months until they became ready to participate Maharnee.

A Jew—he was brought up as Jew—came on the day of the battle of Audh. He said, "O messenger of ALLAH, I want to join you."

Rasool ALLAH asked, "Are you a Muslim or not?"

He read second Kalma. "I bore witness that there is no God but ALLAH, and I bore witness that Mohammad (PBUH) is his servant and messenger of ALLAH." He was allowed to join the army. He did not pray, did not fast. He did not know anything about Islam and he died in the battle of Audh and he was counted as a martyr. Maharnee was the best among the Jews. Rasool ALLAH did not tell him to go and have Nafs of Jihaad for a few years.

However, there is an exception to this rule. The original group that represented the foundation of Islam did go through a special preparation time, and that was Mohajeeren from Mecca because religion was just founded. That lasted for thirteen years, but after that, when laws of Sheria were finalized, that was that—the foundation was already there. One doesn't need another foundation. Therefore, with every generation, they had to take the laws of ALLAH. We cannot tell a new Muslim that you can drink alcohol for thirteen years and after that it will become Haram. Fasting was prescribed on you. Fasting was prescribed on you. Same Ayya.

The family of Abu Bakar Siddique: his first wife was Qatila bin Abdul Uzzah. He divorced in the time of Jahileya. There is a difference of opinion later on whether she became Muslim or not. She was the mother of Asma and Abdullah. He was also married to Umar Ayyan bin Umar. She was one of the early Muslims, and she was the mother of Abdul Rehman and Ayesha. His third wife was Isma binte Ameesh. She was the wife of Jaffar bin Abu Talib. Isma made Hijra with her husband, Jaffar bin Abu Talib. We know Jaffar was the leader of the Muslims in Ibn-e-Seena. They stayed there for a long time. They came back during the battle of Khyber, which was toward the later part of Rasool ALLAH's time in Madina, and then Jaffar bin Abu Talib was second in command in the battle of Motaha.

The eighth year of Jaffar bin Abu Talib Hijra was after Zahid bin Harisa. When Zahid bin Harisa was killed, Jaffar bin Abu Taliba took command. He was carrying the flag or banner. His right hand was cut off. He held it with his left hand, and that was cut off, so he held the flag with whatever arm was left, and that was chopped off. He hugged it until he fell down dead at the end.

Rasool ALLAH said, "ALLAH has replaced his two arms with two wings to fly within heaven." So his wife, Isma binte Ameesh, who was with him was left a widow, but it was a tradition among sahaba not to leave any woman single and in need of help; if a woman is divorced or a woman is left a widow or if a woman did not get married early, Sahaba would not leave a woman of her own. Hazrat Abu Bakar Siddique married Isma binte Ameesh, and she was the mother Mohammad bin Abu Bakar.

The fourth wife of Abu Bakar Siddique was Habiba binte Kharja. She was from Ansaar from the tribe of Al-Kharj. She used to live in a place called Sanna, which is in the suburbs of Madina farther away from the center of the town. That was where Abu Bakar Siddique was on the day Rasool ALLAH passed away, and he had a late arrival because he spent that night with his wife in Sanna. She was the mother of Ume-Kalsoom binte Abu Bakar. These were the wives of Abu Bakar Siddique.

His children—the oldest was Abdul Rehman bin Abu Bakar. He became a Muslim late. In fact, he fought against Muslims in the battle of Badar. He was very courageous and a strong fighter of Quraish. He became a Muslim after Sulah Hudaibeya.

Abdullah bin Abu Bakar played a very critical role at the time of Hijra. Abdullah bin Abu Bakar was injured by an arrow during the siege of Taif, but he died during the Khalafah of Abu Bakar Siddique. His injury was critical, but he lived in that injured state for some time. His death was considered as a martyr's because of the injury of that arrow. Later on, the story went that Abu Bakar Siddique kept the arrow. When he was Khalifah, he met with a delegation from Taif. He brought out that arrow and asked them to whom that arrow belonged to.

One of the persons, part of the delegation, not knowing the reason of that question, after taking a close look at the arrow, said, "This arrow is mine. I sharpened it and prepared it and stuck feathers to it, and I shot that arrow."

Abu Bakar said, "This is the arrow which killed my son Abdullah."

The man said, "Alhamdulillah!" That honored him by killing Abdullah and making him martyr. "Alhamdulillah, then ALLAH guided me and made me a Muslim."

Mohammad bin Abu Bakar Siddique's mother was Asma binte Amees. Mohammad bin Abu Bakar was brought up by Hazrat Ali bin Abu Talib because of the relationship. Asma binte Amees was the one-time widow of his brother Abu Jaffar. They had a very close relationship. At the time of Khalafah of Hazrat Ali, he appointed Mohammad bin Abu Bakar as the governor of Egypt.

Asma binte Abu Bakar was the older daughter of Abu Bakar Siddique. She also played a very important role at the time of Hijra. She was called the woman with two belts—a piece of cloth women wrapped around their waist. When she was delivering food to Rasool ALLAH and Abu Bakar Siddique in Ghar-e-Sour, she did not have anything to put the food in. She had two belts and tied food in them and delivered to Rasool ALLAH and Abu Bakar. Rasool ALLAH called her the woman with two belts. This name was given to her by Rasool ALLAH. Asma binte Abu Bakar married to Zubair bin Awam, one of ten people who were given the glad tidings of heaven. Zubair bin Awam was a warrior. He was harsh with Asma binte Abu Bakar. He would ask her to do a lot of work at home. She complained to her father.

There is a story about Zubair bin Awam. He hit an enemy soldier and he split him into two pieces and the sword went down and cut the saddle of the horse. The saddle fell from both sides. The sahaba saw that. Sahaba said, "You have a powerful sword."

Zubair bin Awam responded, "It is the arm which is powerful not the sword."

There was a well-known warrior from Quraish. They used to call him Al-Qabsh. He was big, well-built. He got into a duel with Zubair bin Awam in one of the battles. This man was covered in iron from head to toe. Zubair bin Awam hit him with his spear into his eye—that was the only opening in his armory. He was covered in steel from head to toe with only small holes for him to see through. Zubair bin Awam hit him with a spear in the opening, but the blade of the spear was big and could not go through. Zubair bin Awam pushed it so hard and pushed it with his foot until he got the blade through. He killed the man, and when he pulled the blade out—it was a thick blade—it bent.

Abu Bakar Siddique wanted to keep it as a souvenir. Zubair bin Awam gave it to him. When Abu Bakar Siddique died, Umar bin Khitab wanted to keep it. He kept it, then it moved on from Umar bin Khitab to Usman bin Unaan. Later on, it was inherited by the son of Zubair, Abdullah, who kept it throughout his life in memory.

Asma binte Abu Bakar went to her father, complaining about her husband. She complained that she had to do all this hard work—cleaning the house, looking after the children, making the flour for food, and then feeding his horse—and that was too much for her. She was asking for a servant, some help. Abu Bakar Siddique could have told her to ask for divorce, but he told her, "If a woman has a righteous husband, she will be his wife in heaven. So, my daughter, be patient."

Abu Bakar Siddique knew Zubair bin Awam was one of those who had been given the glad tidings of heaven, so it was an honor for his daughter to be with such a man. He told her, "Be patient," and she was. Asma binte Abu Bakar passed the age of a hundred years without losing any of her mental abilities. She died in Mecca in year 73 after Hijra, and she narrated fifty-six Hadees of Rasool ALLAH.

Next, Ayesha, the most beloved person to Rasool ALLAH. Ayesha was the narrator of Hadees. This Hadees was narrated by Habiba bin Talhabib, the daughter of the beloved person to Rasool ALLAH. In a gathering, he would look at sahaba in the eye and give them attention. Amir bin Aas was a new Muslim. In a gathering, Rasool ALLAH would look to Amir bin Aas and speak to him directly. Amir bin Aas felt that Rasool ALLAH loves him as out of all these people, "Rasool ALLAH is looking at me," meaning he likes Amir bin Aas.

Later on, Amir bin Aas came to Rasool ALLAH and asked, "Who is the most beloved person to you?"

Rasool ALLAH said, "Ayesha."

Amir bin Aas asked, "Who is the most beloved person from men?"

Rasool ALLAH said, "From among the men, her father."

Ayesha was the most beloved wife of Rasool ALLAH after Khadija. Ayesha was married to Rasool ALLAH at the age of six. It is in Bukhari Shareef, and it was a divine marriage. If one believes that Mohammad (PBUH) is a true final messenger of ALLAH, then he should not have any problem in believing this. There are different opinions. It was the destiny of ALLAH. In order that she becomes the greatest woman scholar for this Ummah, ALLAH had destined that Ayesha would convey the Hadees of Rasool ALLAH to the Ummah. ALLAH married Rasool ALLAH to Ayesha at the same age when we put our children to school—at the age of six. She was to become a student of Rasool ALLAH, and for her to fulfill her duty of teaching the Ummah and conveying the knowledge of Hadees to us, she did not have any children. By the age of eighteen to nineteen, Rasool ALLAH had already passed away. Now she could devote her time to teaching the Hadees of Rasool ALLAH. Therefore, Ayesha ranks number four among the top narrators of Hadees. There is no book of Hadees which does not contain the Hadees of Ayesha. There is no book of Fakka which doesn't have Fakka of Ayesha. There is no book of Tafeer which does not contain the Tafeer of Ayesha. She is the greatest woman scholar who ever lived. Ayesha narrated 2,210 Hadees. Bukhari and Muslims agree on 147. Bukhari narrated fifty-four Hadees from Ayesha; Muslims narrated sixty-nine. Ayesha died at the age of sixty-three—the same age as Rasool ALLAH and Abu Bakar—in the year of 57 after Hijra, Umme-Kalsoom, youngest child of the children of Abu Bakar Siddique. She was born after the death of Abu Bakar Siddique.

Before the death of Abu Bakar Siddique, he was speaking to his daughter Ayesha and said, "These are your two brothers, and these are your two sisters."

Ayesha said, "I know my two brothers and here is one sister, Asam, and who is the other one?"

Abu Bakar Siddique said, "The other one is in the womb of my wife Habiba, and I believe that will be a daughter." That was before he died, and it turned out to be as he thought. Few months after his death, his wife delivered Umme-Kalsoom. Umme-Kalsoom married to Talha bin Ubaid Ullah, another person who was given the glad tidings of heaven. In fact, Zubair bin Awam and Talha bin Ubaid Ullah had a very close relationship like brothers; one is rarely mentioned without the other. Zubair and Talha went together and even died together in the battle of Al-Jamal. Therefore, both Zubair and Talha had a family relationship with Abu Bakar Siddique. Umme-Kalsoom did not live with Talha because he was killed in the battle of Al-Jamal. This was the family of Abu Bakar Siddique.

The statement of Ibn-e-Kheer: the great work of Imaam and scholar of Ibn-e-Kheer, the beginning to the end. He started with creation and ended with people entering heaven. The story of creation, the Ambiya and Seera, the signs of the day of judgment, the day of judgment, and then paradise and naar, one of the best works compiled by Muslims scholars.

About the Islam of Abu Bakar Siddique, Ibn-e-Kheer said,

> The first woman who embraced Islam. The first child who became a Muslim is Hazrat Ali bin Abu Talib. The first slave who became a Muslim was Zahid bin Harisa. And the first free man who became Hazrat Abu Bakar Siddique. And his Islam was more beneficial than all of the above. He became a Muslim when he was a noble man in the society. He used his ability, his strength, his skills and his wealth for the service of the religion and for the service of Prophet (PBUH). He was a noble man and a leader among his people.

When Rasool ALLAH invited Abu Bakar Siddique, Rasool ALLAH told him, "ALLAH has sent me to warn mankind, and I invited you to Islam."

Abu Bakar Siddique immediately, without any hesitation or second thought, said second kalma: "I bore witness that there is no God but ALLAH to be worshipped, and I bore witness that Mohammad (PBUH) is his servant and a messenger."

There is a statement—for every horse, there is a stubble. Every horse, no matter how good it is, one day it will stubble. It happens with the best horses, but with Abu Bakar Siddique, that stubble never came with other invitations that were given by Rasool ALLAH to the sahaba, with some of them taking seconds and with some of them taking days. Some of them took weeks, months, and some of them took years. For example, Khalid bin Waleed took years. Amar bin Aas, even the son of Abu Bakar Siddique, took years. Abdul Rehman bin Abu Bakar during Sulah-Hudeybia. As soon as Rasool ALLAH delivered the message, Abu Bakar Siddique became a Muslim immediately.

The question is how? Was that so that Abu Bakar Siddique could change his mind quickly? Was it that Abu Bakar Siddique could bury the argument quickly? But that was not the personality of Abu Bakar Siddique. If one looks at his Khalafah, Abu Bakar Siddique could be as firm as one could be. Abu Bakar Siddique in few instances which stand up against everyone else. He would hold on to his opinion, and at the end, it would turn out to be the right opinion like what happened to the army of Asma bin Zahid and what happened to Qatil Ibretaneed. Many of the sahaba were against their decisions, and they used every argument to convince Abu Bakar Siddique, but at the end, the argument of Abu Bakar Siddique prevailed.

The original question: How did he accept Islam immediately? The reason is because he was ready for it. He may have thought about it. He did not need to sit on it. He did not need to give a second thought. He did not need to wait and consider it. He was already prepared.

Ayesha said, "My father never ever prostrated to an idol."

Abu Bakar Siddique was not a Mushrik. He said, "When I was young, my father took me to idols, and he told me, 'There are your noble gods.' And then he left me." That is how religion is passed on—parents deliver their religion to their children.

The father of Abu Bakar Siddique, Abu Kufah, took Abu Bakar Siddique to idols: "These are your noble gods, so worship them," and then he left his son.

Abu Bakar Siddique was speaking to idols: "Can you benefit me? Can you harm me? Can you eat? Can you drink?" And then he said, "I am not going to worship idols who cannot hear or sleep." He was a child at that time. Therefore, he was ready for it. Well, normally, people who accepted Islam immediately were at some level of preparation. Some people were waiting for it, but they could not get there because they needed a prophet to deliver it to them.

When Abu Zar-Ghafaar left his people in Ghafaar, they were not business people like people in Mecca nor were they agricultural like people in Madina. Their profession was raiding caravans, stealing. Abu Zar-Ghafaar's natural instinct told him this is wrong. He left his people. When he was passing Mecca, he heard the news that there was someone in Mecca who was claiming to be a prophet. He sent his brother Anees to check it out. Anees came back and told him that some people said he was a magician there (about the prophet Mohammad [PBUH]). Some said he was a poet, and some said he was a liar. Some said he was insane, he was possessed by demons, or he was a fortune teller.

Abu Zar Ghafaar said, "You have not done me any good. I shall go and check out myself."

He went to Mecca. He met with Rasool ALLAH, and he immediately became a Muslim. Why? Abu Zar Ghafaar said about himself: "I used to pray to ALLAH years before I became a Muslim. Two years before I became a Muslim, I used to pray to ALLAH."

They asked to him, "How would you do that?"

He said, "I would face any direction and pray to ALLAH however I could."

He didn't know how to pray because to do that, the guidance of a prophet is required, Mohammad (PBUH), but his Fittana was telling him the truth about ALLAH.

Sulaiman Farsi immediately accepted the message from the Prophet Mohammad (PBUH) because he was waiting for it. That was the stage of Abu Bakar Siddique. He was waiting for it; therefore, as soon as the invitation came, he immediately accepted it. If one was waiting for something, as soon as the invitation comes, response is immediate.

Not in terms of Toheed. The character of Abu Bakar Siddique, his makeup, was good from the beginning.

Ayesha said about her father that "My father did not drink alcohol before Islam or after Islam." He did not drink Hum. In another narration, Hazrat Ayesha said, "My father and Usman bin Unaan called alcohol Haram from the time of Jaheliya." The question is why Abu Bakar Siddique would take that position.

Ayesha said, "Once my father was asked by some Muslims, 'Did you drink wine when you were Mushrik?' Abu Bakar Siddique said, 'I seek refuge in ALLAH.' They asked, 'How could you do that?' Abu Bakar Siddique said, 'I used to guard my honor and my dignity because drinking violates the honor and dignity of a person.' Abu Bakar Siddique says, 'One day I saw a man who was drunk. This man would put his hand in filth, dirt, and he would take some of it and would try to eat it. But when he would pull his hand near to his mouth, he would smell the hand and push his hand away. Then he would draw it closer, and smell would repel him. He would keep on like that. The smell would repel him. Otherwise, he would eat from it.' Abu Bakar Siddique said, 'This man has no sense. He lost his mind. That is what alcohol does to people. People lose their mind.' Abu Bakar Siddique said, 'I used to protect my dignity and my honor that was before Islam.'"

Abu Bakar Siddique also had a character of a Dhaia, a caller to Islam.

This was what Ibn-e-Kheer talked about Abu Bakar Siddique when he came in to Islam. He came in with everything he had, put everything on the line for the service of Islam. Soon after he accepted Islam, he was inviting others to Islam. The people he brought in to Islam were Usman bin Unaan, Zubair bin Awam, Talha bin Ubaid Ullah, Abdul Rehman bin Audh, and Abu Abida bin Jarah. Five of them were given the glad tidings of heaven. They became Muslims through the invitation of Abu Bakar Siddique. Well, everything they did, a copy of that will go in to the account of Abu Bakar Siddique on the day of Judgment, and there are many more people who became Muslims through the invitation of Abu Bakar Siddique.

Also Ibn-e-Arkam became a Muslim through the invitation of Abu Bakar Siddique—that was the house where the Prophet Mohammad (PBUH) would meet in Mecca and many others. Abu Bakar Siddique was a blessed man. This relates to the personality of Abu Bakar Siddique.

He was very social, very likable, very approachable, good in his social skills, had very wide social network, very well known all over Arabia. He knew other people and other tribes, therefore opens the lines of communication with other tribes. He was a scholar of gene-alogy in his time. He knew the names of the tribes, their qualities.

Naturally, Abu Bakar Siddique had to go through the persecu-tions. ALLAH tested them and also tested him like everyone else. When the Muslims' numbers came to thirty-eight, Abu Bakar Siddique came to the messenger of ALLAH and said, "Ya Rasool ALLAH, we should proclaim the message publicly." Up to that stage, invitation to Islam was in secret. The Prophet (PBUH) would invite his close associates, people whom he trusted, and would not make any public announcement of that. There was danger and risk in their early days. Abu Bakar Siddique felt that their numbers were sufficient to give the message openly. Abu Bakar Siddique told the prophet (PBUH), "We want to make this message public."

Rasool ALLAH responded, "We are few in numbers."

Abu Bakar Siddique kept on repeating until the messenger of ALLAH agreed.

Rasool ALLAH would listen to the advice of Abu Bakar Siddique. The relationship between them was very close. Only ALLAH knows the conversation between them. Abu Bakar Siddique has not nar-rated many Hadees because he passed away very early, two years after the death of Rasool ALLAH. Abu Bakar Siddique and Rasool ALLAH spent a lot of time together.

Rasool ALLAH accepted the advice of Abu Bakar Siddique where most of the non-Muslims were gathered. Sahaba gathered around in the Mosque. Rasool ALLAH was sitting next to Abu Bakar Siddique while he was standing. Abu Bakar Siddique delivered the speech—that was the first public speech delivered in Islam. Therefore, Abu Bakar was not only the first Muslim and first person after Prophets to enter heaven and greatest Momineen, the first Khalifah, he was also the first public speaker in Islam. He stood up and proclaimed Kalma-e-Shahadat (First Kalma). The response was that non-Muslims attacked; their point of attack was the speaker Abu Bakar Siddique. Non-Muslims also attacked other Muslims, but the focus was Abu Bakar Siddique.

Among the attackers were Adibeya bin Zubair. He threw Abu Bakar Siddique on the ground and took off his shoes. He started hitting Abu Bakar Siddique in the face and pressing the shoes in the face of Abu Bakar Siddique until Banu Naeem, the tribe of Abu Bakar Siddique, came in and interfered and pushed away the attackers and the attack stopped. Otherwise, Abu Bakar Siddique could have died. They disfigured his face, and he could not tell his nose from the rest of his face. He was covered in blood.

They carried him back home, and the men of Abu Naeem, along with Abu Bakar Siddique's father, standing around him thought he would die. Abu Bakar Siddique became unconscious. His face was disfigured. Tribe people went to Adibeya and said, "If our man dies, we shall kill Adibeya."

That would have started the war between Quraish. As we know the tribal system, you kill one of ours, we will kill one of yours—that is how it works. This is serious among tribes.

Banu Naeem was a small clan in Quraish. By the way, they were all non-Muslims. They said, "If our man dies, we shall kill Adibeya." Hours later, Abu Bakar Siddique regained consciousness. What was the first thing he said? "What happened to Rasool ALLAH?"

One can imagine the response of Banu Naeem. They started cursing Abu Bakar Siddique. They said, "You get into this trouble because you followed Mohammad (PBUH). This man has brought disunity among Quraish, and that made them break ties with their kinship."

The situation was that in one family, there were Muslims and non-Muslims that cannot rift from top to bottom in the families. They used to say, "This is the man who brought disunity."

ALLAH has called Quran as Furqan: "It separates from good and evil." That was happening at the level of the families—some people choose Haq and others Baatin.

Banu Naeem were upset with Abu Bakar Siddique. They said, "You get into this because of Mohammad (PBUH), and if you had died, we're going to fight because of this trouble. Now as soon as you regained consciousness, instead of taking care of yourself and your tribe, you are asking about Mohammad (PBUH) while at the verge of death." They became very angry and walked out.

This was very difficult and a lot of pressure. Abu Kufah, the father of Abu Bakar Siddique, left and told the mother of Abu Bakar Siddique to feed him. His mother brought in some food and water for her son.

Abu Bakar Siddique asked her, "How is the Mohammad (PBUH)?"

She said, "I have no idea about Mohammad (PBUH). You eat some food and drink."

Abu Bakar Siddique asked her to go to Amiya Jameel binte Khitab and ask her about Mohammad (PBUH). She went to Amiya Jameel.

She asked her, "My son is asking you how is Mohammad (PBUH)?"

She responded—amazing response from Amiya Jameel. She was a Muslim in secret. She said, "I have no idea about Mohammad (PBUH), and I have no idea about your son." She had to protect herself because Muslims were few. The mother of Abu Bakar Siddique was a non-Muslim. Therefore, Amiya Jameel said, "I have no idea about Mohammad (PBUH) and have no idea about your son, but if you like, I can go to see your son." She wanted to protect herself but was concerned about Abu Bakar Siddique. She came along with the mother of Abu Bakar Siddique. As soon as she saw Abu Bakar in that state, she screamed and she said, "People who did this to you are evil people."

Abu Bakar Siddique asked, "O Amiya Jameel, How is the Prophet Mohammad (PBUH)?"

Amiya Jameel said, "Your mother is here."

Abu Bakar Siddique said, "Do not worry about her. Speak."

Although the mother of Abu Bakar Siddique was non-Muslim, his family was trustworthy.

Amiya Jameel said, "Mohammad (PBUH) is healthy and fine."

Abu Bakar Siddique said, "I am not going to eat anything nor I shall drink until you take me to him. I want to see Mohammad (PBUH)."

At night, they had to carry him because he could not walk. They had to carry Abu Bakar Siddique on their shoulders. It was late at night. As soon as they came in where Rasool ALLAH was sitting with Sahaba, Rasool ALLAH stood up and, seeing Abu Bakar Siddique in that state, kissed him and felt very sorry for him.

What did Abu Bakar Siddique said? "O messenger of ALLAH, I feel no pain. It is only a small injury in my face." He was doing everything for the sake of ALLAH. Abu Bakar Siddique was an example of sacrifice to the limit, giving everything for the sake of ALLAH. One of the sahaba, Abdullah bin Ameer bin Amar, was asked by Tabeen, "What is the worst thing you have seen in persecution of Muslims by the Quraish?"

He said, "Once I saw Quraish non-Muslims attack Mohammad (PBUH) and yelling at him. Then I saw Abu Bakar Siddique pushing them back and said, 'Are you killing a man just because he says my Lord is ALLAH?" This is Nijarish.

There is another narration, maybe the same incident. Asma binte Abu Bakar said, "We are at home. Somebody came to us and spoke to my father, told him to 'Go and help your friend Mohammad (PBUH).' Abu Bakar Siddique immediately rushed." Asma said, "Abu Bakar Siddique had four braids to tie their hairs. He went to help Mohammad (PBUH). He was pushing the people away from Mohammad (PBUH). That was a group of people, and Abu Bakar Siddique alone pushed them away and said, 'Are you killing a man because he says ALLAH is my Lord?' Then those people attacked Abu Bakar Siddique and left Mohammad (PBUH). He fought with them. When came home, his braids and his hairs, wherever he would touch, they fall away."

Sahaba recognized the status of Abu Bakar Siddique as very high and noble. Hazrat Ali, years after the death of Abu Bakar Siddique, was standing on a pulpit when he was Khalifah (Sahaba were grateful people).

Hazrat Ali bin Abu Talib asked his followers the following question: "Who is the most brave and courageous person?"

Hazrat Ali bin Abu Talib was recognized as the most courageous person, and no one will dispute that. His stories of courage are well known. Sahaba said, "You are the most courageous of men." Hazrat Ali bin Abu Talib said, "I have never faced an opponent and last one to one, but the most courageous of men is Abu Bakar Siddique. In the battle of Badar, we limit a shed for Rasool ALLAH. we asked for a security guard on that difficult day, voluntary, and Abu Bakar Siddique was there. I could see him holding his sword in his hand, going around the tent guarding him from every direction. Abu Bakar Siddique is the most courageous of men." Then he said, "One day in Mecca, when enemies of ALLAH attacked Rasool ALLAH from every direction, no one went to help Rasool ALLAH but Abu Bakar Siddique. He pulling people away, saying, 'Are you killing a man because he says, 'My Lord is ALLAH?'"

There is a story in Quran that talks about a very righteous man—Surat Fakhafir—a long story talking about a member of the family of Feroon who became a believer. Quran gives a long narration of this story. Hazrat Ali bin Abu Talib, after mentioning these two events, one in Badar and one in Mecca, started crying. He covered his face with clothes and soaked the cloth in tears because that brought back the memory of Abu Bakar. One can imagine the love that he had for Abu Bakar Siddique.

He said, "I ask you in the name of ALLAH to tell me who is better—the Momin of Feroon or Abu Bakar Siddique."

Everybody was quiet.

Hazrat Ali bin Abu Talib said, "In the name of ALLAH, one hour of the life of Abu Bakar Siddique is more worthy than the whole life of Momin of Feroon." That was Abu Bakar Siddique.

Ibn-e-Kheer stated,

> When Abu Bakar Siddique became a Muslim, his wealth was for the service of Islam. During the invitation in Mecca, Abu Bakar Siddique would use his money to support Mohammad (PBUH) and to support anybody who is in need among the new Muslim community. Bilal Ibn-e-Arabia was cut off from the society around him. He was a foreigner from Africa. Going through servitudes, difficulties with one of the oppressors in Mecca, Adbiya bin Khalf.

Nevertheless, Bilal became Muslims. A foreigner, a slave of one of oppressor of Quraish, he still had the courage to say, "I have witnessed there is no God but ALLAH, and I have witnessed that Mohammad (PBUH) is his messenger and servant." One of the sahaba says, "Every single one weak among the sahaba did give in at one point or at the other to the demands of the people of the Quraish except Bilal. He never compromised or gave in to their demand even though they excured under enulty." Adbiya bin Khalf would have him starved the whole day and then send him out at noon time to the hot desert around Mecca. Would have him lay on his bare back on the hot sand. Then he would order his servants to carry a huge rock to place it on the chest of Bilal and leave him like that. They would warn Bilal, "You will stay there until you die or give up the religion of Islam." Bilal would say, "ALLAH is one. ALLAH is one." Later on Muslims would ask Bilal, "How was your slogan Audh, Audh. ALLAH is one. How did you choose that particular slogan to repeat again and again?" Bilal answered, "Because I realized that that word angers Adbiya most."

Abu Bakar Siddique went out of Mecca to the punishment place of Bilal. He went to bargain and negotiate with Adbiya bin Khalf and asked him, "How long are you going to persecute this man?"

Adbiya bin Khalf said, "It is because of you. Therefore, you take care of this problem. You have caused this in the first place."

Abu Bakar Siddique said, "Would you sell him to me?"

Adbiya bin Khalf said, "Yes."

"Then how much?"

In one narration, it was for forty pieces of gold.

Abu Bakar Siddique said, "I accept."

Adbiya bin Khalf said, "If you had refused, I would have sold him to you for half that price."

Abu Bakar Siddique said, "If you had asked double that price, I would have paid that."

Now Bilal was the possession of Abu Bakar. He said, "Now you are free." Later on sahaba would say this noble man had freed a noble man. They were both noble men. Muslims considered him noble, the Moazzan of Rasool ALLAH.

There was another slave named "Zaneera" Walla-Alam, but it said that she was a European slave. In Arabia, slavery had no color boundaries.

Zaneera was also purchased by Abu Bakar Siddique. He freed her. As soon as she was free, she became a Muslim but lost her sight. Non-Muslims said, "ALLAH and Uzza, their two gods, took away her sight as punishment for her," but it was a test from ALLAH for Zaneera to see how firm her Imaan was.

Zaneera said, "No, that is ALLAH who gives sight and takes it away and not ALLAH or Uzza." Amazingly, she got her sight back when the test was over.

Mohajeeren Ghafar was another slave. Abu Bakar Siddique bought him, freed him, and later on he became a servant of Abu Bakar Siddique and he died as a martyr.

Nadia and her daughter were slaves with one of the non-Muslim women of Quraish. They had to do a lot of hard work. Abu Bakar Siddique offered to purchase them and later freed them.

Then there was Jareya from Banu Adde, the tribe of Umar bin Khitab. Umar bin Khitab volunteered to punish this woman. She was not his slave, but he hated Islam so much he wanted to punish her. He would beat her when he had a break. He told her, "I am having a break because I am tired not because of money on you."

She responded, "That is ALLAH who is giving me a break. ALLAH made you tired."

Abu Bakar Siddique purchased her and freed her. This became a joke among the people of Quraish. They made fun of Abu Bakar Siddique. They considered him a fool. The tradition was that when one frees a slave, that slave keeps a relationship of loyalty with the one who freed them. If a slave is freed out of gratitude, they keep the relationship of protection and loyalty. Therefore, people would free a strong person so they could protect them who freed the slave.

People of Quraish would say, "Why is he freeing women and weak men?" In fact, the father of Abu Bakar asked him, "You are freeing these weak people. You should free some strong people who will help you in the future."

Abu Bakar Siddique said, "I am doing this for the sake of ALLAH and not for the sake of Duneya." These are in surat in Quran. "The one who will be spared from fie who is the most pious over the one who gives for the sake of ALLAH, seeking no payback in Duneya, and ALLAH will please him." ALLAH will make Abu Bakar Siddique happy—a promise from ALLAH.

Rasool ALLAH had given permission to Sahaba to leave Mecca. If the people wanted to go to Jasheya, they were free to go. Because persecution was coming to a level which was very difficult to handle, very many Sahaba left Mecca and went to Jasheya. Abu Bakar Siddique stayed behind, but he decided to leave for Jasheya. He travelled out of Mecca and reached a few days' distance from Mecca. He reached a place called Burkal Gland where he met Ibn-e-Ghaneya, who was the leader of Al-Kara tribe.

Ibn-e-Ghaneya asked Abu Bakar Siddique, "Where are you heading?"

Abu Bakar Siddique said, "My people have driven me out of my land. I want to travel and worship ALLAH. The earth belongs to ALLAH."

Ibn-e-Ghaneya was not from Mecca. He responded to Abu Bakar Siddique, "A man like you of your status—it is not appropriate for him to leave his land nor is it appropriate for him to be driven out because you are a man who assists the needy and he is kind towards his kinship and you are generous toward the guests and you support the poor and you stand up for every good cause. Therefore, go back, and I shall give you my protection."

There was a system in Arabia called legara where one provides protection for someone. The rule is that "I am not going to allow this to be violated even if it costs me my life." Therefore, people used to honor this rule, legara, because people know blood will be spilled if there is a violation of the protection. Ibn-e-Ghaneya taking that position shows how much respect he had for Abu Bakar Siddique even though he was not a Muslim. The reputation of Abu Bakar Siddique was very high. Everybody knew that Ibn-e-Ghaneya wanted to give protection to Abu Bakar Siddique. Just keep in mind—usually people from outside, not Quraish, would not give legara/protection to somebody from Quraish because Quraish were seen in Arabia as the highest race. Therefore, people did not see this appropriate to give legara for somebody from Quraish, but Ibn-e-Ghaneya was willing to take that risk and took Abu Bakar Siddique back to Mecca and said, "I am giving him my protection."

Quraish came to Ibn-e-Ghaneya, told him, "We will not violate your protection, but we want you to make a condition for Abu Bakar Siddique—that he prays at home. We do not want him to pray publicly outside his home because if he does that, he will deceive our women and children. Make him pray at home. We shall honor your protection."

Ibn-e-Ghaneya told Abu Bakar Siddique that this was the agreement. Abu Bakar Siddique accepted the agreement. Abu Bakar Siddique would only pray at home. This was against the habit of Abu Bakar Siddique. He used to pray in public, in front of everyone. After all, he asked Rasool ALLAH to go public with the message after some time.

In order not to break the agreement with Ibn-e-Ghaneya, he would pray in the front yard of his house. It is still within the house, but the public can see him praying. Abu Bakar Siddique was known to have a very soft heart. Every time he would recite a surah ayyat from Quran, he would cry; tears would roll down his cheeks. This was the reason that Rasool ALLAH told people that Abu Bakar Siddique should lead Salat.

Ayesha said, "My father has a very soft heart, and if he prays, he would cry." There Umar bin Khitab should lead Salat.

When Abu Bakar Siddique prayed in the front yard of his house, many children, women, and youth would gather to see him praying. It was an impressive scene. People of Quraish got angry.

They know the power of Salat. They knew if someone was praying truly with Khushnoo and people see him, that would attract them toward Islam. They went to Ibn-e-Ghaneya and reminded him that the agreement was that he did not pray publicly.

Ibn-e-Ghaneya went to Abu Bakar Siddique and said, "People of Quraish are not going to allow you to pray in public. Either you go back in your room to pray or hand over my protection."

Abu Bakar Siddique said, "I am handing you over your protection, and I am happy with the protection of ALLAH."

Remember when we talked about Zaneera, who lost her sight? That was a test. The same thing happened to Abu Bakar Siddique. As soon as the protection was ended and he went to Alkama to pray publicly, one of the non-Muslims (Quraish) came and hit Abu Bakar Siddique.

Abu Bakar Siddique, speaking to Al-Mukhera, told him, "Can you see what this ignorant man is doing?"

Al-Mukhera said, "You brought this upon you yourself."

Abu Bakar Siddique would only say, "O ALLAH, you are so compassionate and merciful." He was beaten up, but he would say, "O ALAH, you are so compassionate and merciful." He prayed to ALLAH for everything. Whatever happens, we say, "Alhamdulillah, all praise to ALLAH. It is all from ALLAH. We belong to ALLAH. ALLAH can do whatever ALLAH wants."

We have talked about knowledge of Abu Bakar Siddique. Rasool ALLAH took Abu Bakar Siddique with him when he went to introduce himself to different tribes at the time of Hajj. Rasool ALLAH would go to different tribes to invite them to Islam and to ask them for protection. Rasool ALLAH did that for some time because Rasool ALLAH was looking for Nashra, protection for religion. He would take along with him Abu Bakar Siddique.

This story was narrated by Ali bin Abu Talib. Ali bin Abu Talib said, "We were visiting different tribes in their camps. Abu Bakar Siddique was the spokesman. He went to a tribe. Abu Bakar Siddique asked, "Where are you from?"

They said, "From Rabiya."

"From which part of Rabiya?"

Answer: "Hajatil Itman."

Question: "Which part?"

Answer: "Dehal Rakbir."

Rabiya is a tribe in Iroque. Subtribe is Hajatil Itman, meaning "great forehead," and then Dehal Rakbir, which means "Dehal the great" and also "Dabeel the small." All these tribes fall under Rabiya.

Abu Bakar Siddique said, "There is a man named Aaoof who said there is no free man in the valley. Does he belong to you?"

They said, "No."

Abu Bakar Siddique asked, "What about Alooz Azaan, the one who would kill the kings? Does he belong to you?"

They said, "No."

He asked about another man, Zardlaf, who had the unique Turban. "Does he belong to you?"'

The people said, "No."

Then he asked, "Are you the maternal uncles of the king of Lunda?"

Answer was no.

Question: "Are you the relatives of the king?"

The answer was no.

After all that, Abu Bakar Siddique said, "You are not from the great Dabeel. You are from small dabeel."

The question he asked showed that he had knowledge about that area. At the end, Abu Bakar Siddique wanted to leave, but a young man from that camp came to Abu Bakar Siddique and grabbed his camel.

He said, "You asked us a question, and we responded. Now it is our turn to ask questions, and you respond. Where are you from?"

Abu Bakar Siddique said, "I am from Quraish."

He said, "Then you are our leader because Quraish are recognized. What part of Quraish are you from?"

Abu Bakar Siddique's theme was Murraha. Theme was seen as a small and weak clan. It is not like a large clan like Banu Hashim or Banu Nakzoom, the family of Khalid bin Waleed. These were the large families. Also Banu Amiya, Banu Taeem was small in numbers, and in a tribal society, strength depends on your numbers. Taeem was a small branch.

When Abu Bakar Siddique said, "From Banu Taeem," that young man said, "You have shown the target shooter where to shoot." He asked, "Aaosiya bin Khilab, the one who defeated all the invaders who wanted to invade Mecca and brought in Quraish and unified them, therefore he was called unifier, is he from your people?"

Abu Bakar said, "No."

"Next question, what about Abilunaz Abd Kunaf, who inherited everything from his father? Is he from your people?"

Abu Bakar Siddique said, "No."

What about Amar bin Abd Kunaf, who used to crush bread into soup for pilgrims and was called Hashim? Are you from his people?"

Abu Bakar said, "No."

"What about Shibatil Hamd?"

"Abdul Mutlib, the one who used to feed the animals in the land and birds in the sea, the man—if you see his face, it is like the moon in dark night. Are you from the people of Ifahda? The ones who take care of Al-Hajj?"

Abu Bakar Siddique said, "No."

Are you from the people of Hajaba? The ones who hold keys for Kaabah?"

Abu Bakar Siddique said, "No."

"Are you from people of Nadava? The leadership of Quraish, the council?"

Abu Bakar Siddique said, "No."

"Are you from the people who provide water for pilgrims?"

Abu Bakar Siddique said, "No."

"Are you from the people who feed pilgrims?"

Abu Bakar Siddique said, "No."

Abu Bakar Siddique was getting a little agitated with all these questions where he had to say no. Abu Bakar Siddique pulled away his camel and started to walk away and left the young man because it was becoming a little embarrassing.

That young man smiled and said in poetry, "Your stream was overcome by my river that breaks it once and overrides another time.

It means that you proved we belong to Daheal Al-Asghar, small Daheal. If you had waited, we would have shown you where you belong to."

Rasool ALLAH saw all that and smiled, laughed. Ali bin Abu Talib came to Abu Bakar Siddique and said, "This nomad Badoon turned out to be a disaster for you."

Abu Bakar Siddique said, "Yes. For every problem, there is a greater problem, and problems are caused because of what we say. I am the one who got into trouble in the first place."

After that, they moved on to another camp. Abu Bakar Siddique said, "These are great people. Let us go to them." These people were from Banu Shabaan. This is a tribe from Iraq. Imam Ahmad bin Hamal was from Banu Shabaan. They, the Prophet (PBUH), and party went to them. Their leaders were there. Abu Bakar Siddique was the one who was speaking. He was the spokesman for the Prophet (PBUH).

Abu Bakar Siddique walked upto them. He asked one of the leaders, Umm-e-Farooq, a question: "How large is your fighting force?"

He said, "Thousand." That was a large number in the desert.

The next question: "How good is your protection?"

He said, "We do our best."

Then Abu Bakar Siddique asked, "What are the results of wars against your enemies, and how strong are you in war?"

Umm-e-Farooq said, "We prefer our horses over our children, and we prefer weapons over our camels. The results of wars with enemies—ALLAH is the one who gives victory. One day we win, and one day we lose."

Because of these questions, the man thought that the person who was asking the questions was the Prophet (PBUH). They had heard about Mohammad (PBUH) and they knew that he was looking for protection and that was where all these questions were leading to.

He, the leader of the tribe, asked, "Are you the man from Quraish?"

Abu Bakar Siddique said, "If you are referring to the Prophet (PBUH), this is him," and pointed to Mohammad (PBUH).

Umm-e-Farooq responded, "We have heard that he claims to be the messenger of ALLAH."

Although they had not seen the Prophet (PBUH), the news about Prophet Mohammad (PBUH) had spread all over Iraq.

Umm-e-Farooq turned toward the Prophet (PBUH) and said, "What is your message?"

The Prophet (PBUH) said, "My message is to call towards ALLAH and there is no one worthy of worship other than ALLAH and I am the messenger of ALLAH," and he recited some Ayyat from Surah-Al-Inaam, talking about virtues of Islam and some things are Halal and some things are Haram. They were very impressed with the Ayyat of Quran. They wanted to hear more.

He said, "Tell me more."

Rasool ALLAH said some more, and Umm-e-Farooq said, "What you have called to it is a very noble message, and the people who have treated you in an evil way are the truly evil people. If this is your message, then the people who are against you are truly evil people."

He recognized from the beauty of the Ayyat, but Umm-e-Farooq did not want to take a decision and to become a Muslim because he had to consult his people and introduce his religious leader, Hani bin Qaboosa, to get his opinion.

Hani bin Qaboosa said, "Yes, what is that you are calling to is a noble message? However, it is not appropriate to join your religion just after one meeting. It will be hastening and unwise, but we shall go back and consult our people. We shall wait, and you have to wait."

He did not object to Islam but could not make a decision then and there. "We have to think about this? We have left some of our leaders back home." Then he turned out his attention to Mosesna bin Harisa. "Listen what Mosesna bin Harisa has to say."

Mosesna bin Harisa said, "I agree with what he said—that your message is a noble message—but we are people who are between two wings."

Rasool ALLAH asked, 'What is that?"

Mosesna bin Harisa said, "On one side, it is Persia, and on the other side, it is the land of the Arabs."

Banu Shaban are on the border of the Persian Empire, and Mosesna bin Harisa said, "Our agreement with the Persians is that we do not give refuge to anybody who has committed a crime. I think what you are calling to, kings do not like. This is the wisdom, and this was out of one meeting, meaning the religion you are calling to, kings do not like this. Therefore, we can promise you the protection from Arab side, but we cannot promise protection from the side of the Persian because they do not forgive. This is an Empire."

Therefore, it was half a deal but better than nothing. In Mecca, Rasool ALLAH had nothing. It was a dead end. In this case, they provided the opportunity to give invitation to one side and not to the other.

Rasool ALLAH said, "Your response was good, but this is a religion that has to be surrounded from every direction. This religion cannot stand unless you offer protection from every side. This issue needs to be protected from every direction with Islam. One does not pick and choose. ALLAH does not want any partner with him. If one gives to ALLAH and to someone else, ALLAH refuses that. All of your heart goes to ALLAH."

That was the end of the conversation, and Rasool ALLAH left Ali bin Abu Talib said, "I have seen that Rasool ALLAH was well pleased with the conduct of Abu Bakar and his knowledge about people."

Next is a very critical part for the whole Ummah, Hijra. Ayesha, ALLAH be pleased with her, said, "One day at noon, in the heat of the day, we saw Rasool ALLAH coming to our house. He was masked. He had turban wrapped around his face."

"Hijra," Ayesha said. "Rasool ALLAH would visit us every day once or twice, but that particular visit was unusual because it was at noon." In Arabia, people usually take a break at noon because of the heat. That was the time when there was no one in the streets of Mecca. Rasool ALLAH came in.

Ayesha said to her father, Abu Bakar, "Rasool ALLAH would not come at this time unless it is urgent and important."

He met Rasool ALLAH, and Rasool ALLAH said, "Clear your house."

Rasool ALLAH had a secret and wanted the house empty.

Abu Bakar Siddique said, 'This is your family. Consider them as your family. Your secret is their secret."

Rasool ALLAH said, "I have been given permission to make Hijra."

The first thing Abu Bakar Siddique said: "Shall I be your companion?"

Rasool ALLAH said, "Yes."

Ayesha said, "I have never seen anyone cry out of happiness like I have seen my father on that day."

Why did Abu Bakar Siddique cry? Just consider the implication of this journey. This is a journey where one risks his life. If caught, the minimum punishment was death. There was no protection but so ever, why feel happy? Also, it is well known that Quraish have the ability to mobilize everyone to search for them. The chances appear very slim just to agree to go with was a big deal in itself for Abu Bakar Siddique. That would have been a great achievement, but for Abu Bakar Siddique to cry with happiness is on a different level. He could be killed within the next few hours, but Abu Bakar Siddique was looking at this from a different angle. Abu Bakar Siddique was thinking that he would be able to spend time alone—in fact, eleven days for Abu Bakar Siddique to drink from the fountain of prophethood exclusively. For eleven days, Rasool ALLAH spent day and night with him. Therefore, Abu Bakar Siddique was very happy.

Abu Bakar Siddique said, "I have two camels ready." He had already prepared two camels for this journey. Rasool ALLAH hired a guide, a non-Muslim, Abdullah bin Arakat. He made an appointment with him after three days to meet them in the Cave Sour, south of Mecca. At the appointed time at night, Rasool ALLAH, with Abu Bakar, left from the back door of the house of Abu Bakar Siddique. Rather than going north toward Madina, they went south and went into hiding in the Cave Sour. Immediately a massive search effort was started by Quraish in every direction. They mobilized all their forces for this purpose. Looking for the Prophet Mohammad (PBUH) and

Abu Bakar Siddique, Quraish already had planned how to deal with this situation. They knew that Hijra was coming. They held a meeting to discuss how to deal with Mohammad (PBUH). It was said that Shaitaan came into that meet in the human form and sat with them.

Someone said, "We should throw him in prison," but Iblees Shaitaan said, "It is not a good idea because his followers will come and take him out. Saying his messages will come out, they will spread, and his followers will come and take him out. This is not a good solution."

Another man said, "We should exile him."

Iblees said, "The words of Mohammad (PBUH) are so sweet. He will find followers, and they will come and invade you."

What else—it was the turn of Abu Jahil to speak. He said, "We should appoint a strong man from each clan, give them swords, and they will attack all of them at the same time and kill him. His blood will be spread over all the clans of Quraish. Therefore, it will be impossible for Banu Hashim to seek revenge because they will have to fight with everybody."

Shaitaan Iblees agreed and said, "This is it. This is a good and right opinion."

ALLAH said, "Quraish are plotting against you to imprison you, to drive you out of your land, or to kill you. They are planning and ALLAH is planning and ALLAH is the best of the planners."

Mohammad (PBUH) and Abu Bakar Siddique were in the Cave Sour, and a massive search was going all over. They were looking in every direction to find Mohammad (PBUH) and Abu Bakar. Just to show you how seriously they were searching, they did reach to the mouth of Cave Sour, south of Mecca. Madina was in the direction of north, but this shows that non-Muslims Quraish are not going to leave any stone unturned. They reached the Cave Sour and just stood on top of the cave and at the mouth of the cave. They were so close that Abu Bakar Siddique was looking at them and seeing their feet.

Abu Bakar Siddique whispered to Mohammad (PBUH) and said, "O messenger of ALLAH, if one of them just looked down, beneath their feet, they will see us."

Rasool ALLAH said, "O Abu Bakar, we are two, and ALLAH is our third." That was when ALLAH revealed translation:

> If you do not aid him, ALLAH has already aided him, when those who disbelieve have driven him out as one of two when they were in the cave, and he said to his companion.

Abu Bakar Siddique is mentioned in Quran as companion. ALLAH had given him the name Shaib, Shaibeen. He told his companion, "Do not grieve. Indeed ALLAH is with us and ALLAH sent down tranquility on him and supported him with soldiers he did not see and made the word of those who disbelieve the lowest while the word of ALLAH that is the highest. ALLAH is exalted in might and wisdom. ALLAH supported Mohammad (PBUH) with soldiers which he did not see. Who are the soldiers? One of them could be the spider; the story of the pigeon—it is weak—but the story of the spider is strong.

The people of Quraish made it with the opening of the cave. They were about to walk in, but someone told them not to go in. There was a spider web at the opening of the cave. If somebody was there, that spider web would have been torn apart so that we, insignificant, fragile spider web, kept away the enemies of ALLAH from Mohammad (PBUH) and Abu Bakar Siddique. Anything can be a soldier of ALLAH. Water can be a soldier of ALLAH that destroyed Feroon. A mosquito can be a soldier of ALLAH that destroyed Namrood. The earth could be a soldier of ALLAH; it swallowed Karoon. Wind can be a soldier of ALLAH that destroyed Audh. Lighting can be a soldier of ALLAH; thunderbolt destroyed Nahood. No one knows the soldiers of ALLAH but ALLAH.

A spider web blocked the entrance to the cave. One can break concrete, but a spider web prevented them from going in. It is not the weapons and strength but qadar of ALLAH. Three days later, Abdullah bin Adotan came. Well, during those three days, how did they survive? Aamir bin Fahara, with his sheep and goats in the desert, would pass by the cave and provide the milk. There is no suspicion he was a shepherd in the desert.

Asma binte Abu Bakar would bring food for them. She was called "woman with two belts." Abdullah bin Abu Bakar—just look at the family of Abu Bakar Siddique. They were all helping one way or another. Abdullah bin Abu Bakar would go in Mecca from one gathering to another, gathering intelligence information. He would go at night and report all that at night. He would spend the night with them. The people of the desert were good at following their footsteps. They could follow the footsteps of Abdullah bin Abu Bakar. He would have Aamir bin Fahara with his sheep follow him that would erase any footprints. He would do that on the way to the cave and back; that was a very elaborate and sophisticated plan. Three days later, the guide Abdullah, a non-Muslim, brought two camels prepared by Abu Bakar Siddique. Now they started their journey, and rather than going through traditional route, they followed the coastal line. The guide knew that path. They went through that part.

It happened in the middle of summer; it was very hot. They would travel at night and rest during the day. The people of Mecca were the enemies and had driven him out, but the people of Madina were waiting eagerly every day. They would go outside of Madina, waiting for Mohammad (PBUH) to come until the sun would become too hot for them. Every day they would go out in the morning and wait for some hours till it was too hot; they would go back.

One day, they came out waiting. When it was too hot, they went back. On their way back, two men appeared in the horizon dressed in white. Rasool ALLAH and Abu Bakar, dressed in white brand-new clothes, could be seen easily in the desert because Zubair bin Awam came back from a business trip. He met them in the way; he had with him new clothes. He gave two sets of clothes—one for Rasool ALLAH and one for Abu Bakar—therefore, they came into Madina wearing new clothes, white.

There was a Jewish man on top of a palm tree or on top of a building. He could see them in the horizon. He said, "O Arabs, your man has arrived—the one you are waiting for."

All the sahaba rushed to their homes and picked up their weapons to guard. This was a ceremonial tradition. That was to greet Rasool ALLAH when he was coming in. It was very formal. They had their weapons and lived up to meet Mohammad (PBUH). Anees bin Malik, one of the Ansaar, said, "I have witnessed two days in Madina when Rasool ALLAH came into Madina and the worst day—when Rasool ALLAH left us."

They all gathered around Rasool ALLAH and Abu Bakar. Some people knew Rasool ALLAH, and some did not. They would go to Abu Bakar Siddique, shaking his hand, thinking that he is the Prophet Mohammad (PBUH). It was not until the shade moved that they were under the shade. Then Abu Bakar Siddique stood up and held a sheet to provide shade for Mohammad (PBUH). Now it became clear that Mohammad (PBUH) was the one who was sitting.

There was a kind of friendship Abu Bakar Siddique had with the Prophet. He was also his servant. He would stand up, holding a piece of cloth, providing shade to Mohammad (PBUH). We can be his servants, as the sahaba were, but we can try to follow him and do the things that he loved. Naturally if one loves the Prophet, he will do what he did, follow him, and this way we can achieve the love for Mohammad (PBUH).

One of the important points is the preparation. Rasool ALLAH visited Abu Bakar Siddique at an unusual time. He was covered to conceal his identity. During the journey, people would come and ask Abu Bakar Siddique, "Who is this man?" He would reply, "He is guiding me." People would understand he was guiding him through the desert, but he used to mean was that "he is guiding me towards heaven." Rasool ALLAH told him, "Empty the house." They left at night and left from the back door. They followed an unusual path. They hired a guide. Abdullah bin Abu Bakar was gathering intelligence for them. Asma binte Abu Bakar would bring food. Aamir bin Fahara covered the tracks with sheep and provided them milk. All of this was a part of the plan. In terms of hiring the guide who was a non-Muslim, what is the ruling on that? There is a statement seeking the assistance from disbelievers. The general rule is that it is not allowed, but the exception is when the following rules apply: (1)

The existence of a strong need to seek this assistance. (2) That this assistance is not at the expense or compromises invitation or any of its means. (3) There exists satisfactory level of trust in the disbeliever, and finally, (4) that it will not cause doubts among the Muslims. If these rules are satisfied, then it is allowed to seek assistance from disbeliever. In all cases, leadership has the upper hand.

Some lessons from Hijra:

(1) The elaborate organization from Rasool ALLAH, Mohammad (PBUH) is a messenger of ALLAH; perhaps he didn't need to follow all these rules, but Rasool ALLAH is teaching us this is Sunnah. This is the right way. He is our example. He is the messenger of ALLAH; we expect that ALLAH will protect his safety. ALLAH told the prophet Mohammad (PBUH) that ALLAH will protect him from his enemies. Mohammad (PBUH) was protected by ALLAH. Nevertheless, Mohammad (PBUH) went through elaborate planning in detail and worked in and out to show us "this is my Sunnah and this is my way and you will not be following Sunnah if you do not follow my ways." ALLAH has created laws of nature. They are laws of ALLAH; nobody will find any change to the laws of ALLAH. We have to go along with the laws of ALLAH.

(2) Abu Bakar Siddique had no idea that he will be companion, but he was hoping to travel with Rasool ALLAH until the last moment. Nevertheless, Abu Bakar Siddique bought two camels and fed them with special food—although expensive but made the camels strong. He did that because he had hoped that one day he will be travelling with Rasool ALLAH. During the battle of Tabooq, Munafiqeen would come and give reasons to Rasool ALLAH that they will not be able to join, which sounded like valid reasons. They kept on coming with different excuses, and Rasool ALLAH excused them.

ALLAH says, "If they were serious, they would have prior preparations for the journey. They waited until the last moment, and then they had some unfinished business."

(3) The whole plan of Hijra was secret. Rasool ALLAH had both public stage and secret stage, and this is important for invitation. Only ALLAH knows what is the future. In the time of Imaam Mahdi, only three hundred people will give him Baith. Surah-e-Kaaf

is talking about the youth who went into hiding secretly. This surah is to be recited at the time of Dajjal.

The messenger of ALLAH and Abu Bakar settled in Madina. Al-Mohajeeren came from Mecca, the most beloved land to ALLAH. Rasool ALLAH, before he left Mecca, stood in a place called Hazoora and looked back at Mecca, his last view of Mecca before Hijra.

Rasool ALLAH said, "In the name of ALLAH, this is the best land of ALLAH and this land is the most beloved land to ALLAH and if it was not that people have driven me out, I would have never left. I will not leave."

Leaving Mecca was not easy. This is a secret land, and Kaabah is in that land. It is something special. Whoever looks at Kabaah and goes around it becomes attached to Kaabah. A momin, if they go around Kabaah, whenever they leave, they feel homesick. Ibrahim (PBUH) made Dua to ALLAH: "Put the love of this place in the hearts of the people." When Ibrahim (PBUH) left his wife and son there, nobody was living in that place. Ibrahim made Dua: "O ALLAH, make the hearts of people to go towards them."

When Ibrahim built the Kabaah, ALLAH made another command, told him to make Azaan, call people for Hajj. Ibrahim was standing in the desert, no people around except Kabaah. ALLAH told him to call the people.

Ibrahim said, "O ALLAH, my voice will not reach to people. There is no one around."

ALLAH said, "You make the call, and I shall convey the message."

Well, ALLAH did convey the message. The invitation of Ibrahim (PBUH) was given to us by Quran. Therefore, the words of Ibrahim have reached billions of people. All Ibrahim (PBUH) had to do was to make the call, and ALLAH conveyed that call to all of us. People love Mecca, and for Mohajeeren, it is difficult to leave Mecca. In addition to that, Madina was not a popular, pleasant place. It was described to have a lot of stagnant water. Flood water would stay and become very smelly. Many diseases break out in Madina. The residents are used to the environment but a problem for newcomers. When the Mohajeeren came to Madina, they fell sick, and many of them had severe fever. Mohajeeren were home sick, and families were in Mecca; it was a difficult time with difficult feelings.

Abu Bakar Siddique was sharing with Bilal and his servant Fahara. The Prophet (PBUH) told his wife Ayesha to go and take care for them. ALLAH has blessed Mohammad (PBUH). He did not get infected, but other Mohajeeren were going through this.

Ayesha said she went there, and this was before Hijab. "I went to my father and asked, 'O Father, How are you?' My father responded by a line of poetry and said, 'Every one of us is spending the day while the death could be closer to them than the strap on their shoes.'"

Abu Bakar was talking about death, but Ayesha said, "My father does not know what he is saying." The fever was so bad that it was causing hallucinations. Then she went to Aamir bin Fahara, asked him, "How are you?"

He responded, "I have seen death before I can taste it. Even covered will die."

Ayesha said, "He does not know what he is saying." Then she went to Bilal.

He was unconscious. Every time he regained his consciousness, he would sit in the middle of the room and would say, "Will I ever spend the night in valley surrounded by Iskher and Jalil?" These are two plans around Mecca. "Will I ever visit water of Mecca? And will I ever see two mountains of Mecca?" feeling homesick and raising his voice with these lines of poetry.

Ayesha went back to the messenger of ALLAH and told the prophet what she saw, Rasool ALLAH cried because he brought them here. They sacrificed their homes, family, Mecca. They did that for the Prophet Mohammad (PBUH).

Then Rasool ALLAH made dua; it is in Bukhari: "O ALLAH, make us love Madina like we loved Mecca or more. O ALLAH, bless it, and O ALLAH, take the fever out of Madina and take it to Jaffah."

Mecca became blessed through the Dua of Ibrahim (PBUH). At that time, Madina had nothing special to it, but Rasool ALLAH made dua to bless Madina. Rasool ALLAH made dua: "Make Madina more beloved to us than Mecca."

Since then, every believer loves Madina more than Mecca. If you visit Mecca and Madina, once you enter, Madina will feel completely different. Tranquility is in the air. This is in the barkat of dua of Rasool ALLAH. It is a sign of Imaan to love Madina.

Abu Bakar Siddique and other sahaba wanted to go back to Mecca but never went back even when they had the chance to do so. When Mecca was opened, they all went back with Rasool ALLAH to Madina. Abu Bakar Siddique, Umar bin Khitab, and Usman-e-Ghani chose Madina to be their capital, and if the circumstances had not forced Hazrat Ali bin Abu Talib, he would have remained there.

We have finished Mecca era and now the Madina era. We start Jihaad of Abu Bakar Siddique with Rasool ALLAH. Ibn-e-Kheer said it is the consenses among the scholars of history that Abu Bakar Siddique has never missed any of the conquest of Rasool ALLAH. He was there all the time. Many of the other sahaba missed some for different reasons, but Abu Bakar Siddique was always on the side of Rasool ALLAH.

There is another statement by another scholar. He says that Abu Bakar Siddique's name would go side by side with the Prophet Mohammad (PBUH) because he was the friend when he was young and he was the financial supporter when he was old. He carried the Prophet (PBUH) on his own camel, and he provided for the Prophet (PBUH) in that journey. He continued supporting Rasool ALLAH, and he married his daughter to Rasool ALLAH. He was always accompanying him—whether resident or traveler. When Rasool ALLAH passed away, he was buried in the room of his daughter Ayesha. She was the most beloved person to Mohammad (PBUH). Abu Bakar Siddique also led armies that were sent by Rasool ALLAH.

Muslimsa bin Akwa said, "I have been present in seven armies of Rasool ALLAH and nine armies sent out by Rasool ALLAH—sometimes Abu Bakar Siddique as leader, and sometimes he would appoint Usama bin Zaid to be our leader." So Abu Bakar Siddique would lead armies.

Some events happened in the battle of Badar when Rasool ALLAH was seeking the advice of the sahaba whether to go ahead and confront the army of Quraish because they went out for a different purpose. They went to take over a caravan led by Abu Sufyan. This caravan belonged to the people of Quraish, but they ended up meeting the army. Therefore, Rasool ALLAH was seeking the advice of the sahaba on what to do. The first person to speak was Abu Bakar Siddique. Usually when Rasool ALLAH was seeking counsel, Abu Bakar Siddique would speak first. Sometimes other speakers followed him, but sometimes he was the only one to speak, and Rasool ALLAH would follow his opinion.

The most prominent role played by both Abu Bakar Siddique and Umar bin Khitab was as advisors to Rasool ALLAH. Rasool ALLAH was with his army in Badar and Quraish army coming from Mecca. Both armies did not know the whereabouts of the enemy army. There was no appointment. Each army was trying to catch the other. Rasool ALLAH and Abu Bakar Siddique went out to get some information. They walked away in the distance. They met an old nomad, a non-Muslim.

Rasool ALLAH walked up to him and asked, "Have you heard anything about the army of Mohammad (PBUH) and army of the Quraish?"

This man did not know whom he was speaking to. The old man said, "If you tell me who you are, I shall tell you where they are."

Rasool ALLAH said, "If you tell us, we shall tell you."

The old man said, "Someone told me that Mohammad (PBUH) and his army left Madina on such and such date. If the information is correct, now they will be in such and such place." And he pointed out the right position of the Muslim army. That was an indication that he was speaking the truth. "And I have received information that Quraish army left Mecca on such and such date. If the information is correct, they should be in such and such place." After giving this information, now he asked, "Who are you?"

Rasool ALLAH said, "We are from water," and then walked away.

The old man was saying, "What water? Are you from the water of Iraq? River of Iraq?" But what Rasool ALLAH meant was that "We are created from water. ALLAH has made every living being out of water." Then Rasool ALLAH and Abu Bakar Siddique left. In Islam one cannot lie. Rasool ALLAH spoke the truth, but this was the wisdom of Rasool ALLAH that he says something but the listener understands something else. Rasool ALLAH was able to extract the information from the old man. The point is that Abu Bakar Siddique was with Rasool ALLAH. At the time of battle of Badar, Mohammad (PBUH) wanted to fight in the front line with the army, but sahaba said, "No, we shall build a shed for you, and you should remain there. If we lose, you go back to Madina, and there are other sahaba and continue the fight from there."

Rasool ALLAH liked the idea and a shed was prepared behind the lines and Abu Bakar Siddique was the guard, but before that, Hazrat Ali stood at the pulpit and said, "Who is the courageous?" and mentioned the story that Abu Bakar Siddique was carrying a sword and surrounding the tent, protecting Rasool ALLAH from every direction. Rasool ALLAH was making prayer before the battle, standing up, raising his hands, and praying to ALLAH. That was a very lengthy prayer, and Rasool ALLAH was involved in prayer. Rasool ALLAH had a cloth covering his shoulders. Rasool ALLAH raised his hands, praying and very involved in this that the cloth fell down from his shoulders.

Rasool ALLAH was saying, "O ALLAH, fulfill your promise to me because if you decree that this land of Muslims perish, then you will not be worshipped on earth. The only Muslims on the face of the earth are here. This is Islam. If they die, then who will worship you, O ALLAH? The world was very dark, and this was the only beacon of light. The Muslims were in the battle of Badar. O ALLAH, fulfill your promise to me."

Abu Bakar Siddique picked up the cloth of Rasool ALLAH and put it back on his shoulders. Then Abu Bakar Siddique said, "O messenger of ALLAH, that is enough because ALLAH will fulfill his promise to you." Rasool ALLAH went back to the tent, and he fell sleep. Rasool ALLAH slept right before the battle. This happened to Muslims a few times in the battle—they would fall sleep for some time. It happened with them in the battle of Badar. ALLAH says that you slept. This was tranquility from ALLAH. The scholars says if someone sleeps in the battlefield, that is from ALLAH; and if someone sleeps in Salat, that is from Shaitaan.

Rasool ALLAH fell asleep and then suddenly woke up and said, "O Abu Bakar Siddique, rejoice with the victory of ALLAH."

Now Jibraeel came riding his horse. That is the time ALLAH revealed Ayyat. ALLAH says,

> Remember when you asked the help from your Lord and HE answered you. And indeed I shall reinforce you with thousand angels following one and other. ALLAH made it good tidings so your heart is assured thereby and victory is not but from ALLAH. Indeed ALLAH is exalted in might and wise.

ALLAH says, "You ask for help and help with thousand angels," and in other narration, two thousand angels, one following the other. They were led by Jibraeel and Mikaeel, but ALLAH says, "I sent you these angels to give you comfort in your heart."

ALLAH says,

> Victory is from me, you do not need angels for that. I shall give you victory just to please your heart and the hearts of Muslims, I am sending these angels to support you. But victory only comes from ALLAH.

Abu Bakar Siddique joined in the fighting as he would in every battle. Years later, when his son, Abdul Rehman, became a Muslim, he only became a Muslim in the sixth year of Hijra. Abdul Rehman was the last member of the family of Abu Bakar Siddique to become a Muslim. He fought against Muslims in the battle of Badar.

Abdul Rehman told his father when he was a Muslim, "On the day of Badar, you were in my sight." He was an archer, a good one. "You were in my sight, but I turned away because I did not want to kill you."

Abu Bakar Siddique responded: "On the day of Badar, I never saw you. But if I did, I would have killed you."

The Imaan of Abu Bakar Siddique, ALLAH says in Quran,

> Say O Mohammad (PBUH) if your fathers, your sons, your brothers, your wives, your relatives wealth which you have obtained, commerce where you fear decline and dwellings with which you are pleased are more beloved to you than ALLAH and his messenger and his cause, then write till ALLAH executes his commands and ALLAH does not guide the defiantly the disobedient people.

You have to put ALLAH and his messenger and Jihaad for the sake of ALLAH before your sons, your wives, your brothers, your father, your families, your business, your dwellings and relatives. The battle was over; receive victory for Muslims. This was the first battle between Imaan and Kufar when Rasool ALLAH was in the tent, watching the battlefield, and Quraish lost. Saad bin Maaz was with Rasool ALLAH, watching. Muslims were tying non-Muslims in ropes, prisoners of war. The face of Saad bin Maaz did not look pleased.

Rasool ALLAH asked Saad bin Maaz, "It seems you are not happy with what is happening?"

Saad bin Maaz said, "Yes, I am not happy because this was the first day we met Kufar. We should have executed them rather than taking them as POWs."

Seventy of them were taken as prisoners of war, and Rasool ALLAH wanted to know what to do with them. It happened first time.

Rasool ALLAH was seeking counsel from sahaba: "What should we do with these POWs?"

Abu Bakar Siddique was again the first man to stand up and spoke: "O messenger of ALLAH, these are our fathers, brothers, and our relatives. I think we should run some of them because money will strengthen us against disbelief, and maybe one day these people will become Muslims. The battle is over." Abu Bakar Siddique was showing the merciful side. In the battle, he said if he saw his son, he would kill him, but now the battle was over, and he said, "Let us free them. Money will be beneficial for us, and maybe one day they will accept Islam."

The next person to speak was Umar bin Khitab. He said, "O messenger of ALLAH, I do not agree with what Abu Bakar Siddique said. I think you should hand over the relatives of Ali to execute. Hand me over my relatives so that I can execute him, and hand over to Muslims these nonbelievers so that they can execute them until the disbelievers understand that we have no leniency in our hearts towards them."

Umar bin Khitab wanted to execute all these POWs—two different viewpoints opposing each other, difference of opinions. How did Rasool ALLAH deal with them? People have different opinion. This is human nature. The situation is difficult because people disbelieve firmly one side or the other. There is no room for unity or dialogue; it is unfortunate. Differences did exist among sahaba because they were all different. The views are based on knowledge and experience. The experience of Abu Bakar Siddique was different than Umar bin Khitab, and therefore, they saw things in a different color.

The response of the messenger of ALLAH Mohammad (PBUH): "ALLAH makes the heart of some men softer than milk, and ALLAH makes the hearts of some men against the enemies of ALLAH firmer than stone." The analogy of Abu Bakar Siddique is like Ibrahim, who said, "Whoever follows me belongs to me, and whoever does not, ALLAH is forgiving and merciful," and also like Eesa (PBUH), who said, "If you punish them, indeed they are your servants, and if you forgive them, indeed you are exalted in might and wise." Ibrahim and Eesa showed the forbearing and compassionate side toward their enemies.

Then Rasool ALLAH said, "The analogy of you, O Umar bin Khitab is like Nuea (PBUH), who said, "O Lord do not live among nonbelievers inhabiting the earth. Wipe them out. Do not leave any disbeliever," and also like Moses, who said, "Our Lord, indeed you have given Pharaoh and his establishment splendor and wealth in worldly life, our Lord, that they may lead men astray from your way. Our Lord, obliterate their wealth, and harden their hearts so they will not believe until they see the punishment."

Moses said, "Pharaoh and his establishment are using their wealth to mislead people from true path. Therefore, O Allah, destroy their wealth, and harden their hearts so that they do not believe because these people deserve punishment. They do not deserve heaven. These are prophets of Allah, and they view things differently. Personalities are different.

When Ibrahim received the news of destruction of the people of Loath (AS), what did he do? The first thing he did was to argue on behalf of Loath (AS) because Loath (PBUH) was still there and Ibrahim (AS) was worried if the punishment of Allah came on the people of Loath (PBUH). The Prophet Loath (PBUH) and his family were still there. There Ibrahim (AS) was arguing with angels on their behalf. When Sarah (RA) heard the news, the first thing she thought was the people of Loath (PBUH). She laughed. She was happy that the punishment of Allah will come on evil people.

The messenger of Allah then left, and sahaba were thinking, *Maybe he will follow the opinion of Abu Bakar Siddique or the opinion of Umar bin Khitab or maybe he (the Prophet [PBUH]) will follow the opinion of Abdullah bin Rooh.*

Abdullah bin Rooh said, "My opinion is dig a trench, fill it with wood, set it ablaze, and throw them all in."

Rasool Allah came out and said, "We will ransom them."

Rasool Allah followed the opinion of Abu Bakar Siddique.

Next day, Umar bin Khitab came and saw Rasool Allah and Abu Bakar Siddique sitting down and crying.

Umar bin Khitab asked, "Why are you crying? Tell me because if it makes me cry, I shall cry with you. If it does not make me cry, I shall force myself to cry."

Umar bin Khitab did not want to be left out of anything, and remember, in Mecca, when Umar bin Khitab became a Muslim, he wanted to be punished like other Muslims who were being persecuted. Quraish would punish Muslims, persecute them. Well, no one volunteered to torment Umar bin Khitab. He went knocking on doors to find someone to treat him like other Muslims so he could feel like other Muslims, but people would close their doors. Nobody wanted to punish Umar bin Khitab.

Umar bin Khitab wanted to be part of everything that was good. He said, "If I cannot cry, I shall force myself to cry with you."

Rasool ALLAH said, "I have seen the punishment of ALLAH on the top of that tree, and it was about to punish my companions because we have accepted to take the ransom. ALLAH revealed the Ayyat. It is not for a prophet to have captives until he inflicts masacre in the land. You desire the properties in the world and ALLAH wants from you the afterlife and ALLAH is exalted in might and wise. If not a decree from ALLAH that proceeded, you would be touched for what you took by a great punishment. So consume what you have taken as war booty. It is lawful and good and fear ALLAH. Indeed ALLAH is forgiving and merciful."

The Ayyat says it was not appropriate to take captives. Muslims should have killed the enemy because this was the first confrontation between Imaan and Kufar, so Quran supported the opinion of Umar bin Khitab. This is one of the cases where Quran came to confirm the opinion of Umar bin Khitab

Then ALLAH says,

> If it was not decree of ALLAH means that ALLAH says there is no punishment for the people of Badar. This is the decree of ALLAH.

The day of Badar was a special day. There was no punishment for the people who were there on that day.

Later on, Jibraeel (AS) came to Mohammad (PBUH) and asked, "What do you consider the people of Badar among you?"

Rasool ALLAH said, "We consider them as the best amongst us."

Jibraeel said, "The angels who attended Badar are considered the best among the angels. It is not best among humans but also best among the angels. That was a day which witnessed by the creation of ALLAH and the above world. The higher world of the angels—that was a special day. ALLAH has forgiven the people of Badar, and for this reason, ALLAH did not punish them."

Another opinion—why the punishment did not come that ALLAH has made it halal for the messenger of ALLAH and the others the booty of war.

On another Hadees, Rasool ALLAH said, "Five things are made Halal for me, and they have never been made Halal for a prophet before me. (1) I was assisted with fear, a distance of a month (meaning Rasool ALLAH would start marching toward an enemy). The enemy would be terrified even if the enemy is thirty days from me. (2) The whole earth was made a mosque for me. Therefore, pray wherever you can. The other prophets and their followers had to pray in worship places, but for the Ummah of Mohammad (PBUH), ALLAH has made the whole earth a mosque. Therefore, any land is pure. Assume it is pure unless you see filth on it. Unless one sees any filth on the piece of land, it should be considered pure. A Muslim can pray anywhere unless he actually finds filth on it either by smell or by sight of it. Otherwise, assume it is clean. There is a lot of doubt, and that is from Shaitaan. (3) The booty of war is made Halal for me. All the other prophets were not allowed to take it. For example, Bani-Israel—they had to gather it and burn it. For Mohammad (PBUH), it was made Halal. In fact, the messenger of ALLAH says, 'My sustenance comes from beneath my spear.' Sahaba used to consider the most Halal rizq is the booty of war. (4) There are two types of Shifa and greater Shifa. The greater Shifa is only given to Mohammad (PBUH). The minor shifa can be given to the other prophets, can be given to martyr and followers of the Prophet—that is the Shifa. (5) That Mohammad (PBUH) was sent to all mankind while all other prophets were sent to their particular people. These special five qualities were given to Mohammad (PBUH). That was the battle of Badar.

The battle of Audh. Abu Bakar Siddique said, "When we retreated, I was the first person to go back to Rasool ALLAH." Rasool ALLAH and the sahaba were hiding in the mountain of Audh, in a valley. That was how Rasool ALLAH protected the sahaba. They went up to the mountain and Kufaar. Quraish failed to pursue them.

Abu Sufyan came under the mountain, under the place where sahaba were hiding, and he said, "Is Mohammad (PBUH) among you?"

Rasool ALLAH said, "Do not answer."

"Is Abu Bakar among you?"

Rasool ALLAH said, "Do not answer."

Then he said, "Is Umar among you?"

Umar bin Khitab stood up and said, "All three you have mentioned—they are alive and well. ALLAH has saved them to anger you and your people."

The reason for this detail is that Abu Ufyan asked about only three people. He asked about Rasool ALLAH, Abu Bakar, and Umar because they were considered the leaders of the Muslim community—Rasool ALLAH and his two advisers Abu Bakar and Umar.

We move on to Sulah Hudaibia. This was a true agreement between Mohammad (PBUH) and non-Muslims (Quraish). After years of conflict, it happened in the sixth year of Hijra. Battle of Badar was in the second year of Hijra, Audh in the third and battle of Trench in the fifth year of Hijra and Hudaibia happened in the sixth year of Hijra. The people of Quraish sent one delegation after another to negotiate agreement with the Prophet Mohammad (PBUH). The messenger of ALLAH and sahaba came to Mecca with the intention to perform Umrah. The Quraish did not want to allow them in. They said, "We will not allow them to come in by force."

The Quraish insisted to negotiate with Mohammad (PBUH), and this was the first time that Mohammad (PBUH) negotiated with them. Quraish sent delegations, one after another. They sent Urwa bin Masood Istankafi. He was from Banu Sakeef from Taif; he was not from Mecca. He came and saw Rasool ALLAH and sahaba.

He said, "People of Quraish have come out with their women and children and they are dressed in the skins of lions prepared for war and they will not allow you in," and said, "O Mohammad (PBUH), you have gathered around you scum of earth. I can only assume that they will run away from you and will desert you. He had said you have gathered around you scum of earth to go and fight with noble people of Quraish." These were very insulting words.

Abu Bakar Siddique responded by a statement: If you do want to hear it, close your ears. He said, "Go and suck the eliters of Allat"—their God, a very strong statement. Allat is a goddess the people of Sakeef had in the city of Taif. It was a female statue of the goddess. This was a very strong insulting statement. I thought about this statement, whether I should say it as it came or leave it. Then I decided to mention it. Firstly, it is in Bukhari Shareef; one cannot deny the authenticity of it. Secondly, in my opinion, we can learn a lot from this incident. This tells us about the personality of Abu Bakar Siddique, in particular, and something about Sahaba in general.

Ibn-e-Hijar Astalani gave a comment on Bukhari Shareef. He could not skip without commenting on this. He said, "This was a curse that was known among the Arabs. He used a mother instead of Allat in that curse."

Abu Bakar Siddique replaced it with *Allat* that the people of Sakeef used to worship.

People might wonder why Abu Bakar Siddique used these obscene words. When I came to know about this, in the beginning, one might be surprised but when one thinks about this and puts it into prospect, one appreciates what happened. The Sahaba of Rasool ALLAH had certain love for the Prophet Mohammad (PBUH) that we cannot comprehend. Sometimes when we read these stories, we do not understand what is happening.

The statement of Urwa bin Masood was an insult to the Prophet Mohammad (PBUH). He said, "You have gathered the scums of the earth to attack noble people of Quraish." First of all, he was implying that the lowest people were attacking the highest people and also implying the mission of Rasool ALLAH and Rasool ALLAH were failures. When someone says people around Mohammad (PBUH) are O'bash, scums, the scholar is only as good as his students are. You are who your friends are. Anybody who speaks against the sahaba is accusing Mohammad (PBUH) that he is failing in his mission because the sahaba are the product of the invitation of the messenger of ALLAH. The sahaba were harvest of the seeds he planted. Therefore, an attack on sahaba is an attack on the Prophet (PBUH). Sahaba cannot handle anyone insulting Rasool ALLAH.

Another example was when Mardan bin Hukam was the governor of Madina. He was in a gathering, and there was a Jew, Buniya

Moeen; perhaps he was a Muslim at that time because he was in Madina. Mohammad bin Muslimsa, an old man, was also in that meeting.

Mardan bin Hukam asked Buniya Moeen, "What is your opinion about the assassination of Qab bin Ashraf?" Qab bin Ashraf was a Jewish leader in Arabia who had his own fortress closed to Madina. He was one of the mobilizers to distort and fight Islam. He was a great poet. He used all his resources and wealth for this purpose. He was behind the scene to mobilize Arabs and Jews to fight the prophet Mohammad (PBUH). He started crossing the red line. He was describing poetry in which he was describing the women of Sahaba.

To defend the honor of women of sahaba, Rasool ALLAH said, "Who will take care of Qab bin Ashraf? Because he has crossed the line against ALLAH and his messenger."

Mohammad bin Muslimsa volunteered and said, "I will."

Rasool ALLAH agreed and appointed him to go for this special operation to kill Qab bin Ashraf. He went along with five sahaba without going into detail. I have explained in Serat-ul-Nabi. He, Qab bin Ashraf, was killed by these men.

When Murdan bin Hukam asked Buniya Moeen his view on this, Buniya Moeen said, "I think it is treachery." Now he was accusing the sahaba who did this work by being treacherous, but Mohammad bin Muslimsa considered it to be an attack on Rasool ALLAH, and he said, "The one who ordered us to do that was Rasool ALLAH." Then he told Murdan bin Hukam, "Can we accuse Rasool ALLAH for treachery and you are quiet—you do not do anything about it?" Then he told Buniya Moeen, "If I ever see you and I have my sword with me, I shall make you leave without your head."

Mohammad bin Muslimsa was an old man at that time. The narrator of the story says that Buniya Moeen would leave his home unless he knew that Mohammad bin Muslimsa was not in the area. However, the Qadar of ALLAH brought them together in a cemetery graveyard. Mohammad bin Muslimsa did not have any weapon with him. He picked up whatever, like stick, and went to beat Buniya Moeen. He left him motionless but told him, "If I had my sword with me, I would have beheaded you." Sahaba did not tolerate any-body who insulted Rasool ALLAH.

To give you another story, it is difficult to understand. First, we have to appreciate the love of Sahaba for Rasool ALLAH. There was a blind man in Madina. His wife, whom he loved very much, spoke negatively about Prophet Mohammad (PBUH). From time to time, she would insult the Prophet, blame him.

Husband would tell his wife, "Always do not speak against Mohammad (PBUH). Stop that. Do not do it again," but she would not stop and spoke bad about the Prophet.

One day he could not take it anymore, stabbed her with the dagger, and killed her. This story is in Daaud book. Next day people found her dead body.

Rasool ALLAH said, "Whoever loves me should come forward and should speak" because Rasool ALLAH wanted to find out who committed this crime. "Whoever feels he has right towards me, come and tell me who killed this woman?"

The narrator of the story says the blind man stood up, and he was shaking. He came to Rasool ALLAH, but he was in fear, terrified.

Rasool ALLAH asked him, "Why did you do that?"

He said, "O Rasool ALLAH, she used to speak ill about you. I told her many times, but she refused, and this is the reason I killed her."

Rasool ALLAH said, "Her blood is waste. You do not have to pay blood money. You are not punished for that." This shows the love and the sacrifice of the sahaba for Rasool ALLAH.

When Abu Bakar Siddique spoke such words, he was angry and could not tolerate, but this was not his character, and those words he would not use normally. That was once in a life time, and it came out in defense of Rasool ALLAH. Remember, if Abu Bakar was insulted personally, he would not respond in such a way; but because it was targeted at Rasool ALLAH, Abu Bakar Siddique dealt with it in a dif-ferent way. When Abu Bakar Siddique insulted Urwa bin Masood in such a way, this was an insult toward their goddess.

He said, "You have done me a favor in the past. If it is not your favor to me, I would have responded to you."

Favors of Abu Bakar Siddique reached to people even Taif. Rasool ALLAH had done many favors to people—Muslims and non-Muslims—so Urwa bin Masood, said, "If it was not your favors upon me, I would have responded properly."

Urwa bin Masood went back to Quraish and said, "O people of Quraish, I have visited Najashi in his palace, and I have visited Herceles in his palace, Roman emperor, and I have visited Qisra in his palace. I have never in my life seen people who respect their leaders and love them so much. They are willing to give their life for him like the followers of Mohammad (PBUH) treat Mohammad (PBUH). I have visited the courts of the kings around the world. I have seen them, but I have never seen the respect, what sahaba are willing to do for Mohammad (PBUH)."

He did learn a lesson from that. Rasool ALLAH received many delegations, and in the end came Sohail bin Amar, who succeeded signing an agreement with Mohammad (PBUH). The Muslims were not happy with the terms of agreement because they did not see any wisdom behind it, and that was the prevalent view. Muslims were unhappy, and they wished that never happened.

Umar bin Khitab was very outspoken among the sahaba. He went to Rasool ALLAH and said, "O messenger of ALLAH, are you not the messenger of ALLAH?"

Rasool ALLAH said, "Yes."

"Are we not Muslims?"

Rasool ALLAH said, "Yes."

"Are they not disbelievers?"

Rasool ALLAH said, "Yes."

Umar bin Khitab said, "Then why should we negotiate with them such agreement?"

Rasool ALLAH said, "I am the messenger of ALLAH, and I am not going to disobey his commands."

Umar bin Khitab said, "O messenger of ALLAH, didn't you tell us that we will visit Kabaah?"

They were missing Kabaah. They had been away for six years now. Rasool ALLAH promised them that they would make Tawaf around Kabaah.

Umar bin Khitab said, "Ya Rasool ALLAH, you promised us that we shall visit Kabaah."

Rasool ALLAH said, "But did I say you will visit Kabaah this year?"

Umar bin Khitab said, "No."

Rasool ALLAH said, "Then you will visit it, and you will make Tawaf around it."

Umar bin Khitab went to Abu Bakar Siddique and asked, "Is he not the messenger of ALLAH? Are we not Muslims?"

Abu Bakar Siddique said, "Yes."

"Are they not Kufaar?"

Abu Bakar Siddique said, "Yes."

Then Umar bin Khitab said, "Why do we negotiate with them on such terms?"

Abu Bakar Siddique said, "When you ride the horse and that stir up. Stick to the guidance of Rasool ALLAH. Follow him wherever he goes. He is the messenger of ALLAH and he will never disobey ALLAH and ALLAH will never forsake him."

Some scholars have commented on this—that Abu Bakar Siddique was always at the highest status than the rest of the sahaba. Abu Bakar Siddique later on commented on Sulah-e-Hudaibia. Again, sahaba saw this as a loss; but in reality, it was victory for them. Abu Bakar Siddique would not consider it a victory but a greatest victory in Islam—the words of Abu Bakar Siddique.

In the history of Islam, there was no opening greater than Sulah-e-Hudaibia; but people are shortsighted, and nobody knew what was going on between ALLAH and his Messenger (PBUH). There was something going on between ALLAH and his Messenger (PBUH), but sahaba did not know. They were shortsighted, and the nature of people is that they hasten things until they are completed.

ALLAH has its qadar, and ALLAH works in a certain way. People want things to come fast. Rasool ALLAH and Sohail were agreeing the terms, and Ali bin Abu Talib was writing them down.

Rasool ALLAH said, "Write down 'In the name of ALLAH the merciful and beneficial.'"

Sohail bin Amar said, "No because we do not know Al-Rehman Ur-Rahim. We know ALLAH, therefore write in the name of ALLAH."

Rasool ALLAH told Hazrat Ali to erase it, but Hazrat Ali refused to erase it.

The Mohammad (PBUH) said, "This is what Mohammad (PBUH), the messenger of ALLAH, agreed upon."

Sohail bin Amar said, "No. If we accept that you are the messenger of ALLAH, we would not negotiate with you. The issue between us is that we do not approve that you are the messenger of ALLAH."

Rasool ALLAH told Hazrat Ali to erase it, but Hazrat Ali refused. Rasool ALLAH told him to erase it, but Ali bin Abu Talib was hesitating. Rasool ALLAH asked him to show the Prophet where it is written. Hazrat Ali pointed to it because Rasool ALLAH could not read and write. Rasool ALLAH erased it with his finger. Sohail bin Amar was a good negotiator, not easy to negotiate.

Abu Bakar Siddique continued, saying, "I have seen Sohail bin Amar two years later after Sulah-e-Hudaibia in Hijat-tul-Widda. Sohail bin Amar has become a Muslim by now. I have seen with my own eyes bringing camels to Rasool ALLAH so Rasool ALLAH can slaughter them and then Rasool ALLAH shaved his head after Hajj and I have seen Sohail bin Amar going down on his knees, picking up the hair clippings of Rasool ALLAH and putting them on his eyes to get the blessings of Rasool ALLAH. These are the results, and I thank ALLAH for guiding him to Islam."

If we had hastened things, Islam would not have spread the way it did because Sulah-e-Haudaibia war was stopped and that was when invitation was spread all over Arabia. The sahaba could go out and give invitation without fear, and that was when people started to come in Islam in multiples. When Sulah-e-Hudaibia happened, the Muslims were 1,400. Two years later, Rasool ALLAH conquered Mecca with ten thousand. Rasool ALLAH, during nineteen years of invitation, had 1400; but in two years, because of Sulah-e-Hudaibia, these were ten thousand. These were the results of Sulah-e-Hudaibia. People failed to see the wisdom in Sulah-e-Hudaibia when scholars say Abu Bakar Siddique has the best opinion among the sahaba and he had a complete mind among them. Again, Abu Bakar Siddique would lead armies.

Salma bin Aqwa said, "Rasool ALLAH sent us in an army led by Abu Bakar Siddique to Najad. In this kind of war, attacks happened at night, and collateral damage occurs at night. Armies attacking on the villages, eventually some women and children get killed. This is talked in the hood of Fakka—Hukmaltood attacking at night in the dark. It happened during the time of Prophet (PBUH) few times. Sahaba, where there was no chance of army meeting, the army sahaba attacked at night."

Salma bin Aqwa said, "He killed the inhabitants of seven houses. Our slogan was 'Kill, kill.'"

They used to have a different slogan in every battle, used to have certain banners with certain colors. Certain slogans they would repeat in the battleground. Rasool ALLAH used these slogans, and this tradition was carried on by sahaba. In the battle of Salasal, the army was led by Amar bin Aas. The army had leaders and senior sahaba in it. Amar bin Aas was a newcomer to Islam. He became a Muslim after Sulah-e-Hudaibia. In Islam, early Muslims were considered to have senior ranks. Amar bin Aas was a later comer to Islam, but he was appointed leader of the army.

After camping, Amar bin Aas said, "Do not light any night fires." Deserts are cold at night, and fires are necessary to see the directions to be warm, to boil the water, but Amar bin Aas gave clear orders not to have any campfires. Umar bin Khitab wanted to know why he was ordering not to have fires. Umar bin Khitab went to Abu Bakar Siddique and asked about this order.

Abu Bakar Siddique told Umar, "Rasool ALLAH would not have appointed to lead the army unless he has some knowledge with warfare. Rasool ALLAH would not put him in position unless he knows what is he doing."

Umar bin Khitab accepted and did not go to Amar bin Aas. Abu Bakar Siddique was saying that there must be Hukma. Rasool ALLAH appointed Amar bin Aas to lead the army although he became a Muslim recently. Amar bin Aas had the leadership qualities, he had intelligence in warfare, and Umar bin Khitab had realized later on.

When Umar bin Khitab was Khalifah, he once saw Amar bin Aas walking.

Hazrat Umar said, "This man was born to be a leader."

It is not appropriate for Umar except to be a leader—that was the way he walked. Amar bin Aas was appointed in the life of Rasool ALLAH. He was the governor over Oman. When Umar bin Khitab became Khalifah, he was appointed to go and fight in Palestine. Later on, he was appointed to be the governor of Egypt where he stayed for a few decades.

Second incident, the army was going to a faraway land. The army needed some direction. Amar bin Aas asked for a best guide. They brought him Rafay bin Amartai. He was a thief who could raid a caravan alone. There were organized gangs who would raid caravans and also lonely figures who would do their own things. They would attack of their own. They had confidence to do all that by themselves.

Raffay bin Amartai was one of these characters. He would go and raid caravans. This was the best they could find to guide Amar bin Aas, but he was the best. He knew his ways around the desert because that was his job. He spent time with this Muslim army. He was impressed with what he saw.

He said, "I came to Abu Bakar Siddique." He had not met Abu Bakar Siddique but said, "I saw this man who had a cloth on. Whenever he is riding, he would hold the cloth with a pin. Whenever he sits down, he would take out the pin and take off the cloth."

Raffay said he went to Abu Bakar Siddique and said, "O you, the one with the pin. I can see on you marks of intelligence, and I am choosing you out of all these people. I have a question for you."

Abu Bakar Siddique said, "What do you want?"

"I want you to teach me something so that I can be like you, but do not make it long because I shall forget." That fits the profile of a thief; he is not interested in education. "Give me something brief and easy. I want to be like you, but make it easy."

Abu Bakar Siddique made it as easy as he could. He said, "Your hand has five fingers."

The thief said, "Yes."

"First finger, say second kalma. Second finger, pray five times a day. Third finger, pay zakat if you have money. Fourth finger, fast in the month of Ramadan. Fifth finger, make hajj to the house of ALLAH. Did you remember that?"

He said, "Yes."

Then Abu Bakar Siddique said, "At this, never assume the position of authority even over two people."

He said, "We have given position authority to you, the settlers. In Arabia, the Badoom used to have respect for settlers—people of the town, permanent people—and give them position of authority."

Abu Bakar Siddique said, "The time will come when there will be so many positions of authority and that it will reach you and even to people below you, and whenever you are a leader and people are oppressed, you will be asked about that on the day of judgment."

What Abu Bakar Siddique said came true. The Muslim Khalafah grew so fast it expanded with speed. There were so many posts that needed to be filled. It reached to people like him and to people below him.

Lessons from conversation between Abu Bakar and Rafay bin Amartai:

(1) Speak to people according to their level. This is a thief. He did not go to school. He has no educational background. Do not give him Bukhari and tell him to memorize it, and do not tell him he has to go on a Shariya course for a few years and has to study knowledge. People have different capabilities. Not everybody will become a great sheikh and scholar, and not everybody will become Imaam. Not everybody will be a scholar. Just imagine if Abu Bakar told him Surah-e-Bakra and told him to memorize it. He could barely remember the five fingers. That is about it. Therefore, for gangsters and brothers from that background, teach them, and take it easy with them. Praise be to ALLAH, these brothers are wonderful when ALLAH guides them to truth. The spirit that they have—the spirit that you cannot find with a scholar. It happens, for example, Imaam Hanabil heard someone speaking about Bushra Al-Afi. He said, "He is not a scholar. Bushra Al-Afi was not a scholar in terms of he did not know a lot of Hadees compare to Imam Ahmad bin Hanabil." But

what did Imam Ahmad bin Hanabil say? He already has the fruit of knowledge that is fear of ALLAH. What does the Ayyat say? The ones who have fear of ALLAH are scholars. Fear of ALLAH is fruit of knowledge, fear of ALLAH. If you have all the knowledge of the world but do not have fear of ALLAH, this is worthless. Ahmad bin Hanabil was saying this man has already fruit of knowledge; therefore, in a situation, knowledge is important. In that sense, he is a scholar; he has the fear of ALLAH. The prophet of ALLAH (PBUH) would speak to people according to their knowledge, and sahaba would understand that. Although he was a child, Ibn-e-Albas had a mind of a scholar, and therefore, Prophet (PBUH) would speak to him at a higher level while a nomad would come to the Prophet (PBUH), and the Prophet (PBUH) would give him very brief order that is easy to remember. There one must have Hukman in invitation to speak to people according to their abilities.

(2) Secondly, you have to be honest. Abu Bakar Siddique did not hold back and said, "Do not be a leader." And that was the first conversation with the man. He did not know him well. He told him, "Don't be a leader," but Abu Bakar Siddique saw some things in this man that were not fitting for a position of authority, so he was very honest with him. Also, if you see something wrong with the brother, correct them, but do that nicely.

Fateh-e-Mecca, the Prophet (PBUH) had an agreement with Quraish—truce, no war. That was in the agreement of Fateh-e-Mecca. One term in the agreement started that if anyone wants to enter into agreement and go with Quraish, he could do so. Co-elation and if anyone wanted to go with the Prophet, co-elation they had the right to do so. According to agreement, both sides are free to make alliances. Banu Bakar entered into alliance with Quraish. Khaza entered into alliance with the Prophet (PBUH). Khaza had a special relationship with the grandfather of the Prophet (PBUH). They carried on a relationship with the Prophet (PBUH) even though they were non-Muslims, but they wanted to be on their side. They had the alliance with the grandfather and wanted to continue the alliance with the Prophet (PBUH) even though they were non-Muslims.

There was a feud between Banu Bakar and Khaza. They were angry with each other. Banu Bakar made a secret agreement with some men of Quraish. If they provide weapons to Banu Bakar, then they will make an ambush on Khaza at night, kill them, and disappear. Some men of Khaza were killed. Umar bin Salim came to the Prophet Mohammad (PBUH), and he narrated lines of poetry, asking the Prophet (PBUH) to fulfill the agreement and give him victory, that "we have been betrayed by Banu Bakar and have been betrayed by Quraish."

The Prophet (PBUH) immediately said, "Ya Umar bin Salim, I shall give you victory." The Prophet (PBUH) went home and told Ayesha to prepare his luggage for battle, food, and everything he needed for this journey, but the Prophet (PBUH) wanted to keep this expedition secret. Why? Because the Prophet (PBUH) wanted to avoid bloodshed in Mecca. The Prophet (PBUH) wanted to mobilize his army and attack Mecca suddenly so that people of Mecca were surprised and it was too late for them to fight back. Therefore, their blood can be protected. The Prophet (PBUH) did not want to give them time to prepare for war. The Prophet (PBUH) wanted to make his move clandestine and keep it quiet. Therefore, he told Ayesha to prepare everything for him.

She was grinding some grain. Abu Bakar Siddique, ALLAH be pleased with him, saw that Ayesha was preparing some luggage. He said, "Is the Prophet (PBUH) thinking of attacking an enemy?"

She did not respond.

Abu Bakar Siddique asked her, "Is he (the Prophet [PBUH]) thinking of attacking the Romans?"

She did not respond.

Next, "Does he intend to fight the people of Najit?"

She did not respond.

"Does he intend to fight the people of Quraish?"

She did not respond, and then the Prophet (PBUH) came in.

Abu Bakar Siddique asked, "O messenger of ALLAH, are you planning for war?"

The Prophet (PBUH) said, "Yes."

He asked, "Is it with Romans?"

The Prophet (PBUH) said, "No."

"Is it with the people of Najit?"

The Prophet (PBUH) said, "No."

Then Abu Bakar Siddique said, "Is it the people of Quraish?"

The Prophet (PBUH) said, "Yes."

Abu Bakar Siddique responded, "Don't we have truce between us?"

The Prophet (PBUH) said, "Didn't you hear what they did to Banu Tayyal (Khaza)? They have broken the agreement."

We have to look at the conduct of Ayesha, ALLAH be pleased with her. She kept quiet to protect the secret of the Prophet (PBUH) even from her father, the closest man to the Prophet Mohammad (PBUH). The Prophet (PBUH) did not keep secrets from Abu Bakar. He told him, but Ayesha kept quiet.

The battle of Honaine. Abu Qatada (Al-Ansaari) said, "I saw Muslims fighting with non-Muslims. There was another nonbeliever who was trying to get around the Muslims and wanted to attack from behind, so I attacked that nonbeliever to protect my brother. When he saw me, he lifted up his arm to hit me with his sword, but I was faster and chopped off his arm, but then he hugged me and he terrified me with his hug and then became weaker. Therefore, I killed him. Then we retreated. I had to leave."

The Prophet (PBUH) said, "If you kill someone, you can take his armors." Take whatever is with the fighter. There are spoils of war, booty of war, heavy armor, food stuff, camels, horses—that is all booty of war. There is a different order with booty. The leader divides it four out of five to fighters, and one out of five is divided into five sections, but with the armors—that all goes to the fighters. The personal weapons that are found on the dead soldiers are taken by the one who killed him.

The Prophet (PBUH) said, "Whoever has killed will take armor." There is a difference of opinion on what is included in the armor—any cash, their clothes—but that is something we have to look in the book of Feeka.

Abu Qatada went and found that there was nothing on that dead man; it was all taken. Weapons were very expensive, and Abu

Qatada was very poor. He went to the messenger of ALLAH and said, "O messenger of ALLAH, I have killed that man but cannot find his weapons."

One of the Quraish who was there said, "I am the one who took the weapons."

That man said, "O messenger of ALLAH, ask Abu Qatada to allow me to keep it." This was the man whom Abu Qatada defended.

Before the response of the Prophet (PBUH), Abu Bakar intervened. He said, "No. In the name of ALLAH, a weak bird from Quraish is not going to take away the weapons belonging to the line of ALLAH, who is defending ALLAH and his messenger."

Now the man who took the weapon, he was from Quraish. The people of Abu Bakar and Abu Qatada was from Ansaar, and Abu Bakar was saying, "A weak bird from Quraish is not going to keep weapon which should go to the line of ALLAH, who is defending ALLAH and his messenger."

The messenger of ALLAH approved the Fatwa of Abu Bakar and told the man to give these weapons back. The point is that Abu Bakar was at a level where he could Fatwa in the presence of the messenger of ALLAH, where he could make the judgment in the court of the Prophet (PBUH). He could give his ruling while the Prophet (PBUH) was there. That was how close the relationship was. This was because Abu Bakar Siddique was drinking from the fountain of prophethood for years and years. The Hukman and wisdom, justice the messenger of ALLAH approves.

In the Battle of Honaine, there was a lot of spoils of war, booty of war. There were many new Muslims in the army. The Prophet (PBUH) gave to these new Muslims the booty of war and held it from Ansaar and old Muslims in order to draw these new Muslims closer to Islam, but still there was greed among new Muslims. Al-Abas bin Mardas was one of the chief of clan. He made long poetry because he was upset because he received his share equal to other well-known people. The messenger of ALLAH gave them a certain amount, but Al-Abas bin Mardas did not like that. He thought it was a matter of status. However, his day cannot be raised.

He thought, *That is my status, and I cannot go up, so you have to give me equal to them.*

There was a line of poetry, it says. When the messenger of ALLAH heard this poetry, he went and cut his tongue, but it did not mean literally. What was said by the Prophet (PBUH)? "Give him until he is satisfied and will be quiet"—meaning "make him happy so that his tongue would not say something like that."

At that time, poetry was powerful. One would say Qab bin Ashraf made poetry against the women of sahaba. At that in Arabia, poetry would have more effect than a blockbuster movie of today or a front-page article on *New York Times* or primetime TV with BBC. At that time, poetry was the media of the day. There have been incidents where one-line poetry brought the end to the reputation of a tribe.

The messenger of ALLAH said to "go and cut his tongue." They gave him camels until he was happy. Later on, the Prophet (PBUH) met with Al-Abas and said, "Are you the one who said Al-Yana and then Ada-Kari in the line of poetry?"

When the Prophet (PBUH) said the line of poetry, he switched the names. He said, "Al-Yana and Ada-Kari."

Abu Bakar Siddique corrected the messenger of ALLAH, and it was not Al-Yana and Ada-Kari. It was Al-Ayana and Iqra.

The Prophet (PBUH) said, "It is the same thing."

Abu Bakar Siddique smiled and said, "You are truly as ALLAH said, 'We have not taught him poetry, and it is not appropriate for him.' It is only remembrance of ALLAH and manifest book."

The messenger of ALLAH only changed the words or names, but the meaning was the same.

When Abu Bakar Siddique corrected it, the Prophet (PBUH) said, "It does not make any difference," but for the listeners of poetry, one has to follow the rules.

Then Abu Bakar Siddique said, "As ALLAH said, 'We did teach him poetry. It is not appropriate for him, but it is Quran.'"

In the siege of Taif, when Muslims were laying siege of Taif, an arrow injured the son of Abu Bakar Abdullah. That injury was the cause of the death of Abdullah, but he died a long time after injury. He died after the death of the Prophet (PBUH). Abu Bakar was Khalifah (king). He received the delegation from Taif. This was after the long time after shooting the arrow. The shooting happened during the life of the Prophet (PBUH).

Abdullah, the son of Abu Bakar when he was Khalifah (leader), Abu Bakar kept the arrow with him. It was the cause of death of his son Abdullah.

When he received the delegation from Taif, he brought the arrow to show them and asked, "Does anybody know the source of this arrow?"

One of the men who was present said, "I am the one who prepared this arrow. I sharpened it. I am the one who attached feathers to it, and I am the one who shot it."

Abu Bakar, ALLAH be pleased with him, said, "This is the arrow that killed my son Abdullah."

What was the response of Abu Bakar? He has lost his son. He said, "Alhamdulillah, praise to be ALLAH who honored him through you and did not dishonor you and made you a Muslim—that is better for both of you. ALLAH honored my son through you. You are the one who made him martyr. ALLAH did not dishonor you. ALLAH made you a Muslim. It is good for you."

There is a narration which says that two people who love in heaven are a Muslim and a nonbeliever who killed a Muslim and then became a Muslim himself. They end up loving each other in heaven because the martyr knows that "this is the person who killed me, and I received this status," and the person prays that he was not punished for this because he became a Muslim.

The battle of Tabooq—this was the first time the messenger of ALLAH (PBUH) went himself to fight the Romans. There was an initial encounter in the battle of Motha. This time, the messenger of ALLAH wanted to go and lead the Muslim army and make an incursion into the Roman Empire. This was a very special event. It needed some special preparations different than any other battle the messenger of ALLAH participated in. In the battle of Tabooq, the Prophet (PBUH) gave the banner flag to Abu Bakar Siddique, ALLAH be pleased with him. When the army marched out, that was a long journey, and they were camping out in the desert at night.

Abdullah bin Masood said, "I saw fire in the distance. I wanted to go to see what was happening." He went there, and he said, "I saw Abdullah bin, one of the companions of the Prophet (PBUH). With him were the Prophet (PBUH), Abu Bakar, and Umar."

The Prophet (PBUH) was in the grave and was telling Abu Bakar and Umar to lower the body of Abdullah. The Prophet (PBUH) said, "Bring down your brother."

The Prophet (PBUH) placed him with his own hands in the grave and then he said, "O ALLAH, I am going to bury him tonight, and I am pleased with him, so, O ALLAH, be pleased with him."

Abdullah bin Masood said, "I desired and wished that I was in that grave to receive this prayer of the Prophet (PBUH): 'O ALLAH, I am pleased with him so ALLAH be pleased with him.'"

Again those were the Prophet (PBUH), Abu Bakar, and Umar. It was a difficult time, a hot summer.

Umar said, "We reached the level where we had no water left. We would slaughter our camels and drink from inside the camels and eat the digested food." They would drink that. They were thirsty. They would take whatever was left and put them on their bodies to cool down.

Abu Bakar went to the Prophet (PBUH) and said, "Your prayers are accepted. Pray for us."

The Prophet (PBUH) asked, "Is that what you want?" meaning "I shall do that for you. Is that what you want?"

Abu Bakar Siddique said, "Yes."

The messenger of ALLAH made prayer. The narrators of the Hadees said the Prophet (PBUH) did not bring his hands down until the clouds were over their heads. The expense in the battle of Tabooq was special. That was where the Prophet praised Usman bin Unaan we have covered in our first session.

Umar bin Khitab said, "When the Prophet (PBUH) was asking for donation at that time, I had some money. Therefore, I told myself today I shall be ahead from Abu Bakar. If ever I am going to be ahead of him, this is my head. I had the chance."

Umar said, "He carried half of his wealth. I went to the Prophet and gave it to him."

Rasool ALLAH asked, "O Umar, what have you left for your family?"

Umar said, "I have left half of my wealth at home."

And then Abu Bakar came. He gave his money to the Prophet.

Rasool ALLAH asked him, "What have you left for your family?"

Abu Bakar said, "I have left at home ALLAH and his messenger." He brought all his wealth.

Umar bin Khitab said, "I shall never try to compete with you. I shall never try to be ahead of you." This was in Tabooq. Umar bin Khitab persisted all the way until the battle of Tabooq, but then, he said, "Never again."

Al-Hajj, in the ninth year of Hijra, which is Hajat-tul-Widda. The year before Hajat-tul-Widda, the messenger of ALLAH appointed Abu Bakar to lead the Hajj. The messenger of ALLAH wanted to go to Hajj himself, but he said, "It is not appropriate for me to perform Hajj when people are going Kabaah naked."

There was a belief among the Arabs that only the people of Quraish are pure; they can make Tawaf with their clothes on, and because we commit sins and our clothes are unpure; therefore, we have to take off our clothes, and they would go around Kabaah, Tawaf naked. Not everyone would do that. They used to believe if they had to make Tawaf with clothes, they had to borrow clothes from someone, from Quraish because they are the pure people. Therefore, if they had money, they would buy clothes; and if they didn't have money, they would make Tawaf naked. The messenger of ALLAH said, "It is appropriate for me when this is going on." Therefore, the Prophet (PBUH) asked Abu Bakar to lead Al-Hajj. This is an indication that a leader needs to stay away from some things which are allowed for the rest of the Ummah because of the important position of leadership. The messenger of ALLAH did not go himself but allowed the rest of Ummah to go and make Hajj. A leader has to follow strict rules than ordinary people, to uphold higher standards. Abu Bakar Siddique left for Hajj. The Prophet (PBUH) received the revelations, first Ayyat from Surat-e-Tobah. These Ayyats are announcing the end of the agreement between the Prophet (PBUH) and the non-Muslims and the end of the era of Shirk in Arabia. Now it is either Islam or sword—no other choice at that time.

The Prophet (PBUH) told Ali bin Abu Talib to take his camel to go fast and follow Abu Bakar, ALLAH be pleased with him, and convey to the people to recite Ayyats of Surah-e-Burra. Please note this is the only Surat which does not start with the name of ALLAH because this is an announcement of war. Therefore, it does not start with *merciful, beneficial,* and *compassionate.*

Ali bin Abu Talib went very fast until he reached Abu Bakar Siddique Khalifah.

Abu Bakar Siddique saw him riding the camel of Prophet (PBUH) and asked, "Are you leading, or are you a follower?"

Ali bin Abu Talib said, "I am a follower."

Abu Bakar Siddique thought, *Maybe Ali, ALLAH be pleased with him, is the new leader of Al-Hajj,* but he said, "I am a follower."

They went to Mecca. Abu Bakar would take people in different positions in the Hajj. The rituals of Hajj and Ali bin Abu Talib would follow him wherever he goes and he would recite the Ayyats of Surah-e-Burra to everyone and after that, he would announce four things—four points. The Prophet (PBUH) told him to tell people the following: (1) No one will enter heaven unless they are believers. (2) No one should make Tawaf naked. (3) If anyone has any agreement with the Prophet, it will end after the agreed term/period and will not be renewed. (4) Finally, no nonbeliever will make Hajj after this year. Therefore, the era of Shirk associating with ALLAH is over/finished. Shirk associating with ALLAH is behind our backs. Ali bin Abu Talib made these four points clear. This was to prepare the ground for the Prophet (PBUH) to lead the Hajj next year with no Mushrik around. Mecca will be purified now. Please make a note—only believers will enter heaven. This was made clear. Secondly, no more naked Tawaf of Kabaah (house of ALLAH). The truce agreements—the Prophet (PBUH) did not break any agreement but said after four months, all agreements will be finished, then either Islam or sword. This happened when Abu Bakar, ALLAH be pleased with him, was leading the Hajj.

Hajat-tul-Widda is the only Hajj the Prophet (PBUH) performed. This will be mentioned here. An incident happened, and Asma, daughter of Abu Bakar, is narrating:

> The Prophet (PBUH) was sitting and Ayesha was sitting next to him. Abu Bakar Siddique was waiting for Mac, his camel. He was waiting for a long time. The servant was late. Then suddenly his servant came but no camel. Servant came without the camel. Abu Bakar Siddique asked the servant, "Where is the camel?" Servant replied, "I lost the camel yesterday." "What?" Abu Bakar Siddique attacked the servant and started beating him. The Prophet (PBUH) smiled and said, "What is he doing in the state of Hajj clothes, Ahram." But that was the only camel Abu Bakar Siddique had. He was very upset that his servant lost his camel. This is the end of Jihaad of Abu Bakar Siddique with the Prophet (PBUH).

We move on to the next session. Inshallah, in this session, we go through some events involving Abu Bakar Siddique in Madina. In the previous topics, we have seen participation of Abu Bakar Siddique in battles where the Prophet (PBUH) participated. In this session, we shall talk about Abu Bakar in battles where the Prophet (PBUH) did not participate. Abu Bakar Siddique would protect the secrets of the Prophet (PBUH). The daughter of Umar bin Khitab, ALLAH be pleased with him. His daughter Hafsa was married to one of the companions of the Prophet (PBUH), sahaba who fought in the battle of Badar. Later on, he died. Umar bin Khitab wanted to see his daughter married to one of the best persons. He went to Usman bin Unaan and offered his daughter to him.

He asked Usman bin Unaan, ALLAH be pleased with him, "Do you want to marry my daughter Hafsa?"

Usman bin Unaan replied, "Let me think this over." He returned later and said, "I have decided that I do not want to marry at this time. I am not interested in marriage now."

Umar bin Khitab may have disliked that, but he went to Abu Bakar Siddique and said, "I am offering you my daughter. Do you want to marry her?"

Abu Bakar Siddique did not respond. He did not say anything.

Umar bin Khitab said, "I was more upset with Abu Bakar Siddique than Usman bin Unaan because Usman, although negative, but gave me an answer."

Abu Bakar Siddique was silent, no response. Umar offered his daughter to him, and he did not answer. A few days later, the Prophet (PBUH) married Hafsa. After the marriage, Abu Bakar came to Umar and said, "I think you are upset with me because I did not give you an answer."

Umar said, "Yes, I was upset with you."

Abu Bakar Siddique said, "The reason I did not respond back was that I heard the Prophet (PBUH) mentioned her name and I was not going to be the one who would disclose the secret of the Prophet, but if the Prophet (PBUH) had not married her, I would have married her."

Abu Bakar Siddique said, "The Prophet (PBUH), by mentioning her name, was interested to marry her. This is the reason I kept quiet. Wait and see. If the Prophet had not married her, I would have married her, but I am not the one who would disclose the secret of the Prophet (PBUH)."

The Prophet (PBUH) wanted to have a relationship—the marriage relationship—with four very close companions. We know the Prophet married the daughter of Abu Bakar Siddique. Also, he married the daughter of Umar bin Khitab, then the Prophet (PBUH) married two of his daughters to Usman bin Unaan. First he married his daughter to him, and when she passed away, he married him his other daughter. There is a statement; God knows how strong. This is the statement:

If I had ninety-nine daughters, I would have married them to Usman bin Unaan. If they were dying, I would keep on marrying with him.

That was how much love the Prophet (PBUH) had for Usman bin Unaan. Then he married his daughter Fatima to Ali bin Abu Talib. Now the Prophet (PBUH) had family relationship with four close friends and leaders, ALLAH be pleased with them. There are two things to note here: (1) Marriage in those days was very easy. Now marriage is very complicated; so much bureaucracy. Unfortunately, Haram is easier than Halal. In the time of companions of the Prophet (PBUH), things were very simple. First of all, the nature of companions, said Abdullah bin Masood, they were the least superficial among people. They did not like complications. They lived a very simple life. They loved simplicity. They were far away from complication or sophistication. The companions were simple in their dress. Their food was simple—simple furniture, simple houses, simple in everything. They loved and cherished their simplicity. They had knowledge.

Umar bin Khitab said, "I had knowledge about the fancy dishes and food, but this is how I want to live—a simple life." That was not because of ignorance, lack of knowledge. They simply viewed it as a better way of living. Merit was simple. We know Umar bin Khitab was offering his daughter for marriage. Who would do that today? Who would go to a riotous person and offer his daughter like that? Now it may be shameful, embarrassing, not good; it is lowering one's status.

Umar bin Khitab did not have any problem with that. He went and offered his daughter to Usman and Abu Bakar Siddique because he wanted the best for his daughter. In those days, because marriage was simple and easy, there were hardly any unmarried women deprived from the blessing of marriage. There was a general rule to take care of every woman in society. Every woman will be taken care of. The problem of polygamy, the whole society, was taken care of. Nobody was left out of this important relationship because ALLAH has created us in pairs. It is a part of nature to be in such a relationship. Therefore, nobody in the society will be left out and deprived of this. The Prophet Mohammad (PBUH) said, "Whoever wanted to take a different path, that is not my Sunnat." The ones who wanted to practice celibacy—getting away from marriage—because this was the practice of Christian monks, the Prophet (PBUH) said, "This is not my Sunnat. My way is the way to get married. Whoever does not follow my way does not belong to me." Therefore, marriage in Islam is worship. This is a form of worship and will please ALLAH. The message for parents is to encourage children to get married because this is the way in Islam. At the time of the sahaba, Halal was easier than Haram. It was difficult to commit Haram. The path to Halal was easy, honest living. These are just comments. In Western society, everything is available—both Halal and Haram. Sometimes indecent things are promoted because we are living in times where sometimes good is evil and evil is good. As the scholars say, Biddaha replaces Sunnat. Whatever is wrong has uprooted something which is right. Therefore, we should go back to the ways of sahabas and encourage Halal and discourage Haram. The Prophet (PBUH) said, "Marriage should be done at early age." What is early age, around twenty years? We ask ALLAH to make it easy on our brothers and sisters who are seeking marriage to make Halal and open doors for them and to close their doors on Satan's face.

The Prophet (PBUH) was giving Friday's sermon when a caravan came into Madina. They used to send caravans to Syria and Yamen to bring back merchandise. These caravans would come back a few times a year. The caravan would be led by a group of men, but it would include the money of the whole community. Everybody would invest in that caravan. They would go out and all wait for the caravan, eager for its return—that was their livelihood. Therefore, it was the big event when the caravans arrived. Everybody jumped in to get the best deal.

It happened that the caravan arrived when the Prophet (PBUH) was giving Friday's Ceremon. The rules of Jumma were not clear like not allowed to move and not allowed to speak. Everybody left the mosque. Only a very few remained with the Prophet (PBUH). Well, we assume it was not mandatory for them to remain. We assume that

167

sahaba would remain—that is mandatory. It must have happened before the final rules of Jumma were given; they left. ALLAH revealed in Surah-e-Jumma; ALLAH says,

> When they saw diversion, O Mohammad, they rushed to it and left you standing. Say, what is with ALLAH is better than diversion and transaction and ALLAH is the best provider.

"They left and you, the Prophet (PBUH), is standing." ALLAH is saying what ALLAH has is better than this business. ALLAH is the one who gives sustenance. You left Sulat-tul-Jumma while the Prophet (PBUH) was giving ceremon. In the narration, the statement was only twelve people remained. Among those twelve, there were Abu Bakar Siddique, ALLAH be pleased with him, and Umar bin Khitab, ALLAH be pleased with him. The point is that they were always on the right side. Although both of them were businessmen and had a lot of interest to go and meet the caravan, they stayed behind until Rasool ALLAH finished his ceremon. Therefore, they were not included in this Ayyat.

Hadees in Bukhari, the Prophet says,

> If your trouser sheet is dragging under the ankle of pride, showing off, ALLAH will not look at you on the day of Judgment.

Abu Bakar Siddique was very slim when he would tie or tuck up his trouser, It is like loongi type sheet from both half dress. That would slip and go down. Since he was slim, it would not hold on his waist.

He came to the Prophet (PBUH) and said, "My dress would not hold and slips down and go below the ankle. The only way I can keep it up—tucking or tugging it up."

The Prophet (PBUH) told him, "You are not one of those who would do that out of pride." The messenger of ALLAH told him, "You are not included in this hadees." This is a witness statement from the

Prophet that Abu Bakar is free from arrogance. We know how great a sin is arrogance. The Prophet (PBUH) said, "Whoever has a single grain of arrogance, he will not even smell heaven."

We ask ALLAH to keep us away from evil sin. This has brought the demise of Satan Iblees. That was how Satan Iblees lost his very high status among the angels—because of arrogance. Satan Iblees said, "I am better than him (Adam). Why should I make Sujood for him? I am better than him."

This is why it is said that the worst thing for Satan Iblees is when he sees a human making Sujjod to ALLAH. Refusal to make sujjod brought ALLAH's anger on him, ALLAH's wrath on him. Then Satan Iblees sees Muslims making Sujjod; he knows this will bring the mercy of ALLAH on that person. Therefore, he (Satan) hates the sight of Sujjod. It angers Satan when we make Sujjod to ALLAH. Satan was ordered to make Sujjod. He refused, and Adam was ordered to make Sujjod, and he did make sujjod (sons of Adam).

(4) During Eid, Abu Bakar Siddique went to see his daughter Ayesha. He came in and saw two young girls from Ansaar singing for her—a special performance for Ayesha, ALLAH be pleased with her. According to this particular narration, no instruments were used. They were singing.

When Abu Bakar Siddique saw this, he was angry and said, "You are using influence of devil in the house of the Prophet, singing in the house of the Prophet (PBUH)."

He was very upset with his daughter, but the Prophet (PBUH) was there. Rasool ALLAH was facing the wall. He did not see Ayesha and did not see Abu Bakar.

The Prophet (PBUH) spoke to them without looking back and said, "O Abu Bakar, all nations, all people, every people have celebration, and this is our celebration, Eid, a day of celebration."

The Prophet (PBUH) approved what Ayesha was doing and told Abu Bakar in a situation like this, it is appropriate and fine to celebrate. In another hadees, the Prophet (PBUH) said "We want non-Muslims to know that there is room for entertainment in our religion." There is room for entertainment as long as it is done in Halal fashion. As a human being, there is a compartment of needs for entertainment. Your soul, your heart, and your body needs this. It is different according to different people. Some people have larger compartments than others, but everybody has some need for this. In Islam, we are encouraged to be serious because this is a serious religion. ALLAH says,

> O Ya Ya, hold the book with strength and power.

ALLAH says to Bani Israel,

> Take the commands which we have given you with strengths.

The religion is serious, but these are times to entertain themselves. But we should not turn all the time in entertainment and fun. ALLAH says about nonbelievers they have taken their religion entertainment and fun. Sometimes the church groups would come to the mosque to pray Salat. They are impressed with Salat. They see Muslims praying in the mosque; often they ask a question: "You do not have any singing in the mosque, so no groups to sing and perform for you. Well, no, this is our worship. They knew it simple and plain—that is because they are used to singing and entertainment in their church.

There was a professor in social sciences who was an atheist; he did not believe in God. He said, "I still like to go to church because I love the songs." Even if there is no singing and entertainment in the mosque, ALLAH puts peacefulness in the heart just by being in the mosque. When Quran is being read, lining up in the Salat, the moment Inquohein with everybody else, the whole sight of Salat is impressive when two million people are gathered in Kabaah for Salat, making Sujjod together, Rukoo together, and listening to the recitation of Quran. It is a very powerful scene. Look at Hajj. There is no singing, but it is a powerful image. A Muslim is looking this. Just imagine how deprived a person is if they do not have salat in their lives. Could you imagine a Muslim living without making Sujjod?

Can you imagine living without Salat-tul-Jumma? Can one live without having concept of Ramadhan, no fasting, no taraweeh? No breaking of fast? Happiness and pleasures come with eating the first date when hungry. Just imagine how deprived the person may be when they don't have the concept of Hajj. They do not know what Hajj is and what Hajj is. They do not see it, and they do not experience it without having the celebration of Eid. Even though there is no singing and no entertainment in Islam, it is so fulfilling. Islam makes life full with joy and happiness.

Ibn-e-Tania was jailed for a day, and he was threatened. He said, "What can my enemy do with me? My heaven is in my heart. If they put me in jail, I shall find time to remember ALLAH. If they kill me, I am a martyr. What can they do?"

A momin is carrying his heaven, peace and tranquility in his heart. For people who have experienced in Masjid-e-Nabi in Madina, there is a patch in the Masjid which is part of heaven. People who have been there must have experienced this. ALLAH has blessed us, but we should not take it for granted but must thank ALLAH and praise ALLAH. We do not have musical instruments going in Masjid, but it is more fulfilling and enjoyable than the best musical concert in the world. ALLAH has blessed us, and we should praise ALLAH, but still we need to fulfill deep desire for entertainment. That is one of the purposes of marriage. ALLAH has made between men and women mercy, compassion, patience, and many types of entertainment which serve dual purpose. Like sports, it is not only entertainment but also preparation. We ask ALLAH to give us a correct understanding of our religion because both extremes are very dangerous. We also notice that this was not a habit. Otherwise, Abu Bakar Siddique would not have said what he said; it was not a habit that always singing was going on. It was once in a while. Most of the scholars agree that all instruments are not allowed with the exception of Tanree. In this incident, Ayesha had two young girls who were singing for her.

The generosity of Abu Bakar Siddique in Bukhari and Muslims. We have mentioned the poor sahaba named Al-Soofa, most of them Mohajir from Mecca and from other places. They did not have any houses in Madina. They ended up staying in the corner in

171

the mosque. They were poor, unable to buy a house. The Prophet (PBUH) allowed them to stay in the mosque in the corners; there were some living quarters in the mosque. Sometimes young people and other sahaba would join them.

Abdullah bin Umar said, "I spend two years in the mosque before I get married." People wanted to stay in the mosque to be close to the Prophet (PBUH) to learn the teachings of the Prophet (PBUH). Abdullah bin Umar stayed two years in the mosque, but he was not poor. Umar was well off. He wanted to be close to the Prophet (PBUH).

One particular night, the Prophet (PBUH) said, "If you had food for two, take a third person with you. If you had food for three, take a fourth person. You have food for fourth, take a fifth person." The Prophet (PBUH) wanted to provide food for Al-Soofa for that night. The Prophet (PBUH) told the sahaba that food for two is enough for three and food for three is enough for four and food for four is enough for five. Abu Bakar Siddique took three people to his house and entrusted them to his son Abdul Rehman, and he left and went to join the Prophet (PBUH) and had his dinner with the Prophet (PBUH).

Noone, a scholar, said that "this shows that Abu Bakar Siddique would consider any time spent with the Prophet (PBUH) was more valuable than time spent with his family and the rest—even his children and his guests."

He took the guests, and instead of having dinner with them, he went to have dinner with Prophet (PBUH). The Prophet (PBUH) brought ten guests with him from Al-Soofa, and Abu Bakar took three. Abu Bakar Siddique told his family to feed them, and his son, Abdul Rehman, was at home. He stayed with the Prophet (PBUH) and came home very late.

The wife of Abu Bakar asked, "Why were you so late? And you did not feed you guests?"

Abu Bakar Siddique was surprised and asked, "You have not provided food to them until now?"

The wife said, "No, because they refused."

Abdul Rehman said when he heard that, he ran away because he knew his father would be upset. Abdul Rehman was grown up at that time and fought battles but still was afraid of his father. Abdul Rehman went into hiding.

When his father called, first time he didn't respond. Second time, he didn't respond. Third time, he responded.

Question: "Why didn't you feed them?"

He took his father to the guests and asked to the guests, "Did I not offer to provide you dinner but you refused?" Abdul Rehman had insisted that guests should eat, but guests refused and said, "In the name of ALLAH, we shall not eat until Abu Bakar comes back. We shall wait for him."

Abdul Rehman told his father, "I tried my best, but they refused."

Abu Bakar Siddique was upset and asked, "Why didn't you eat until this time? I am your host, but I didn't know. No one told me when I was in the house of the Prophet (PBUH). But did you spend so many hours waiting for me? I have eaten, and you go ahead and have your food."

They replied, "In the name of ALLAH, we will not eat until you eat with us."

Abu Bakar Siddique said, "This is from Satan Iblees," and sat down. Please note Abu Bakar Siddique had said he was not going to eat—that was his oath. Now he had to break his oath. That was what he meant that "this is from Satan," meaning he breaks his oath. He was Siddique. Well, in Islam, if one makes an oath and then something better comes along, you take the better and make it clear to pay for the oath which was made.

Abu Bakar Siddique sat with them to eat. This hadees is in Bukhari and Muslims.

Abdul Rehman, the son of Abu Bakar, said, "Whenever we take a mouthful, more food would appear. People take food, and more food appears. The food was growing in the pot. They all had their fill. I took the plate to my wife and said, "Look at this." She was also amazed to see that there was more food in the plate, then she sent it.

Abu Bakar Siddique took the plate to the house of the Prophet (PBUH) and some other Soofa ate from it and food was increasing. This was the one of blessing to the prophets and blessing to the valley of ALLAH. Miracles happened to the Prophet of ALLAH and blessings to the friends of ALLAH. This was a blessing that happened to Abu Bakar Siddique, ALLAH be pleased with him.

Abu Bakar Siddique was very generous, and his generosity is very well known. He was the one who would take care of the bills when he was with the Prophet (PBUH) when the Prophet (PBUH) was inviting people to Islam in early days in Mecca.

Abu Zar Ghafari had heard that a man was claiming to be a prophet in Mecca. He came to Mecca, making inquiries. He wanted to know more. He was searching for truth. Abu Zar Ghafari came into Mecca because invitation was secret in Mecca. At that time, it was against the law to preach Islam or to practice Islam. It was not allowed to meet with Prophet (PBUH).

Abu Zar Ghafari spent an entire month in Mecca but was unable to meet with the Prophet (PBUH). Later on, he met the Prophet (PBUH) and Abu Bakar Siddique.

The Prophet (PBUH) asked him, "How did you survive for the whole month?"

Abu Zar Ghafari said, "I survived on nothing but water of ZamZam." He said, "I was putting on weight, and flesh on my body was folding."

The nomads were fit people—flat tummies, no fat.

Abu Zar Ghafari said, "The water of ZamZam was not only satisfactory for me, but I ended up gaining weight. Flesh started to fold on my stomach."

Nowadays, it is not a big deal; we all are fat enough to have folding skin on the stomach, but at that time, it was an achievement. Those people were very fit.

The Prophet (PBUH) said, "Water of ZamZam is food if you want to be so"; in another narration, "This water is also healing, depending upon your intention. If the intention is for supplication, prayer, ALLAH is listening. If the intention is for medicine, it is medicine; and if one drinks as food, it is food as long as one is a Momin, believer."

The Prophet (PBUH) told Abu Bakar to take him and feed him. Abu Bakar Siddique took him to his house and gave him some rosins to eat. These rosins came from Taif, a special treat. Abu Bakar Siddique would be always on the side of the Prophet (PBUH) to take care of his expenses. It was a fancy for sacrifice.

One day in a battle—this was a Gazwa. Ayesha lost her necklace. She went around looking for her necklace, and it was time for the army to leave. She could not find her necklace. The Prophet (PBUH) was waiting for her patiently. His young wife was looking for her necklace, and she could not find it; but it was getting very late, nightfall. People ended up staying there. Everybody knew the reason why the Prophet (PBUH) camped in that place. They knew it was because Ayesha, ALLAH be pleased with her, had lost her necklace.

They went to Abu Bakar Siddique and said, "Look what your daughter has done to us. She made us spend the night in a place where there is no water. We have no water."

Abu Bakar Siddique went to Ayesha, and Ayesha said, "I was sitting and the Prophet (PBUH) was sleeping and his head was on my thigh."

Abu Bakar Siddique was poking her waist, saying, "What have you done to us? You made us stay in a place where there is no water with us."

Ayesha said, "The only reason I was not moving—because the Prophet (PBUH) was sleeping on my lap, and my father was poking me in my waist." She said, "We ended up spending the night there. Next day, in the morning, we had to leave. I had to find my necklace. We could not find it. I went on my camel, and when my camel stood up, the necklace was underneath it."

People went to Abu Bakar Siddique to complain that it was because of Ayesha. Now they stayed in a place where there was no water, and they had no water with them. That was when the revelation of Tozimum came down.

The sahaba came back to Abu Bakar Siddique and said, "This is the blessing of ALLAH of your household. This Ayyat of Tozimum came down because your daughter lost her necklace."

It is the blessing of household of Abu Bakar Siddique. The point to note here is how the Prophet (PBUH) would treat his family. With his wife, children, and servants, the Prophet (PBUH) was very accommodating.

Anas bin Malik, ALLAH be pleased with him, said, "I have served the Prophet (PBUH) my entire life. I don't remember a day when he beat me or chastise me or reprimand me for anything for my entire life." He was the servant of the Prophet (PBUH).

When the Prophet (PBUH) came to Madina, the mother of Anas bin Malik came and said, "I want to be assistant to you. Here is my son. Keep him as your servant."

God is great. She came and gave her son to serve him. Well, that was the best for her son. Anas bin Malik grew up in the house of the Prophet (PBUH) and learned all that knowledge and to become one of the greatest narrators of the Hadees. He is one of the top seven people who narrated Hadees. That was because of the decision of his mother, which was to serve the Prophet (PBUH).

Parents need to influence their children in the right way. She could have sent her son to be a great businessman or a great farmer. She made a good decision. She chose what was pleasing to ALLAH. ALLAH has blessed her son. Anas bin Malik, one of the greatest of Ansaar, well, we should not be concerned about children's rizq. ALLAH gives them rizq. When a child is born, his rizq also comes with him. Every child comes with his own rizq. We cannot provide rizq for ourselves; how can we provide rizq for our children? Rizq is coming from ALLAH. Therefore, care for them the most, save them from hellfire. Save yourself and your families from hellfire.

During the difficult time, when rumors were going around and people were accusing Ayesha, ALLAH be pleased with her, the poor relatives of Abu Bakar Siddique who were sponsored financially by Abu Bakar Siddique got involved in this rumor. They spoke against Ayesha. Abu Bakar Siddique was upset because people were talking about his daughter negatively.

He said, "I am not going to spend any more money on them."

Abu Bakar Siddique would take care of total expenses of some families, and the family of Musta was one of them. The following Ayesha was revealed. Let not there among you of virtue of these who serve not to give to the needy and poor in the cause of ALLAH. ALLAH will pardon them and overlook. Would you not like that ALLAH should forgive you and ALLAH is forgiving and merciful?

ALLAH says, "Let not those among you of virtue." ALLAH is saying Abu Bakar is a man of virtue. ALLAH is saying, "You do not want to spend on them, so you do not want ALLAH to forgive you."

As soon as Abu Bakar heard the Ayyat, he said, "Yes, I want ALLAH to forgive me." From then onward, he started to care of Musta again. Abu Bakar Siddique was doing business in Madina. He travelled to Syria and other places. He continued to earn his living even though he wanted to be close to the Prophet (PBUH), but he travelled to make a living seeking rizq. Even though he became very busy in his life in Madina, every moment he would spend in business was rewarded because everything he earned, he would spend for the sake of Islam. In fact, his business was worship. His wealth was for the service of the Prophet (PBUH) and the religion. It was exactly like he was doing other worship. The following narration will show that the Prophet (PBUH) was grateful to his friendship with Abu Bakar Siddique:

> He said to the Prophet (PBUH), "Give me a piece of land," and the Prophet (PBUH) gave a piece of land to Abu Bakar Siddique "next to mine. Then we had a dispute on a palm tree. I claimed it to be in my land, and he claimed it to be in his land. We had an argument. He then said something to me that made me upset. He spoke some harsh words that made me upset, but then he immediately regretted that and said, 'O Rubya, reply back to me so that we can get even.' Look at his nature. You respond back so we could be even." Abu Bakar Siddique did not

have hard feelings against anyone. Rubya said, "I would not reply back." Abu Bakar Siddique said, "Reply back to me, or I shall go and complain to the Prophet (PBUH)." That is how serious it was for him. He doesn't want to face ALLAH on the day of Judgment owing anything to anyone. Abu Bakar Siddique wants to be clean. He doesn't want any hard feelings in anybody's heart about him. He told Rubya to respond back, but he refused. Abu Bakar Siddique left angrily. He was going to the Prophet (PBUH), but Rubya said, "I followed him, but then a man from my clan, Aslam, said, "Why is that he is going to complain about you when he spoke ill about you in the first place?" Rubya said, "Do you know who this is? The second of two, he comes second after the Prophet (PBUH). I do not want you come around me. Otherwise, he will think we are grouping up against him. If he gets upset, then the Prophet (PBUH) becomes upset; and if the Prophet (PBUH) is upset, then ALLAH's wrath will be upon me, and that will be the end of Rubya. Get away from me. Go away." Rubya knows who Abu Bakar Siddique is. Rubya did not want to have any people around in case. Abu Bakar would think they have come to support him. Although Rubya knows that Abu Bakar spoke ill about him but he refused to respond and also refused to receive any help from his family. Then he went to the Prophet (PBUH) and saw Abu Bakar Siddique was sitting next to him. Rubya says, "The Prophet (PBUH) was sitting and looked up at me: 'O Rubya, what is your issue with Siddique?" That was the name the Prophet (PBUH) would call him. Rubya said, "O messenger of ALLAH, we had this argument. He said something to me and I was upset, then he asked me to respond and I refused." The Prophet (PBUH) said, "Yes, do not respond back but say, 'O Abu Bakar Siddique, may ALLAH forgive you.'" The Prophet (PBUH) said, "You did right. You should not respond back to Abu Bakar Siddique even if he commits wrong against you. Do not respond. Rather, say, 'May ALLAH forgive you.' Not only that you stay quiet, but make supplication that ALLAH forgives Abu Bakar Siddique." That shows the love and gratitude the Prophet (PBUH) had for Abu Bakar Siddique. The Prophet (PBUH) shows extreme loyalty to the ones who are with him from early days. The Prophet (PBUH) later on, when he opened Mecca, all those of great positions and leaders wanted to have close relationship like Abu Sufyan and other great men of Arabia, but the Prophet (PBUH) would consider the best who were with him from early days even though they were slaves. The Prophet (PBUH) remembered the service they showed to Islam, and the Prophet (PBUH) was very grateful for that.

When the Prophet (PBUH) was on his deathbed, near to death, he went to the battleground of Audh. He spoke to the Shauhda of Audh and said, "I am going to be your witness on the day of Judgment. You gave up your lives for the service of this religion. I shall be your witness." And when the Prophet (PBUH) was about to leave this world, he said, "Close all the doors except the door of Abu Bakar."

One day, Abu Bakar Siddique had an argument with Umar bin Khitab. The Prophet (PBUH) was sitting with sahaba, and Abu Bakar Siddique came running. The narrator of Hadees said he had lifted up his dress, and his knee was uncovered. The Prophet (PBUH) looked at Abu Bakar Siddique's face and said, "Your friend has been involved in a dispute. I can see on his face."

When Abu Bakar Siddique came in and gave his Salam, the Prophet (PBUH) said, "What is the problem?"

Abu Bakar Siddique said, "I had an argument with Umar bin Khitab. I spoke ill about him, then I regretted that and asked Umar, 'O Umar, forgive me. Umar bin Khitab said, 'I am not going to forgive you.' I asked him to forgive me. He refused, and he left. Umar bin Khitab regretted that.'"

Umar went to the house of Abu Bakar Siddique. Please note sahaba were very fast in forgiving. Umar bin Khitab went to the home of Abu Bakar Siddique and found out he was not there. He felt Abu Bakar was with the Prophet (PBUH). He went there. When Umar bin Khitab was coming, Abu Bakar Siddique saw that the face of the Prophet (PBUH) changed. One can tell when the Prophet (PBUH) was angry; his facial expressions would change.

Abu Bakar Siddique said, "I felt sorry for Umar bin Khitab."

Now Abu Bakar Siddique was worried that the Prophet (PBUH) would be upset with Umar bin Khitab. Abu Bakar Siddique went down on his knees and said, "O messenger of ALLAH, I am the one who transgressed against him."

Abu Bakar Siddique felt that the Prophet (PBUH) was angry and anger was directed against Umar bin Khitab. He wanted to make clear that he was the one who spoke ill against Umar bin Khitab. Even though Abu Bakar Siddique mentioned it twice and clarified the situation, the facial expression of the Prophet (PBUH) was still angry.

The Prophet (PBUH) said to Umar bin Khitab, "When I came to you, you said I am a liar and Abu Bakar Siddique said that I was telling the truth. He consoled me with himself and his wealth. Leave my friend alone. Are you going to leave my friend alone and Prophet (PBUH) it twice?" The Prophet (PBUH) wanted to make it clear to the sahaba: "Do not harm my friend Abu Bakar Siddique. He is greatest among you. Leave him alone, and do not harm him because I am going to stand for his defense. I shall be on his side." The narrator of the Hadees said we never saw anybody dare to harm him after that. This Hadees is in Bukhari.

The Prophet (PBUH) was delivering a speech. He said, "The Prophet (PBUH) said, 'ALLAH has given one of his slaves two choices—the first choice to stay in this world. The second choice is to leave this world, to die so to go to what ALLAH has for that person, the afterlife, and that slave chose the later one. That slave chose to go to what ALLAH has for him in the afterlife.'" Abu Bakar Siddique started crying.

Abu Saeed-ul-Khudry, one of Ansar, said, "We looked at Abu Bakar Siddique and could not figure out why he is crying. There was nothing emotional about that statement." ALLAH gave the choice to one of his slaves to live in this world or to leave this world, giving the choice of living longer or dying. Why was it that Abu Bakar Siddique was crying?

Abu Saeed-ul-Khudry said then, "We found out why he cried. Abu Bakar Siddique was one amongst us who understood what the Prophet (PBUH) meant. The Prophet (PBUH) was, in fact, talking about himself. He was that slave of ALLAH, but Abu Bakar Siddique, ALLAH be pleased with him, because he has spent so much time with the Prophet (PBUH) more than anyone else among the sahaba, he was able to understand the Prophet (PBUH) better than anybody else. He was able to understand the message even or before the Prophet (PBUH) speaking about it because they had been friends for their entire lives. Abu Bakar Siddique was weeping, and then the Prophet (PBUH) said the following: 'The one who had done me the greatest favors through his friendship to me and his wealth is Abu Bakar Siddique.'"

Just imagine the Prophet (PBUH) saying that toward the end of his life in front of sahaba—admission and recognition of his close friend Abu Bakar Siddique. The Prophet (PBUH) was saying that "he had done me so many favors."

There is another Hadees. The Prophet (PBUH) said, "Everyone who has done me a favor, I have paid them back except Abu Bakar Siddique." Then the Prophet (PBUH) said, "If I was to take a Khalifah, Khalifa is higher than Shaikh. Shaikh is a friend, Khalifah is a higher level than friendship, very close." The Prophet (PBUH) said, "If I was to take a Khalifah besides ALLAH, that would be Abu Bakar." The Prophet (PBUH) was saying, "I am the Khalifah of ALLAH." The Prophet (PBUH) is the Khalifah of ALLAH. The Prophet (PBUH) said, "If I was a Khalifah of someone else, that would be Abu Bakar Siddique, but between us, there is a brotherhood of Islam and the love of Islam. That is the relationship between me and Abu Bakar Siddique."

Then the Prophet (PBUH) said, "In this Masjid-e-Nabi, if the sahaba, particularly Mohajeeren, who came from Mecca, they were given small pieces of land next to the Mosque to build their houses next to the walls of the Masjid-e-Nabi. They would open for themselves very small gates so they can walk into the Mosque. There were private doors for the sahaba, and there were quite a few of them."

The Prophet (PBUH) said, "I want all of these private doors to be closed except the door of Abu Bakar. That is a privilege only for Abu Bakar Siddique—to have a private door opening into Masjid-e-Nabi."

Just imagine to have a private gate; no one gets in but you.

The Prophet (PBUH) said, "All those gates should be closed except the gate of Abu Bakar Siddique." This Hadees is in Bukhari. Abu Bakar Siddique got the message of the Prophet (PBUH) was toward the end of his life.

After a few months, the Prophet (PBUH) came back from the Hajj-tul-Widda, last Hajj. He fell ill. The illness of the Prophet (PBUH) was getting bad to worst, and he was not able to join in to Salah-tul-Jhumma. The Prophet (PBUH) said by instinct, "Abu Bakar to be the Imaam in Salah."

Ayesha, ALLAH be pleased with her, when she heard that, she tried to change the mind of the Prophet (PBUH). She said, "My father is very soft hearted. If he stands in your place, he will break down. It is not easy to replace the Prophet (PBUH). If he stands in that position, he might break down. He is softhearted. Therefore, why not ask Umar bin Khitab to take that position?" In fact, Ayesha, ALLAH be pleased with her, had another reason for not wanting her father to be there. Imagine, people came from a far distance to hear

Khutaba from a well-known scholar. It is advertised that well-known scholar is giving Khutaba, and people are coming, travelling a long distance, and then you find out that there is someone else giving Khutaba, speech. People will not like that.

Ayesha was thinking this is a place where people are expecting the Prophet (PBUH) to be. Therefore, when people will see her father, they will not like that. People are used to see that the Prophet (PBUH) is leading in that position. Therefore, she wanted to change the mind of the Prophet (PBUH). She said, "Let Umar bin Khitab lead the salah."

The Prophet (PBUH) said by instinct, "Abu Bakar Siddique to be the Imaam." She again suggested otherwise, third time. The Prophet (PBUH) said, "You are like the woman of Yousaf (PBUH). Tell Abu Bakar to lead the Salah."

The Prophet (PBUH) meant by saying woman of Yousaf (PBUH)—woman of Yousaf had different motive when they invited women to a party. The Prophet (PBUH) was saying that here, there was a different motive that she did not want her father to be the Imaam. Abu Bakar Siddique became the Imaam of Muslims for a few days. He was leading in Salah.

Abu-ul-Hashar-ul-Shamsi used this evidence to say that "Abu Bakar Siddique is the greatest scholar for this Ummah because the Prophet (PBUH) says, 'Who has greater knowledge of the book of ALLAH should lead the Salah.' Then Abu Bakar Siddique was asked to lead the Salah not only because he is the friend of the Prophet (PBUH) but also he has the most knowledge of the book of ALLAH, the deepest understanding of Islam."

Ibn-e-Kaseer commented on these words of Abu-ul-Shamsi and said, "This should be written in gold letters. These are very valuable words supporting that Abu Bakar Siddique is the most scholarly person in this Ummah."

One day, the Prophet (PBUH) felt better although still very weak and tired. One day Abdullah bin Masood came and touched the Prophet (PBUH). He saw that the temperature was very high. He said, "O messenger of ALLAH, you have a very strong fever."

The Prophet (PBUH) said, "Yes. We the prophets, our fever is double the fever of everyone else." The Prophet (PBUH) said, "The people who go through severe test are the prophets, and then it goes down according to the level. Therefore, the greater the person close to ALLAH, the test will be more difficult."

Example: When taking an exam, there are some questions only a few students will be able to handle—not everybody. Then there are some questions only A-plus will handle.

ALLAH puts the Ambia through difficult tests. The narrator of the Hadees said, "I could see the Prophet (PBUH) being carried by two men—Al-Abbas and Ali bin Abu Talib, ALLAH be pleased with him. His feet were dragging on the ground—that is how ill the Prophet (PBUH) was. He could not move his feet and was carried by two companions. They had already started the Salat. When Abu Bakar Siddique saw the Prophet (PBUH) coming, he retreated, wanted to go back. The Prophet (PBUH) waved to him and told him to stay where he was. Then the Prophet (PBUH) came and sat next to Abu Bakar, and he started leading him Salah. Abu Bakar Siddique was following the Prophet (PBUH), and sahaba are following Abu Bakar Siddique. After Salah, the Prophet (PBUH) went back inside his house. Abu Bakar Siddique carried and led the Momineen in Salah. It was Monday 12th Rabi-ul-Awal. In Salat-e-Fajr, the Prophet (PBUH) opened his curtain, and he was standing. He looked at sahaba in salah. The room of Ayesha was touching the mosque only. Curtain was separating the room from mosque. The Prophet (PBUH) uncovered that curtain and looked at sahaba praying Salat-ul-Fajar. The mosque is full, and Abu Bakar is reciting Quran in Salah. When the Prophet (PBUH) saw that, he smiled. There was happiness on his face."

The narrator of this Hadees said, "The face of the Prophet (PBUH) became like a plate of silver. It was shining with light. The Prophet (PBUH) was so happy because now he is realizing fruits of his harvest. He is watching the sahaba performing Salat, the greatest duty in Islam. The prophet (PBUH) is looking at the success of his message."

The Prophet Mohammad (PBUH), the final messenger of ALLAH, is the most successful among the Ambiya of ALLAH. The other Ambiya—once they leave this world, their nations were not able to carry on after them. They went down and down until they reached the bottom. Well, ALLAH would send another Prophet to bring them up again with Bani Israel; at one time they had seventy prophets to keep them on the straight path. The Prophet (PBUH) had been so successful that there is no need for another prophet after him. His students were also successful, as ALLAH says,

> That you are the best Ummah brought for mankind.

This ummah will carry on with his message, coming the honor of Islam until the day of Judgment. The Prophet (PBUH) said, "There will be a group in my Ummah who will stay on the straight path until the day of Judgment. They end up fighting Dajjal." The Prophet (PBUH) was so happy that he felt he was ready to leave. Mission completed. The sahaba can be trusted with the responsibility, appointing their own leader, coming on the message of Islam. This was the reason that the face of the Prophet (PBUH) was shining. The Prophet (PBUH) was happy and smiling.

One of the Sahaba said, "When we saw the face of the Prophet (PBUH), we nearly forgot about our Salah. That was such an emotional for us—we were about to forget our Salah, meaning it was going to be a fittana in our Salah.

Abu Bakar Siddique, after completing Salah, went to his daughter Ayesha and said, "It seems the Prophet (PBUH) is getting better."

At that time, Abu Bakar Siddique had two wives and told his daughter that he was going to his wife in Sunnia; the other wife was in Madhina. Sunnia was in the outskirts of Madhina. When Abu Bakar Siddique saw the Prophet (PBUH) standing up and looking at the sahaba performing salah, he felt that Prophet (PBUH) was getting better; therefore, he could go to his wife in Sunnia, but the Prophet (PBUH) was toward the last few hours of his life.

After the Prophet (PBUH) saw the sahaba and ALLAH provided comfort to his heart in seeing the fruits of his invitation, the burden of the illness was taking its toll. Samma bin Zada came in, the Prophet (PBUH) now unable to speak.

Ayesha said, "The Prophet (PBUH) would raise his hand and then put the hand on Samma bin Zada again and again. We knew that the Prophet (PBUH) was making Duah for him."

The Prophet (PBUH) loved Osama bin Zaid so much he said, "He is beloved, the son of beloved. I loved his father, and I loved him."

The Prophet (PBUH), in fact, adopted his father as his own son until adoption was abandoned in Islam where the person changes his name, but the Prophet (PBUH) loved Osama so much he was making Duah for him.

Then Ayesha said she held the Prophet (PBUH) in her arms. He was between the bottom and top of her chest. She was holding the Prophet (PBUH) in her lap. Then she said, "My brother Abdul Rehman came in, and he had Muswaq with him. The Prophet (PBUH) was looking at Muswaq, and I realized that the Prophet (PBUH) wants it. I asked him, 'Do you want it?' and the Prophet (PBUH) nodded yes."

Ayesha said, "I took the maswaq from Abdul Rehman and chewed it until it was soft then gave it to the Prophet (PBUH), and he held it in his hand. He brushed his teeth as he was healthy. Throughout while using the Muswaq, he was saying, 'The highest companion, the highest companion, the highest companion.'"

The Prophet (PBUH) was speaking to whom? He was speaking to the angel of death. The Prophet (PBUH) said, "Every prophet before their death, the angel of death comes and seeks permission from them before taking their soul."

With us, the angel of death would come unannounced and would take the soul and leave, but for the prophets of ALLAH, out of respect, he would ask the permission first—that was when Moses (PBUH) punched the angel of death; this is a well-known story in Bukhari.

The Prophet (PBUH) was saying, "The highest companion, the highest companion, the highest companion." The Prophet (PBUH) was answering the question from the angel of death and was saying, "I want to be with ALLAH. I am ready to leave. I have finished my mission. The deed is complete."

Ayesha said, "Then the Prophet (PBUH) says, "O ALLAH, for-give me and have mercy on me and make me join the highest companion that is ALLAH."

Ayesha said, "Then the Prophet (PBUH) raised up his hands and would say, "The highest companion, the highest companion, the highest companion" until his hands went down. These were his last words."

The one who loves to meet ALLAH, ALLAH will love to meet him. The Prophet (PBUH) was eager to meet his Lord, and ALLAH is also eager to meet Mohammad (PBUH), the final messenger of ALLAH. This is the greatest disaster that occurred to Ummah. In a narration, it states,

> When ever one of you is inflicted with a calamity, remember your calamity losing me. Your calamity will become insignificant to you. If you ever go through trouble, problem in your life, remember that the biggest problem of all, the biggest disaster that happened is that the Prophet Mohammad (PBUH) passed away. If you remember that, your problem will be insignificant.

How did the sahaba, ALLAH be pleased with them, deal with this? The sahaba are very solid men. They were very strong. They were capable of taking on any situation, but the death of the Prophet (PBUH) was something beyond.

Rajh-ul-Humlay said,

> When the Prophet (PBUH) died, a inca-hatic state issued. Some of the Muslims were ellecinated and did not know what they were say-

ing while some of them sat down and could not stand up. Some of them—their tongues would not move and could not speak—and some of them refused the fact that the Prophet (PBUH) has died.

Abu Bakar ul Arbi stated, "A cahatic state happened. The death of the Prophet (PBUH)—this event broke their backs. This was the biggest disaster in their lives."

Ali bin Abu Talib went in hiding in the house of Fatima and Usman could not speak and Umar bin Khitab said, "The Prophet (PBUH) did not die." He was saying, "The Prophet (PBUH) has gone to meet ALLAH for forty days, and he will come back. When he will come back, he will cut the arms and feet of those who say he (the Prophet [PBUH]) has died. It was a very difficult situation—a difficult time in their lives.

Anas bin Malik said, "I have seen two days in Madina. One day was the best day—that is when the Prophet (PBUH) came in to Madina. Everybody was happy and Madina was full of light and then I witnessed and lived through the day when the Prophet (PBUH) died. Madina became dark. The light was of the Prophet (PBUH), and when he died, the light went out of Madina."

Abu Bakar Siddique was at Sunnia. He came straight in the room of Ayesha. He came to the Prophet (PBUH) and uncovered his face. He kissed him on the forehead and said, "You are pure when alive, and you are pure when you are dead. You have gone through death that ALLAH has destined for you."

Then Abu Bakar Siddique went into the mosque. Umar bin Khitab was speaking when Abu Bakar Siddique started to talk. People left Umar and came to listen to Abu Bakar Siddique. Abu Bakar Siddique, ALLAH be pleased with him, made a brief speech, but it was a turning point in the history of this Ummah. Just a few words, Abu Bakar Siddique said, "If you were worshipping Mohammad (PBUH), the Mohammad (PBUH) is dead. But if you are worshipping ALLAH, then ALLAH is alive and ALLAH never dies." Then he recited the Ayyat 144 of Surah-al-Imran:

Mohammad is not but a messenger, other
messengers have passed on before him, so if he
was to die or he killed would have turn back on
your heels and he who turns back on his heels
will not harm ALLAH, but ALLAH will reward the
grateful.

Umar bin Khitab said, "When I heard that Ayyat from the
mouth of Abu Bakar, it felt that this was the first time I heard this
Ayyat."

Even though Umar bin Khitab was Hafiz of Quran, knew
Quran by heart, he did not imagine that the death of the Prophet
would be at that moment. The ayyat was revealed at the time of the
battle of Audh, where there was a rumor that the Prophet (PBUH)
was killed in the battle.

Some of the sahaba sat down when they heard that rumor and
said, "Why should we fight when Mohammad (PBUH) is killed?
Just stay here." Therefore, ALLAH was telling them "If Mohammad
(PBUH) is killed or dies, would you go back to unbelief? Even if he
dies, you have to carry on with the message."

Umar bin Khitab said, "When I heard Abu Bakar recite that
Ayyat, my feet and legs failed to carry me and I fell down on my
knees and I realized that the Prophet (PBUH) was dead."

Just imagine Umar bin Khitab, a strong powerful man; his feet
could not carry him, and he fell down on his knees.

The narrator says,

Then one can only hear crying in the
mosque. Abu Bakar Siddique, ALLAH be pleased
with him, is the one who brought them back to
reality. Al-Qurtbe says this is the evidence that
Abu Bakar Siddique has the strongest heart. Who
is the one closest to Mohammad (PBUH)—that
is Abu Bakar Siddique. If there was anyone who
could have failed in this situation because of the
weight of it, that should have been Abu Bakar

Siddique because he loved Mohammad (PBUH) and had been associated with him more than anybody else. Nevertheless, he was the one who brought them back and unified the sahaba and made them to realize that this is the Qadar of ALLAH and it has happened. Remember, this is one of the most outstanding moments in the life of Abu Bakar Siddique. A short speech but a turning point for the Ummah. This was Monday. Later on that day, the same day the Ansar, ALLAH be pleased with them, started gathering in Saqafit Bani Saada. This was a shed belonging to Bani Saada, a meeting place. In the beginning, there were Al-Auash and Bani Khuzarg, but Al-Auash left. Only Bani Khuzarg were there. What were they discussing? They were Ameer for Muslims. Umar bin Khitab was busy with burial, proceedings, but someone came and called him.

Umar bin Khitab said, "I am busy."

The man said, "Come out because something important has happened."

Ansar have gathered in parties in Saqifa of Bani Saada, and war was about to break out between Al-Auash and Al-Khuzarg. They fought each other for a long time. The Prophet (PBUH) brought them together. We know this very well—that Satan Iblees could cause fittana among people anytime.

In one narration, Umar bin Khitab went out. Another narration in Bukhari—that Abu Bakar Siddique and Umar bin Khitab both went to Saqif Bani Saada. When they were going there, they met with two men from Al-Auash.

They asked, "Where are you going?"

Abu Bakar Siddique and Umar bin Khitab said they were going to the meeting place of Ansar. They said, "Do not worry, you the Al-Majroon, go ahead and decide. You make a decision and do not worry about Ansar gathering"—meaning "this affair belongs to Mohajereen."

But Umar bin Khitab said, "But we shall go there because it is Shaura. We will not make decision of our own. The decision will be through Shaura."

They went to the meeting place, Al-Khuzarg. There was a man sitting there covered with blanket.

Umar bin Khitab asked, "Who is this man?"

They said, "Saad bin Abida. He is ill."

He had a fast fever. Saad bin Abida was the leader of Al-Khuzarg. He was the one they wanted to appoint Ansaar over Muslims. Saad bin Abida was very well known among Ansaar. The Prophet (PBUH) liked him very much. They wanted to appoint him the leader for the Muslim community. Abu Bakar Siddique and Umar bin Khitab went in and sat down.

Umar bin Khitab said, "I was preparing a speech while walking toward the meeting place in his mind, bringing together a speech to present."

One of the Ansaar stood up and started to speak. This was a formal meeting. They would start by praising ALLAH and making Salah on the Prophet (PBUH).

He said, "We Ansaar are the helpers of ALLAH"—*Ansaar* means "the helpers"—"and we are the Battalion of Islam. We are the army of the religion while Majhroon fear immigrants, are small in number, who left their people, but now they want to ship away from us this authority." In fact, this man was saying that the leadership of the community should be transferred to Ansaar after the Prophet (PBUH). He was saying Mahjar were few in numbers compared to Ansaar. In all the battles, Ansaar were the majority, and Mahjjaroon were minority. This Hadees is in Bukhari. He was asking that Bia Baat should be given to Saad bin Abida.

Umar bin Khitab stood up to speak because he had already prepared the speech in his mind, but Abu Bakar Siddique said, "Umar! Take it easy and sit down until I deliver my speech and complete it. Then you can say whatever you want."

Umar bin Khitab said, "Because of the temper of Abu Bakar Siddique and because I do not want to anger him, therefore I sat down."

Abu Bakar Siddique stood up and started to speak. Among the things, he said, "Perhaps all of his speech survived. We have got it in bits and pieces." He said, "What you have mentioned about yourself, meaning Ansaar, it is undeniable. That is the truth. When you say you are the army of Islam, that is truth. When you say you are the helpers of ALLAH, that is truth."

Abu Bakar added to that by narrating the Ayyat and Hadees, which praise Ansaar. Abu Bakar Siddique said, "The Prophet (PBUH) said, 'If Ansaar would take one way while all the other people take another way, I shall follow the Ansaar.' The Prophet (PBUH) said, 'I am with you'. The Prophet (PBUH) said, 'My life and my death will be with Ansaar.' When the Prophet (PBUH) opened Mecca, he did not stay in Mecca but went back with Ansaar to Madina."

Abu Bakar Siddique brought up all these Hadees, praising Ansaar, but then he said, "But the Arabs will never accept leadership but in the hands of Quraish. The Arabs were divided tribes, and every tribe had its own pride. It is very difficult to bring them together."

Abu Bakar Siddique was saying the only people whom the Arabs will be willing to submit to—the people of Quraish because it had been established in their hearts that Quraish are the mobility of Arabia. They are protectors of Al-Harm.

Abu Bakar Siddique then held up the hands of Umar and Abu Abida and said, "I would be satisfied with either of these two men being the Ameer. Therefore, give Biea to whoever you want."

Umar bin Khitab said, "Everything I wanted to say in my prepared speech, Abu Bakar has said it in his impromptu speech." He said, "I was preparing and thinking about the speech all the way until I got there. Abu Bakar Siddique said it in a better way and in a complete way and added the things which I had missed in his impromptu speech."

Umar bin Khitab said, "The only thing to my disliking was his last statement asking people to give Biea to me."

Then Umar bin Khitab said, just looking at what he said, "ALLAH be pleased." He said, "In the name of ALLAH, I be rather taken and beheaded than become Ameer over people and Abu Bakar is one of them. I would never want to be a leader over Abu Bakar Siddique. I would rather die than be a leader over Abu Bakar Siddique."

Umar bin Khitab saw it as inappropriate. "How could I be in a position of leadership and Abu Bakar is behind me?" He said, "I rather die. They cut my neck."

Al-Habab bin Munder stood up and said, "I have a solution." He was one of Ansar. "How about Mohajereen appoint an Ameer and we Ansaar appoint an Ameer?"

Umar bin Khitab said, "You cannot have two swords in one sheath. Two swords cannot go together. There has to be one leader." Then an argument happened, and voices were raised.

Umar bin Khitab said, "I feared Fittana. Therefore, I went ahead and told Abu Bakar, 'Extend your hand forward, and I shall give you Biea.'"

Then Umar said, "I gave my Biea to Abu Bakar Siddique, and after that, Mohajereen followed. They were doing this with such emotions. They came to realize who could we appoint an Ansaar and Abu Bakar is around."

Later on, Umar bin Khitab said, "Oh, people of Ansar, you should know that the Prophet (PBUH) has appointed Abu Bakar Siddique to be our Imaam. Which one of you can stand and be an Imaam while Abu Bakar is there? The Prophet (PBUH) has appointed Abu Bakar Siddique to be Imaam, and Khalifah would be the Imaam in Salah. Can you lead Abu Bakar in Salah?"

They said, "We seek refuge in ALLAH." They came back to realize that Abu Bakar should be Khalifah. They all jumped forward to give biea to Abu Bakar, and doing that, some of them were stepping over Saad bin Abida. He was ill and lying there. Some people were saying, "Be careful. You will kill Saad bin Abida."

This was not a nationalism or tribalism. They were searching for the truth. Whenever they would find it, they would hold on to it.

Few important notes on the affairs of Saqifa. First of all, both Abu Bakar Siddique and Umar bin Khitab were not seeking leadership. Umar bin Khitab said he would rather like to be beheaded rather than seeking leadership over Abu Bakar while Abu Bakar Siddique said in a Khutabah, "I have never been eager to become a leader in any night or in any day and I have never wanted this to come to me and I never prayed to ALLAH to make me a leader— public or private—but I was afraid that it will become a fittana. I am afraid of disunity among Ummah, and that is the reason I have accepted it. I accepted it for the benefit of the Ummah. I am having no rest, no peace of mind for this position of leadership."

He said, "I have no ability to take on this responsibility unless ALLAH gives me strength. I have designed someone stronger than me to take it from me."

They did not want to become leaders. They were not seeking authority.

Abu Bakar Siddique said, "He accepted it to keep away from fittana." When Abu Bakar Siddique said, "People will not accept except Quraish," in fact, there is a Hadees that narrated among forty sahaba. There are many narrations but one of them in Quraish. This affair is in the hands of Quraish. That is because of their status. The Prophet (PBUH) said that the position of Khalifah was only Khalifah; there were other positions of leadership. This is strictly talking about the position of Khalifah, the highest position.

The Hadees that indicated the Khalafah of Abu Bakar Siddique. There are many indications and hints to the Khalafah of Abu Bakar Siddique:

(1) This Hadees is in Muslim. Attatumara, a Prophet (PBUH). A woman came to the Prophet Mohammad (PBUH). Mohammad (PBUH) told her to come back. She wanted to ask a question or something else. The Prophet (PBUH) told her to come back, made an appointment for her. She asked, "O messenger of Allah, what if I did not find you?" The Prophet (PBUH) said, "'If you do not find me, then go to Abu Bakar."

Ibn-e-Hajar Askalani said, "In this Hadees, there is evidence that the appointments of the Prophet (PBUH) are to be carried on by the Khalifah after him. The Khalifah after him is Abu Bakar Siddique, and the response is to claim that Khalifah should have been

Ali bin Abu Talib or Al-Abbas." This was an important point made by Ibn-e-Hajar Askalani. He said, "This is clear evidence that the Prophet (PBUH) considers his deputy to take responsibility in his absence is Abu Bakar Siddique. The Prophet (PBUH) made it clear. The Imaam in Salah is Abu Bakar, and Salah is religion."

This woman came to the Prophet (PBUH) maybe for a different issue. Maybe she wanted Sadaka or she may have a question. The Prophet (PBUH) was telling her, "If you do not find me, go to Abu Bakar." Abu Bakar was a leader for religious and other issues. Therefore, it is clear evidence that the Prophet (PBUH) was saying, "The one who should assume the responsibility after me is Abu Bakar. If you do not find me, go to Abu Bakar Siddique."

(2) This Hadees is in Tirmisey. Hadefa said, "We were sitting with the Prophet (PBUH) in a gathering. The Prophet (PBUH) said he did not know how long he would be among the sahaba but "follow the two who will come after me." The Prophet (PBUH) pointed to Abu Bakar Siddique and Umar bin Khitab. Also said, "Hold on to the covenant of Umar, whatever Ibn-e-Masood narrates of my Hadees." Believe that the Prophet (PBUH) was pointing to Abu Bakar and Umar bin Khitab; follow their ways—meaning "these are the leaders after me."

(3) This Hadees is in Muslim. Abu Hurrairah narrated, "The Prophet (PBUH) saw a dream. In the dream, the Prophet (PBUH) was sitting next to a pool, and he was drawing water for people to drink. In old days, there used to be a pool next to the well. People would draw water out of the well and pour the water into the pool and people would directly drink from the pool. The Prophet (PBUH) said he was drawing water out of the well, "then Abu Bakar Siddique wanted me to rest, and he took over and started pulling out the water from the well, but his pulling was weak, may ALLAH forgive him." The Prophet (PBUH) said, "Then Umar bin Khitab came and took over the bucket from Abu Bakar." The Prophet (PBUH) said, "I have never seen a man strong and pulling out water like Umar bin Khitab." When he left, the pool was full and splashing.

A Shaffi gave an interpretation to this dream. He said, "The dreams of the prophets are a form of revelation. When the Prophet

(PBUH) said the drawing water by Abu Bakar was weak, it means that his Khalafah will be short. It will not be long and he will not make many conquests. He will not spread the water all over."

The water from the well is a religion of Islam. The Khalafah of Abu Bakar was short. He did not have the chance to spread the religion very far. His Khalafah was just over two years. His Khalafah was not as long as Umar's Khalafah, and Umar devoted his time spreading the message and the religion of ALLAH—that is what it means that the pool of water was full and water was splashing out. It is also evidence that the Hadees is saying that the next Khalifah after the Prophet (PBUH) is Abu Bakar Siddique followed by Umar bin Khitab.

(4) This Hadees is in Muslims' Shareef. Ayesha, Allah be pleased with her, said the Prophet (PBUH) told her when he was ill, "Call your father Abu Bakar and call your brother Abdul Rehman so that he, the Prophet (PBUH), can make a covenant because he was afraid that someone may desire that and say it is more appropriate for him to be in that position." But Allah and the believers only want Abu Bakar Siddique. The Prophet (PBUH) was saying, "Give me a paper. To that I shall write down a document that the Khalifah after me is Abu Bakar because someone may come and claim this and say that it belongs to me when Allah and believers want Abu Bakar Siddique." We know that did not happen. The Prophet (PBUH) did not write the covenant. It will be talked about later, also about the implications of that.

(5) Hadees in Muslims when the Prophet (PBUH) was ill. He was asked to pray, but they said, "No, people are waiting," and the Prophet (PBUH) said, "Put some water on me." The Prophet (PBUH) had a high temperature, fever, and poured cold water on his body, but he, the Prophet (PBUH), fell unconscious. When he regained consciousness, he asked, "Did they pray?"

Answer was, "No, he asked for water, wanted to prepare for Salah, but every time, he would fall unconscious." That happened three times.

Then the Prophet (PBUH) said, "Tell Abu Bakar Siddique to lead the Salah."

Abu Bakar asked Umar, "Why do you not lead people in Salah?"

Umar bin Khitab said, "No," and told Abu Bakar, "You should be the one leading Salah."

Here is another evidence that Abu Bakar considered Umar bin Khitab should be after him, second after Abu Bakar. That is the reason Abu Bakar Siddique asked Umar bin Khitab to lead Salah, and Umar bin Khitab said, "No, but you are the one who should be the Imaam." This is another evidence that Khalifah of Muslims should be the Imaam, and the Prophet (PBUH) clearly said that was Abu Bakar Siddique.

(6) The conversation took place at Sakeefa between Ansaar and Abu Bakar Siddique and Umar bin Khitab where Ansaar said, "Have two leaders, one from each side."

Umar bin Khitab simply told them, "Oh, people of Ansaar, do you not remember that the Prophet (PBUH) told Abu Bakar Siddique to lead the Salah? Now, who would like to be the Imaam while Abu Bakar Siddique is praying behind you?" and they said, "We seek refuge in ALLAH. We would never want be ahead of Abu Bakar Siddique, ALLAH be pleased with him."

Ali bin Abu Talib narrated, "When the Prophet (PBUH) passed away, we found that the Prophet (PBUH) has, in fact, appointed Abu Bakar the Imaam in Salah. We said, 'If the Prophet (PBUH) is pleased to have Abu Bakar lead us in our religion, then he should also be our leader in worldly affairs because religious affairs have higher status. Since Abu Bakar is appointed to lead in religion, then it makes sense that he should also lead in our worldly affairs.'" This is the statement made by Ali bin Abu Talib, ALLAH be pleased with him. "Intahqat Insanat."

Ale-Summa have two opinions regarding Abu Bakar Siddique whether the Prophet (PBUH) appointed Abu Bakar Siddique Khalifah explicitly or implicitly. Some scholars point out the appointment of Abu Bakar Siddique as Khalifah and implicitly apply that this is opinion of Imam Hussan-ul-Bassary and also the opinion of Imam Ahmad bin Humel.

Some scholars consider the Khalifah of Abu Bakar explicitly appointment by the Prophet (PBUH) because he appointed him to lead the salah. This is the opinion of Ilim Al-Hazari, also the opinion of Ale-Hadees. Their evidence is if you do not find me, then go to Abu Bakar. They consider this as a clear appointment by the Prophet (PBUH) Abu Bakar Siddique as Khalifah.

Ibn-e-Tamia commented on this by saying, "The Prophet (PBUH) has hinted and applied without explicitly writing it or mentioning this." Ibn-e-Tamia said it is the wisdom of ALLAH that the appointment of Abu Bakar Siddique should be done through a document or will by the Prophet (PBUH). Ibn-e-Tamia said, "If it was done through a document, then people would say Abu Bakar was appointed because of that document. The way he is appointed, the implication of Hadees and also by the choice of Muslims because they gave him Biea. Therefore, it is combined, stronger, and raises the status of Abu Bakar Siddique." Ibn-e-Tamia said, "This is expected thing to do that it does not even need to be written down. It was clear, and that is what happened. There was no dispute on the issue."

Abu Bakar was given Biea and then public Biea in the masjid, private Biea in Sakeefa; and then later on, when Abu Bakar Siddique gave his first Khutba in the Masjid as leader, Khalifah, the rest of the people came and gave Biea.

The Question by Ali bin Abu Talib was "Why is that he did not give his Biea in Sakeefa, in the portaces of bani Saad!" The answer was simple—because Ali bin Abu Talib was entrusted with the funeral arrangements for the Prophet (PBUH). He was the twelfth male family relative of the Prophet (PBUH). Therefore, he was given this responsibility of organizing the burial of the Prophet (PBUH). Also, the Biea of Abu Bakar Siddique happened on the same day, the day the Prophet (PBUH) passed away. That was Monday. That was one of the reasons that Ali bin Abu Talib was late for giving his Biea to Abu Bakar Siddique, but Abu Bakar Siddique called him in the mosque, and Ali bin Abu Talib came and gave his Biea. According to the above, all other stories are not true. Ali bin Abu Talib had reasons for not giving Biea on the first day because he was busy with organizing burial of the Prophet (PBUH).

Ibn-e-Tamia stated, "If this had been an issue and confusion, the Prophet (PBUH) would have clarified and would have written it down." He said this issue had no confusion. The status of Abu Bakar Siddique was so high there was no confusion. Abu Bakar Siddique was the Khalifah. Ale Sunna considered the consensus of sahaba that Abu Bakar Siddique was the Khalifah.

Saeed bin Ayaz was asked when he gave his Biea. He said, "The same day the Prophet (PBUH) passed away, because sahaba did not want to stay even for one day without Jhamah, they did this on the day even before the burial of the Prophet (PBUH).

When we talk about the importance of the Khalifah, the Prophet (PBUH) passed away. They had to be wash and buried. We also know the Sunna is to bury the person as fast as possible. The burial of the Prophet (PBUH) was delayed. He died on Monday, but he was buried on Wednesday night because sahaba wanted to clear the issue of Khalafah first. Sahaba, before the Prophet (PBUH), they were Arabs and usually a disorganized people, fighting with each other. They were independent. They did not want to commit to any one leader, but now this collective work was so much ingrained in them they considered this inappropriate to stay even for one day without having a leader who would run their affairs, and they gave that trust before washing and burying the Prophet (PBUH) even though their hearts were broken. They were discussing this issue on the same day the Prophet (PBUH) passed away. This shows the importance of Khalafah in our lives, Muslims in a Jhamad, and a leader to run their affairs.

Asklani said that was the Jahamah of Muslims to obey Abu Bakar Siddique.

The issue of Khalafah, Imam Abu worthy, he was one of the great classical scholars of Islam in political issues. He wrote a book, *Ahaqoam- Sultania, The Laws of Governance.* He said the issue of having an Imam—Imam means leader—is one of the fundamentals of religion. He says, "ALLAH wants Ummah to have a leader to succeed the prophethood." Therefore, the issue of leader is so important that he is a successor of prophethood. He should try to fulfill the roles the Prophet (PBUH) used to fulfill in his life. That was one of the reasons Abu Bakar Siddique was called Khalifah-tul-Rasool ALLAH, the successor of the Prophet (PBUH). "If you do not find me, then go to Abu Bakar"; he was the deputy to the Prophet (PBUH).

What is the order of Khalifah? It is sunnah. Is it Wajiha? Ibn-e-Hajar Askalani commented on a statement made by Doady—he is also a scholar—that establishing Khalifah is Sunna Mohukida. Ibn-e-Hajar responded to that—the evidence Dahoody used was that Biea to Abu Bakar Siddique was not given until hours passed. He stated that they stayed a few hours without a Khalifah. It means it is a Sunna Mahukida.

Asscullani commented on this and said, "But that is not the view of the scholars. The consensus of scholars is that it is mandatory, the fact they waited for few hours." He said waiting to bring the unity among the Muslims is acceptable. If waiting for some hours to unify the Ummah is acceptable, and this is the fastest possible time, they could establish Khalifah within hours. Ibn-e-Hajar made it clear that it is the duty compulsory. It is consensus of the Sahaba because they did it even before they buried the Prophet (PBUH). Sometimes we establish our religious views based on what is the dominant case around us. We think because this is how we are now, this is the right way to be. In some places, there are rich and no Khalafah in Islam today. People think there is no problem in that. The sahaba in early days in Mecca, the total population of Muslims was thirty-eight only.

Abu Bakar Siddique went to the Prophet (PBUH) and said, "We should have invited in public, not in secret."

As soon as sahaba reached one hundred, the Prophet (PBUH) was searching for a base to establish a proper community; but then, the Prophet (PBUH) moved to Madina. If he had wanted to stay in Mecca, his uncle Abbas was giving protection. The Prophet (PBUH) was not harmed physically. There were threats to his life, but invitation was going on. But the Prophet (PBUH) was asking for support in the last few years of his invitation in Mecca. Sahaba did not like Islam being humiliated.

Some points from the meeting: (1) Shaura in Islam. Umar bin Khitab said whoever asks to be in a position leadership without the Shaura, it is not Halal for him to accept it. The Biea of Abu Bakar was through the Shaura of Muslims, some with the Khulafah after that. We also know that Khalfah is established through Biea.

The Prophet (PBUH) said, "If one dies without beit to an Imaam, he will die in a state of Jahaliya."

Abu Bakar Siddique said, "People would not accept a leader outside Quraish. We have to consider what is possible and what is not possible."

After the Biea given to Abu Bakar Siddique, ALLAH be pleased with him, the postika in Saqeefa of Banu Saada. The next day, Tuesday, they met in the mosque. That was the time when everybody was going to give Biea to Abu Bakar Siddique. Umar bin Khitab had Abu Bakar stand on the pulpit. Umar bin Khitab made praise to ALLAH and salah to the messenger of ALLAH (PBUH). Umar bin Khitab, ALLAH be pleased with him, said, "Yesterday, I said something that is not in the book of ALLAH, and that was my own opinion." He was referring to what he said—that the Prophet (PBUH) did not die and other words relating to the statement.

Umar bin Khitab said, "This is not in the book of ALLAH. That was my own opinion."

He was apologizing for what he had said the day before, then he asked Muslims to stand up and give Biea to Abu Bakar Siddique, ALLAH be pleased with him, the one who would carry the initiative. In many major events of Muslims' Ummah was Umar bin Khitab. He was the first one to give his hand to Abu Bakar Siddique and gave Biea in Saqeefa. Now he was the one who was arranging the general Biea of Muslims.

Muslims were standing one by one, placing their hand in the hand of Abu Bakar, and were giving Biea. What does Biea mean?

The literal meaning of *Biea* is transaction, like in a sale. If one sells something, that transaction is called Biea. That word is borrowed in this context to give it a new meaning, and that is covenant between two parties just like a financial transaction; there are two parties, and they both consent to this trade. There must be consent when a financial transaction happens, meaning "I cannot sell you if I do not want to sell you, and you do not buy this if you do not want to." Therefore, both parties need to agree. They would shake hands to finalize the agreement. Shaking of hands symbolizes the consent from both sides. It means both parties agree; they do that by shaking of the hands. This tradition carries on among Muslims and non-Muslims.

This is honored to show the position of the leader and the followers. This is convenient between them. This is called Biea. This is a pledge between the leader and the follower. The Prophet (PBUH) took Biea from the Ansaar in Bina Tul Aqha. The Prophet (PBUH) took a pledge of allegiance from woman. He took a pledge of allegiance from individuals. He took a pledge from one man that you do not ask anything from anybody. The pledge could be on different issues. There is a minor biea, and there is a major biea. A minor biea is on a particular issue while the major biea is on the Khalafah.

Hadees said, "If you die and do not have Biea on your neck, then you are doing on the way of ignorance." Biea is something one cannot get out of if entered. There is no way of breaking this. If one commits to it, they commit to it as long as they live. This is the reason the Prophet (PBUH) said, "It is tied around your neck, cannot get out."

When sahaba gave biea to Abu Bakar Siddique, they knew this was serious. Likewise, when they gave biea to the Prophet (PBUH), they knew this was serious.

When the Prophet (PBUH) asked the Ansaar, "I want you to give me the Biea that you will protect me as much as you protect your families and your wealth," the Ansaar knew the implication of that. One of the Ansaar stood up before they gave the Biea. He told them, "Do you know what you are getting into? This is something that will cause you a lot of enemies, and people are going to point their swords towards you." Then he said, "If you do not think you will carry it out, pull out now before it is too late. Because once we have given the Biea, we cannot walk out."

At that time, they asked the Prophet (PBUH), "If you want this from us, what is for us in this because this is two-way traffic? It is not only one-way relationship." They said, "That is your part of the agreement. What is for us?"

The Prophet (PBUH) did not promise them wealth, salary. The Prophet (PBUH) said, "I promise you paradise."

Ansaar said, "What a profitable trade. We shall never give up. What is better than paradise?"

Therefore, the Biea we are referring to is Hadees—that is Biea of Khalfah. This type of Biea is only given to the Khalifa, not to anybody else. Major Biea only goes to the Khalifah. Minor Biea on other issues can be given to other people. For example, in the battle of Yarmooke, some of the sahaba said, "We pledge to die"—very famous martyrs, the biea to die in this battle. Therefore, this form of biea is acceptable in the absence of the Khalifa, but the Major Biea only belongs to the Khalifah of the Muslims. I hope the issue of Biea is clear.

After the Biea, Abu Bakar Siddique, ALLAH be pleased with him, stood up on the member and delivered his inauguration speech. This was the first speech as Khalifah. He said, "O people, I have been put in authority over you, but I am not the best of you. If I do the right thing for you, then help me. If I do wrong, then put me straight. Truthfulness is a secret trust, and living is a betrayal. The weak one among you is strong until I restore his right, Inshallah, and strong one of you is weak until I take from him what is due. Inshallah. No people forsake Jehad for the sake of ALLAH but ALLAH inflicts them with humiliation, nor does the indency spread among the people that ALLAH develops them in punishment. Obey me as long as I obey ALLAH and his messenger. If I do not obey ALLAH and his messenger, you do not owe me obedience. Stand up for your prayers. May ALLAH have mercy upon you."

This is a masterpiece when it comes to politics or governance. Abu Bakar Siddique, ALLAH be pleased with him, was now entering into a new territory. He was the first Khalifah. No one has any experience in that. Before that time, there was the Prophet (PBUH) himself.

Now it was obvious there would be some changes between a Prophet (PBUH) leading his people and a man from people leading the people. There were bound to be some differences. From now on, that would be Abu Bakar Siddique laying down some ground rules for the Khalifah after him. He was the one who would sit the Sunna of Khalafah. No one had done it before. He was the one who was going to lay down the groundwork for Khalafah Islamia. This fell under the Sunnah of the Prophet (PBUH). He said, "Follow my Sunnah and Sunnah of righteous guided Khalifah after me." Therefore, what Abu Bakar Siddique was doing is part of the Sunna that we are commanded to follow. There are a lot of issues that could be debated how to deal with these issues.

Abu Bakar Siddique, from his first day, was telling them how we shall proceed. First of all, he was saying, "I have been put in authority over you, but I am not best among you." We know he is the best among the sahaba—there is no doubt about that—but this could also mean that there could be a situation where the Imaam may not be the best out of the community. If that is the case, do you change the Imaam, or do you follow the Imaam? And this is called Imam-ul-Mufzoal, meaning "Imam is not the best over the best."

The scholars say, "If the Imaam is following the law of ALLAH and establishing the limit of ALLAH, then the people should not pull out their hands from his hisa. Even though he might not be the best, he may be the second best. But as long as he is establishing the Sheria of ALLAH, people should follow that Imaam and should avoid Fittana. That could be implied from the statement of Abu Bakar Siddique—that he is not the best among them. Even though he is the Khalifah, he is not the best among them. Abu Bakar Siddique said that out of humbleness. He established the sources of law.

At the time of the Prophet (PBUH), he was receiving the revelations from ALLAH and would govern the Ummah accordingly. The Khalifah after him had no revelation. What should he do? What are the sources of laws? Abu Bakar Siddique said, "Obey me as long as I am obeying ALLAH and his messenger."

(1) The sources of law, ALLAH and his book, Quran, and the Sunnah of the messenger of ALLAH. "Follow me as long as I am following ALLAH and his messenger."

(2) About the speech of Abu Bakar Siddique, the rights of the Ummah hold the leaders accountable. Does the Ummah have the right to hold the leader accountable? This issue was not clear yet at

the time of the Prophet (PBUH). It is obvious that they, the people, could not. At the time of the Prophet (PBUH) could not, the Ummah could not and were not able to hold the messenger of ALLAH accountable. Who is the Ummah? He holds the Prophet (PBUH) accountable for what he does. The Ummah does not have the right to question the leadership of the Prophet (PBUH) because the Prophet Mohammad (PBUH) was being corrected by ALLAH through angel Jibraeel. There are so many examples where ALLAH was correcting through Jibraeel, but people did not have the right to correct the Prophet (PBUH). This is an issue to be clarified.

Abu Bakar Siddique was not a prophet. Could the people correct him or not?

He said, "If I do right, then help me and support me. But if I do wrong, then put me straight." Now the leadership is not in the hand of the Prophet (PBUH). People can make mistakes, and if people see a mistake, it is their responsibility to put the mistake right. Abu Bakar Siddique knew that his way will be followed. He was saying, "It is your responsibility to fix my mistakes," meaning put him on the straight path even with some force is needed. If something is twisted, bent, strength is needed to put it right.

Umar bin Khitab once said, "If I failed to follow the path of ALLAH and his messenger, what will you do?"

One man said, "We will straighten you with our swords."

Umar bin Khitab said, "Praise be to ALLAH, among the people, there is someone like you." He appreciated that there are people who can speak the truth. Therefore, the accountability of the leadership is necessary. This should be on every level. In luxurious politics and in religion, this is the leadership in Islam which now we are diverted from.

(3) The Islamic state will be established on justice and equality.

> The weak one among you is strong as for
> as I am concerned, until his right is restored.
> Inshallah. And strong one of you is weak until I
> take from him what is due. Inshallah.

This means there will be no favoritism. There will be no pref-
erence of one over another. "For weak people, I shall give them what
is due to them. From strong, I shall take away what is due to others."
Abu Bakar Siddique decided to pay every member of the Muslim
community a fixed payment. In those days, every Muslim used to
receive salary from the government not for any work they do for the
government, but this was something which was paid to every member of the Islamic nation. Abu Bakar Siddique decided to pay ten
dinars each. Ayesha, ALLAH be pleased with her, would say that Abu
Bakar would pay every free man ten dinars, including slaves, likewise
ten dinars to women and their slave women also ten dinars. All of
them are equal.

Some of the scholars came to Abu Bakar Siddique and said,
"We see that you have made equal payments for everyone when
there are people more pious and one serving Islam more than others.
Therefore, they should be paid more."

Abu Bakar Siddique said, "What you say about the righteousness of the people, only ALLAH knows, I do not know. Then I cannot
decide who should be paid more. Anyway, these are the provisions
of this world, and the beneficial reward for righteousness is in the
life hereafter. It is not in this world. Let everybody live in this world
because the reward will come on the day of Judgment."

Next year, Abu Bakar Siddique raised the payment to twenty
dinars. More money was coming to the Muslim treasury; therefore,
he started to pay more to Muslims. They would receive that payment. Even the children would receive.

When Umar bin Khitab became Khalifah, he changed the payments for valid reasons as he saw. But when Umar bin Khitab was
leaving this world, he said if he could reverse something that he had
done, he would have followed the way of Abu Bakar and would pay
the people equal amount.

(4) Truth: the relationship between the leader and the follower
is a relationship of trust. There must be trust. Without trust, there is
no relationship between the leader and the follower.

Abu Bakar Siddique said, "Truthfulness is a sacred trust, and
lying is a betrayal. I want my followers to be truthful to me, and

I shall be truthful to them." That is the relationship. In Islam, it is emphasized that a leader should be honest and truthful. The Prophet (PBUH) said, "There are three people whom ALLAH will not speak to on the day of Judgment and they will not be purified. ALLAH will not look at them, and they will have severe punishment: (i) an old man who is committing adultery, (ii) a king who is a liar, (iii) a dependent who is destitute but still arrogant.

The Prophet (PBUH) said, "These three people, ALLAH will not look at them, will not speak to them, and will not purify them. Why? Because these three people are committing sins which are inappropriate for them."

An old man who is committing adultery—the urge for this desire becomes less when a person is older. For an old man to commit such a sin shows the perversion of such a heart. This is indecent. Although the same sin by a young man is different, but punishment is the same for both. But the weight of the sin is greater when a person is older. Question—what is the age limit? Who is old?

A king who is telling lies—normally people lie out of weakness. People lie out of fear. A king who is not in that position, a king is in a position of strength should not be afraid. The king is not weak. Why should he lie? That also shows evilness. That shows the personality and character of a person.

The third one, someone who is dependent on others for food and shelter and he is still arrogant against that person. Poverty makes a person humble, but a person who is poor and still arrogant—he is a disaster. Lying when it comes from a person in position of leadership is a major sin. God only knows about the rulers in the Muslim world because it is doubtful if they are strong. They are more puppets than kings and leaders.

But Abu Bakar Siddique was saying that "the relationship between me and you is a relationship of truth."

(5) Jehad said, "No people forsake Jehaad for the sake of ALLAH, but ALLAH inflicts them. ALLAH governs the life of people."

The Prophet (PBUH) said this is in Abu Dahood, The Prophet (PBUH) said, "If you trade and follow the tails of cows and you are busy with agriculture and leave Jehad, then ALLAH will punish you with humiliation, and that will not be lifted until you go back to your religion." The foreign policy at the time of Abu Bakar Siddique was Jehaad.

(6) War against voice, evil, indecency. Abu Bakar Siddique said, "Nor does indecency spread among the people but ALLAH develops them in punishment."

In Ibn-e-Maja:

> The Prophet (PBUH) says, "When every indecency, prevails in society, then ALLAH will punish them with diseases which did not exist among their forefathers.:

The word we have is *Tul-her*. It means "publicly practiced when indecency." Indecency is publicly practiced. Even at the time of Khalifah, people were committing sins in secret. There is a miracle of the Hadees of the Prophet (PBUH). When sins are committed publicly, ALLAH will inflict diseases which did not exist in their forefathers. AIDS is one of the testimonies of that. AIDS was not known generations before, but it happened because of practice of indecency. A nation and people who are indecent become weak. They cannot fight and cannot defend themselves.

ALLAH says,

> When we intend to destroy a city, we command its affluent but they defiantly display there in.

So the word becomes, in fact, up them which we destroy completely. The affluent, the high class—that is where the corruption starts. That is where indecency starts. When that happens, their way becomes a role model for the rest of the society. Seeds of evil are planted there, and fruits extend all over the society. Well, no nation was destroyed until the high class was corrupt and their corruption spread to the society, and that when the punishment of ALLAH came upon the society. That happened to the Roman, Greek, and Persian

Empires, and it happened to Muslims. These rules do not exempt anyone. Muslims committed indecency and did not stay with the book of ALLAH, and therefore, they were wiped out.

The Prophet (PBUH) said, "I do not fear poverty on you, but my worry is that you will become wealthy. When you become wealthy, then you start competing over this world. When you do that, you will be destroyed like people before you."

ALLAH says,

> Also ALLAH presents an example a city, which safe and secure, its provisions coming from every location in abundance but it denied favors of ALLAH. Therefore ALLAH made them taste hunger and fear for what they had been doing. (Surah-e-Nahal vv. 1–12)

That was the speech of Abu Bakar Siddique for Khalafah. He set the rules for Islamic government: (1) sources, Quran, and Sunnah, (2) to hold the leaders accountable, (3) justice and equality, (4) trust between the leader and the followers, (5) Jehaad for the sake of ALLAH, (6) war against biased favoritism.

One day, after Abu Bakar Siddique became Khalifah, Umar bin Khitab and Ibn-e-Jaraha saw Abu Bakar Siddique carrying some garment on his shoulders, walking toward the marketplace to do business.

Umar bin Khitab asked him, "What are you doing?"

Abu Bakar Siddique said, "I am going to trade—buying and selling."

Umar bin Khitab said, "But you have some duties towards Ummah, and you are buying and selling garments?"

Abu Bakar Siddique said, "I have to provide for my family."

Umar bin Khitab said, "Let us pay you a salary."

Well, Umar bin Khitab and Abu Abida took Abu Bakar Siddique along. They decided to pay him 250 dinars per year and to give him daily allowance for food. How much food did they give him? They gave him one-half of sheep every day. A little while after that, Umar bin Khitab took responsibility.

The prophet (PBUH) told Umar bin Khitab, "You are similar to Moses (PBUH). Moses (PBUH) could not see anything going wrong and ignored it. Moses (PBUH) would interfere, could not ignore it. That was the personality of Moses (PBUH). He just could not walk away from an event. When Moses (PBUH) saw an Egyptian beating and fighting an Israeli, he interfered and paid very dearly for that. Moses (PBUH) had to leave Egypt because of that because he was accused of committing a murder because of that even though he ran away from Egypt for helping someone who got him into trouble. After running away from Egypt, when Moses (PBUH) reached Murdyan after a long journey by foot, his shoes were torn apart. He was walking on his bare feet and the skin of his soles peeled off. He had no food and survived by eating tree leaves. His lips were green and dry, cracking. When he arrived, he was tired. He threw himself under a tree for rest. He prayed to ALLAH. He said, 'O ALLAH, I am in need of any good that you send down to me. Anything that comes from you, I need it.' That showed how desperate Moses (PBUH) was. What did he see? Even in that situation, he saw two women with their sheep and goats standing behind many men who were fighting over water. Moses (PBUH) saw the men were getting the water and these two women staying behind. Even though he was tired and exhausted, he walked to those women. He asked them, 'What is the matter with you?' The women said, 'We cannot drink water until these men are satisfied and leave. We are not strong to push our way through those men.'

"Moses (PBUH) went in, pushed his way through, and got water for their animals, sheep. He was still helping and correcting any wrong in front of him. ALLAH be praised, there was response to his supplication. He said, 'O ALLAH, whatever good you send, I need it.'

"Those two women went to their father and said, 'We found a man honest and trustworthy. Please hire him.' Moses (PBUH) got a job and also got married."

Umar bin Khitab had a similar personality. He could not see something out of place and let it go. He would not stand there and watch. He would intervene even though that would cost him his life. Umar bin Khitab was working. He found some women sitting.

Umar bin Khitab asked, "What is the issue? Do you want anything?"

These women said, "We are waiting for the Khalifah to come and judge between us."

Abu Bakar Siddique did not go to office on that day. Umar bin Khitab was looking for the Khalifah but did not find him. He found the Khalifah in the market, trading.

Umar bin Khitab grabbed the hand of Abu Bakar and asked him to come with him and asked him, "What are you doing?"

Abu Bakar said, "The salary you gave me is not enough to feed the children."

Umar bin Khitab said, "Fine, we shall give you pay rise." Umar bin Khitab here was making decisions. He said, "We shall give you pay rise."

Abu Bakar Siddique said, "Pay me three hundred dinars per year, and give me the whole sheep per day.

Umar bin Khitab said, "No, we shall not give you that," but Ali bin Abu Talib, ALLAH be pleased with him, said, "Yes, give that to him. Give him that."

Umar bin Khitab said, "Do you think so?"

Ali bin Abu Talib said, "Yes."

They agreed a sheep every day and three hundred dinars per year. Then Abu Bakar Siddique goes in the mosque, calls the Muslim scholars, stands on the pulpit, and said, "You paid me 250 dinars for a year and half of a sheep every day, and that was not enough for me. Well, Umar bin Khitab and Ali bin Abu Talib gave me a pay rise, three hundred dinars for the year and one whole sheep every day" and asked them, "Do you agree?"

All of them said, "Yes, we agree." He had to get the consent of his people. God is great. Today, it looks, we are talking about a dream world.

The imitance of Umar bin Khitab—he would take the imitiave to keep things moving. We should not expect that everything should come from the leader. Abu Bakar Siddique could not ask for pay rise; therefore, he went to the market to trade. But Umar bin Khitab brought him back and gave him the pay rise. People have to play their part.

The need for full-time Islamic workers. Umar bin Khitab asked Abu Bakar Siddique to take this job full time. There can be no market trade have to served the Muslim community full time. At present, our problem is we are sitting and waiting. Muslims are going through problems, family, job, or other issues. Not enough help. Muslims are in need of Islamic education. The field of Islamic work falls short. Umar bin Khitab wanted full time Khalifah, and therefore, he said to Abu Bakar Siddique, "If that is not enough, we will give you more."

Ali bin Abu Talib said, "Give him more." In Islamic work, any salary will be less than the other work. That is one of the reasons if there is more income somewhere else, people go there instead of Islamic education. Still needs and bills have to be paid from the work one does. We have to understand Abu Bakar Siddique was not asking for pay rise for the role of the Khalifah. He was asking to receive what he get without being a Khalifah. He was saying these are my qualifications. I can trade in the market and can make my living. He was simply asking pay should be equal to that, or he would not be able to do the job.

When Umar bin Khitab held the hand of Abu Bakar and asked him to come with him, at that, Abu Bakar Siddique said, "I do not need this position of authority you have put me in. It is not paying me enough to take care of my family."

Well, Islamic work will remain unprofessional and weak, but the needs of the Muslim community are not going to be fulfilled unless the Muslim community comes together and pays for best professionals to take care of those needs. Bring the best teachers and bring the best Imaams, also good and successful administrators.

Abu Bakar Siddique was very active in the community. He had two wives, one in Madina and another in Samna. This was a village outside Madina. Before he became Khalifah, he used to milk the goats. Abu Bakar Siddique would go to their families and milk their goats in the village.

When he became Khalifah, a young girl said, "Abu Bakar is not going to milk our goats anymore. Now he is the Khalifah."

When Abu Bakar Siddique heard that, he said, "I shall still milk your goats," also prayed to ALLAH to not prevent him from doing what he used to do before he was appointed Khalifah. "I do not want this new position to change my Khulabs." He would go around milking people's goats. He would ask people, "Do you want milk with foam on the top or without foam?"

His armies were shaking the thrones of the Persian Empire and the Roman Empire, but he was milking the goats of old women.

Khalifah was comfortable in Madina, going around serving the people while his shabgers are shaking the world powers.

Abu Bakar Siddique would wear regular clothes just like ordinary people.

Umar bin Khitab said, "Stay away from people who use expensive and fancy clothes. Continue to wear clothes like your forefathers, normal clothes." Two pieces of clothes. At that time, Umar bin Khitab was the Khalifah himself, and he was speaking to his army in Azhar Bijohn.

One day Umar bin Khitab went to visit Umma Aimin like the Prophet (PBUH) used to visit her. She was a slave from Abey Scenia. The Prophet (PBUH) freed her and used to love her very much. She also nursed the Prophet (PBUH) at birth. She was like his mother.

Abu Bakar Siddique said, "Let us go and visit her as the Prophet (PBUH) used to do." Abu Bakar Siddique and Umar bin Khitab went to visit her (Umma Aimin). As soon as they sat down, she started to cry.

Abu Bakar Siddique asked her, "Why are you crying if ALLAH has given him what is best for him." Abu Bakar Siddique thought she was crying because the visitor was not the Prophet (PBUH) but Abu Bakar Siddique and Umar bin Khitab.

Therefore, he said, "ALLAH has given him what is better for him. Question, why are you crying?"

She replied, "I know ALLAH has given to his messenger what is best for him. I am not crying because of that. I am crying because there is no more revelations after the death of the Prophet (PBUH)."

That stirred the emotions of Abu Bakar Siddique and Umar bin Khitab, and they started crying with her.

Abu Bakar Siddique saw a woman. He did not know that woman. Her name was Zenib. After a little while, he asked, "What is the matter with this woman?" because she was not speaking. He was told that she had taken an oath that she will make Hajj without speaking.

Abu Bakar Siddique advised her to speak because this is not allowed, and furthermore, this is an act of Jaheiliya "ignorance."

She spoke and asked Abu Bakar Siddique, "Who are you?"

Abu Bakar Siddique said, "I am a man from Mohajereen."

She asked, "Which part of Mohajeeren are you from?"

Abu Bakar Siddique said, "I am from Quraish."

She asked, "Which part of Quraish?"

Abu Bakar Siddique replied, "You ask too many questions. At first you were not speaking and now asking too many questions. I am Abu Bakar Siddique."

She said, "Khalifah-tul-Rasool ALLAH, successor to the messenger of ALLAH. This age is good we are living in that came after an age of ignorance. How long will it last?"

This woman lived in the time of Jahelia, and she lived in the time of Islam. She saw the blessings of ALLAH and Burka of the rule of ALLAH, the order of ALLAH. She said, "This time of good, how long will it last?"

Abu Bakar Siddique, ALLAH be pleased with him, said, "It will last as long as your Imams stay with straight path. This affair will last."

She asked a simple question: "Who are the Imaams?"

Abu Bakar Siddique said, "Among your people, are there any leaders who give the orders and those orders are obeyed?"

She said, "Yes, there are people, yes."

Abu Bakar Siddique said, 'Those are the Imaams. Anybody in that position of authority is an Imaam. Anybody people listen to—

214

he is an Imaam. As long as the Imaams will be on straight path, Ummah will be on straight path. He would join in good and would forbid evil. He would educate the Ummah."

There is an Ayya in Quran where ALLAH says,

> Oh you who believed there is a responsibility upon you about yourself. Those who have astray will not harm you when you have been guided. Take care of yourself, no matter what happens to people around you that will not harm you.

Some people might interpret this in a negative sense, that take care of yourself and forget about the rest. Abu Bakar Siddique said, "He gathered people and said, 'I heard the messenger of ALLAH (PBUH) say, "If people see evil happening in front of their eyes and they do not prevent it, they all will be punished."'" Therefore, we have to understand the Ayyat correctly.

Noviee, a scholar, said, "When ALLAH says that, 'Oh, you who believe if you are doing right, it will not harm you,' the misguidance of others, it does not mean that you should enjoin good and forbid evil, but it means if you forbid evil and enjoin good and then the people do not follow this, that will not harm you."

An important concept the Prophet (PBUH) talked about was a victorious group; they will be harmed by the ones who disagree with them. Because they have already done and, therefore, anybody who disagree would not harm them as long as they have done their role in enjoining good and forbidding evil. But if you do not forbid evil, then you will be harmed by that. No one bearer of burden will bear the burden of other. He would fix the mistakes of others. For example, Abu Bakar Siddique was sitting in a gathering. He said, "Asalam-o-Alaka ya Khalifa-tul-Rasool ALLAH. Asalam-o-Alaka oh khalifa of the messenger of ALLAH." He said, "You give me salam out of these people mean you did not give salam to other people sitting here. Say Salam-o-Alaikum to everyone."

Abu Bakar Siddique told his son Abdul Rehman, "Do not fight with your neighbor because this will remain and people will die.

Your neighbor will die and you will die, but your deeds will remain. Therefore, be good to your neighbor. What you do—that is permanent, and it will be remembered. It will be brought up on the day of Judgment."

Abu Bakar Siddique, ALLAH be pleased with him, regarding governorship of the Muslim states, followed the policy of not changing any governor or general that was appointed by the Prophet (PBUH). All of "Amara al Gin" and "Amara al Baldan"—there were two types of appointments. One was a general over the Muslim army, and the other was a governor over the Islamic state. The ones who were appointed by the Prophet (PBUH), Abu Bakar Siddique did not change any of them unless he was going to appoint in a better position or give them choice. For example, Amar bin Aas was appointed by the Prophet (PBUH) the governor over Oman.

Abu Bakar Siddique sent him a letter informing him that he was thinking to appoint him over the army and send him to Palestine. "Therefore, you have a choice—either you want to stay where you are appointed or you would go and lead that army."

Amar bin Aas went with the recommendation of Khalifah. He left Oman and took charge of the army going to Palestine. Abu Bakar Siddique sent Al-Majhor bin Abu Omea a message, asked him whether he would like to be a leader of Sunma or leader of Hazara Moat. He had been appointed by the Prophet (PBUH) in Yemen. Al-Majhor bin Abu Omea chose to be the leader of Sunma. Other than that, he did not fire anyone that was appointed by the Prophet (PBUH).

The responsibilities of these Umara? *Ameer* meaning "a leader or the head of something." Responsibilities: (1) Heading the prayers and Jhumma prayers. Part of the responsibility of the leader is the Imaam of Salah—that meant, in return, leader in religion. Since they are leaders, therefore, to deal with issues, affairs of this world. Now it is the other way around. Now we know the role of an Imaam is less than the political or military responsibility.

Sahabas, ALLAH be pleased with them, when Abu Bakar is the Imaam in Salah, that was the indication that he would take over after the Prophet (PBUH). Leader would lead the salah and Jumma in the mosque and would deliver Khutaba-tul-Jumma. Well, Khalifah would deliver Khutaba-tul-Jumma in the capital, and leader would deliver Khutaba in Muslim states in a major mosque in their area. Khutaba-tul-Jumma, a message to people to teach them religion. This also provided the chance for the leader to speak about the situation of the Ummah to his followers. Khutaba had a comprehensive role of teaching the people Fiqa, teaching people their religion and also informing the people about the affairs of the Ummah.

(2) Second responsibility of leaders—everything relating to Jehad would be their responsibility. For example, Abu Bakar Siddique wanted to reinforce armies which were sent to the Persian and to the Roman Empires. He sent a leader to Yemen, asking them to recruite soldiers and send them. Therefore, the leader would play the role of recruitment, also would undertake financial responsibilities—help with booty of war, food for soldiers, salaries, etc.—that was also the responsibility of the leader. Negotiate with the enemy, any peace agreement or truce—that is also what leader would do on behalf of the Khalifah. Anyway, there will be two-way communication between the two, but Abu Bakar Siddique gave the leader a lot of independence and authority to make decisions. But in major issues, they would always send a message to the Khalifah to consult with him.

(3) The appointment of judges and Zakat collectors and the collectors of Jazeya—that was also something done by the leader.

(4) They will take the Biea for the Khalifah. In those days, the communication system was slow. Therefore, it was not possible to take Biea from everyone at the same time. Therefore, in Madina, Umar bin Khitab took Biea for Abu Bakar Siddique. He was the one who mitigated in Khutaba, but Abu Bakar Siddique was present, standing on the member, the pulpit, and people gave Biea, but that was not possible in faraway states. Therefore, in other states, people would give Biea to the leader on behalf of the Khalifa.

(5) They would establish the Ahdood and would enforce the law. Example, there were two women in Ahzaramoth who used to sing. One of them was singing against the Muslims. Al Mohajar made an issue, but there was no clear order or limit, Ahdood, that he knew of,

but he broke their front teeth. He reported to the Khalifah what he had done. Abu Bakar Siddique told him that the woman who used to sing against the Prophet (PBUH) should have been executed and the woman who used to sing against the Muslims—there was no need to break her teeth but some minor punishment because the first case is a Kuffar, and the second case is a sin. Abu Bakar Siddique connected the judgment of Al-Mahjor.

(6) The Ahumena would hold steady circles in the mosques. The leader who is a political leader or an army general would sit in the mosque and hold the people, teaching the Quran and Hadees of the Prophet (PBUH). They view this as part of their responsibility. Maz bin Jubble was a leader who would sit in the mosque and teach the people. Abu Darjah and other sahaba had these political and military responsibilities. They would do that as a leader and to teach religion.

There are stories that Ali bin Abu Talib and Zubair were late in giving Biea. The truth is that Ali bin Abu Talib was not present in the Sakeefa of Banu Saada because he was busy with the funeral arrangements of the Prophet (PBUH). However, the next day in the mosque, when Abu Bakar Siddique was taking Biea from general public, he looked around and did not see Zubair bin Awaam, ALLAH be pleased with him. Abu Bakar called him, and Zubair came.

Abu Bakar Siddique said, "Do you want to disunite the Muslims?"

Zubair responded, "We have nothing against the Khalifah-tul-Rasool ALLAH." He came and gave his Biea to Abu Bakar Siddique. He also said, "I was late but not because I had anything against you." He gave his Biea to the Khalifah, then Abu Bakar Siddique looked around and did not see Ali bin Abu Talib.

Soon after, Ali bin Abu Talib came in, rushing.

Abu Bakar Siddique said, "Do you want to disunite the Muslims?"

Ali bin Abu Talib said, "O Khalifah-tul-Rasool ALLAH, I have nothing against you." Then Ali bin Abu Talib gave his Biea to Abu Bakar Siddique. This Hadees is mentioned by Ibn-e-Kheer. Ibn-e-Kheer also said that Imaam Muslims went to the Sheikh Ibn-e-

Khazima to teach him this Hadees and wrote it down, and then Imam Muslims said, "This Hadees is equal to a camel," meaning "it is a very valuable Hadees."

He told him it was not only equal to a camel but equal to a big pile of money, gold coins. This hadees is very valuable because it tells the truth, what happened. Ali bin Abu Talib was at home when the Muslims were gathering in the mosque. Someone came and told him that the Khalifah was taking Biea in the mosque. Ali bin Abu Talib went out in a hurry because he did not want to be late. Therefore, he went without shirt. They delivered his shirt when he was in the mosque because he did not want to be late when the Biea was given to the Khalifah-tul-Rasool ALLAH.

Knowing this, how can anybody say that Zubair and Ali bin Abu Talib did not want to give Biea to Abu Bakar Siddique, ALLAH be pleased with him, when these two scholars know Abu Bakar the best? This was Ali bin Abu Talib, who said about Abu Bakar Siddique, "He is the one who is always ahead of us. We never tried to compete with him in any good unless he would come out the first."

Ali bin Abu Talib loved Abu Bakar Siddique so much that when Abu Bakar Siddique passed away, Ali bin Abu Talib asked for Mohammad bin Abu Bakar to be brought up his own house. Ali bin Abu Talib took the child Mohammad bin Abu Bakar and raised him. Ali bin Abu Talib loved him so much that he made him leader, the governor of Egypt.

Zubair bin Awam, ALLAH be pleased with him, married the daughter of Abu Bakar, "Asma." They had family relationship with Abu Bakar and loved him so much, but the other claims are false; there is no truth in them. The scholars say that all Muslims gave Biea to Abu Bakar Siddique. None of the scholars broke out the agreement.

One of the sahaba, Saeed bin Zaid, was the one of the ten people who were given glad tidings of Genna in their life. He was asked a question: "Did you witness the death of the Prophet (PBUH)?"

He said, "Yes."

"When the Biea was given to Abu Bakar?"

He said, "The Biea was given to Abu Bakar the same day the Prophet (PBUH) passed away because Muslims did not want to stay even for one day without a Jahmah."

"Was there anybody against the biea of Abu Bakar Siddique and refuse Biea except a Murtud," meaning a Muslim who changed his religion or somebody who was about to become a Murtad. ALLAH saved the Ansaar. ALLAH protected them and made them all to give Biea to Abu Bakar Siddique.

Next question, "Was there anybody from among the Mohajereen who did not give him Biea?"

He responded and said, "No, all of them came and gave him Biea." Therefore, it is a clear issue.

There was another issue which was brought up—the issue of inheritance. The uncle of the Prophet (PBUH) Al-Abbas and the daughter of the Prophet (PBUH) Fatima, ALLAH be pleased with her, both came to Abu Bakar Siddique, asking for their inheritance from the Prophet (PBUH).

Abu Bakar Siddique, ALLAH be pleased with him, said, "I heard the Prophet (PBUH) say, 'The Ambiya of ALLAH, the prophets of ALLAH are not inherited. Whatever they leave, that is Sadaqa. The prophets of ALLAH are excluded from the laws of inheritance. A prophet of ALLAH is the father of his Ummah.' Question, what do we call the wives of the prophet? The mothers of the believers? Also about prophet Ibrahim (PBUH). He is your father. He is the one who named us Muslims. Therefore, the prophets of ALLAH do not leave any inheritance."

When Ali Abbas and Fatima came to Abu Bakar Siddique, they did not know this Hadees. Abu Bakar Siddique told them this Hadees, and they accepted that. Therefore, they did not receive any inheritance. Abu Bakar Siddique also said, "I am not going to disobey any order of the Prophet (PBUH). I will follow him. If I do not follow him, I shall go astray."

Attadia, a scholar, said when Fatima, ALLAH be pleased with her, heard that from Abu Bakar Siddique, she had no hard feelings at all, and she accepted that. Even later on, when Ali bin Abu Talib became the Khalifah, he did not change what Abu Bakar Siddique had done regarding the inheritance of Prophet (PBUH) although he was the member of the family of the Prophet (PBUH).

Next, the army of Osama bin Zaid, just after three days of the death of Prophet (PBUH) and the appointment of Abu Bakar Siddique as Khalifah. Abu Bakar Siddique said, "The army of Osama should go out. No one from the army of Osama should stay in Madina, and they should go to the camp in Al-Jurf 'Background.'" In the eight years of Hijra of the Prophet (PBUH), appointed an army to go for the first time and face the Romans. The Prophet (PBUH) appointed his beloved Zaid bin Harisa to lead that army.

Second in command was Jaffar bin Abu Talib, and third in command was Abdullah bin Rohaa. He was from among the Ansaar. The total army was three thousand strong and had to go to show Syria. This was the very first time Muslims were going to meet the Romans. That army marched out. To their surprise, they saw the enemy army in front of them, filling the horizon—soldiers as far as one can see. The Muslim army was three thousand and the enemy army two hundred thousand. Sahaba had never seen a crowd like that in their lives. In Arabia, there was not enough population to have an army of two hundred thousand. Arabia was sparsely populated; tribes were small; they did not have these huge numbers. Sahabas saw an army of two hundred thousand they never saw before. The Muslim army was only three thousand. They made Shaura. Some of them said, "The enemy army is huge, very large. Therefore, we should go back."

In Quran, ALLAH says about Muslims,

If you are strong, then one will face ten; and
if in a weak position, then one will face two.

The Muslim army had an excuse to go back.

But Abdullah bin Rohawa said, "We have come here to be martyrs. Therefore, why should we go back? If that is the reason we have come, therefore, why should we retreat? If we are looking for martyrdom, then why should we go back?"

Well, they decided to go forward. They fought for the first day, the second day, and the third day. Zaid bin Harisa was killed.

Jaffar bin Abu Talib took over—he was killed—and then Abdullah bin Rohawa was also killed. The three of them were killed. The appointed leaders were killed. Then the Muslims chose Khalid bin Waleed as their leader. He made a successful retreat with the Muslim army. Next year, the Prophet (PBUH) wanted to go out himself. He prepared the army for Ghazara of Tabook. The Muslim army went out, but the Romans did not come to face them. There was no fighting, and the Prophet (PBUH) went back without any harm. On the third year, the Prophet (PBUH) wanted to send out Osama bin Zaid to lead the Muslim army. The Prophet (PBUH) told him, "I want you to go and step over with your horses the same place where your father was killed." The Prophet (PBUH) wanted Osama bin Zaid to lead the Muslim army and step over where Zaid bin Harisa was killed. A few days after that, the Prophet (PBUH) passed away.

Now for three years, the Prophet (PBUH) was arranging a campaign to conquer the Romans, Motha, Tabook; and on the third year, the army of Osama bin Zaid was no professional army the way they used to gather the army. Everyone of sahabas were expected to participate in Jehaad. They would have their campground outside Madina and soldiers would come in the camp and when the army was ready, it would leave this campground. This campground was Al-Jurf. The Prophet (PBUH) told the army to go to Al-Jurf. Some people could get ready in a day; others may take little longer. The army was outside of Madina. The leader of the army would know the number of the army, and they had to be separate from the people of Madina. When the Prophet (PBUH) passed away, all the soldiers in Al-Jurf came back to Madina. Three days later, Abu Bakar Siddique told them to go back. Osama bin Zaid obeyed the order and went back and some of the soldiers went back to Al-Jurf with him, but now some of the sahaba came to Abu Bakar.

Just imagine the situation only three days after the death of the Prophet (PBUH). Abu Bakar Siddique was telling the Muslim army to go out and fight the Romans. Ibn-e-Kheer narrated this:

> Sahaba told Abu Bakar, "This army is majority of Muslims and Arabs have cut their

ties with you." Therefore, they told Abu Bakar, "It is not appropriate to disperse the group of the Muslims. This army is the major group of Muslims, and now you want to send them out while all the Arabs around us are thinking about attacking us. Well these delivation were going on. They tried to convince the Khalifah, and front-line spokesperson was Umar bin Khitab. Osama bin Zaid was in Al-Jurf. Umar bin Khitab was carrying a message from him for the Khalifah. Osama bin Zaid had asked Umar bin Khitab to convey the message to the Khalifah. He said, "I have with me the leadership of Muslims and majority of Muslim men. Also, I do not feel safe and also the family of the Prophet is not safe from non-Muslims." Osama bin Zaid is saying, "This army has the leadership of the community and this army has fighters." Osama says he is worried that non-Muslims may come and take away the Khalifah and family of Prophet (PBUH). Well, scholars are finding the weight of the responsibility of protecting the family of the Prophet (PBUH). Now the Prophet (PBUH) is dead, and the responsibilities lies with sahabas to protect the wives of the Prophet (PBUH), to protect his family.

Osama bin Zaid was saying also the opinion of the sahaba; the priority was to protect the Khalifah and to protect the family of the Prophet (PBUH) and the city of Muslims of Madina because all around, there was a movement of Redha. The Muslim estate is Madina; therefore, the army should stay in Madina. This is a valuable argument under this situation. It should not be a priority to go and fight the Romans at this time because the Romans were not posing a threat at that time. Leaving Madina unprotected was not wise; non-Muslims could attack at their free will.

Abu Bakar Siddique, ALLAH be pleased with him, after listening to all these different views and arguments and under pressure from scholars and especially Umar bin Khitab, even the leader of the army, Osama bin Zaid, presumed all the opinions were against going out. Abu Bakar Siddique gathered Muslims in the mosque, stood up, and delivered the following speech. It was a brief speech:

> With the name of ALLAH in whose hand is the soul of Abu Bakar, even I thought that the hearts will snatch me away, I would carry out the sending the army of Osama just as the messenger of ALLAH ordered. Even if no one else remained in the villages except myself, I would carry it out.

Abu Bakar Siddique was putting an end to all the argument. He was saying, "Not only if they take over Madina, even if they succeeded in destroying the whole community and no one survived except me, if I am the only person left, I shall still send this army out."

Abu Bakar Siddique was not talking here about a strategy or what is most beneficial. Abu Bakar Siddique was talking about the Sunna of Prophet (PBUH): "I am a follower of Sunna of the Prophet (PBUH), and I am not an invader." Abu Bakar Siddique was making it clear his government will follow the sunna of the Prophet (PBUH)—whatever the case may be. "Even if it means that the whole community is destroyed, I shall still follow the way of Prophet (PBUH) even if I am the only person left behind." Well, this was a very difficult position to take. Just imagine the mindset of the sahabas. The Prophet (PBUH) just passed away.

Ayesha, ALLAH be pleased with her, said, "When the Prophet (PBUH) passed away, all of the Arabs apostated and left Islam, and the necks of munafeeqeen started sticking up. In the name of ALLAH, my father was carrying a burden. If it was placed over mountains, this would destroy them. The companions of the Prophet (PBUH) which was filled will wolfes situation."

She was talking about the scholars of the Prophet (PBUH). Because the shepherd has passed away, this scattered goats in a dark, rainy night, and the whole area was infested with wolves. This was how Ayesha described the situation of the sahabas. There was fear. There was difficulty, enemies from every direction, but Abu Bakar Siddique was saying, "I do not care. I am going to follow the Prophet (PBUH), and you have to follow me."

Ibn-e-Hijar lasani said,

> The position of Abu Bakar Siddique shows the majority opinion is not always right. Sometimes a lone person could have the right opinion.

In this case, Abu Bakar Siddique was going against the majority's opinion, but he was right.

Imam Al-Kurthee said,

> He had the best opinion among all of the sahabas of the Prophet (PBUH) because of the time Abu Bakar had spent with the Prophet (PBUH) and drinking from the fountain of prophethood. Well, this is the position of trust and belief. One cannot take that position without deep trust and belief. This is something based on Imaan. It cannot be based on intelligence. This depends on how deep the faith is.

It is similar to the Prophet Moses (PBUH) when he was running away from Pharaoh with his nation and there was a sea in front and Pharaoh was passing with his powerful army. Moses (PBUH) had told his nation, Israelis that "ALLAH will give us victory. ALLAH will save us."

But the real world was telling something else. Eyes were seeing the sea was in front and Pharaoh, with his army, was following and catching up. The ears were listening—nothing but complaints of Bani Israile, the nation. What they were saying: "You have lied to us that we shall be safe. Now, sea is in front, and Pharaoh, with his army, is following. Nowhere to go and nowhere to hide." Well, it is a fact of life that people get affected when the same thing is repeated time and again.

Another example, the information minister of Hitler. He said, "We shall keep telling lies until people believe. Keep on lying, and people at the end will buy that."

But Moses (PBUH) had deep faith and trust in ALLAH. Moses (PBUH) said, "No, ALLAH is with me, and ALLAH will guide me." Moses (PBUH) said, "I do not believe my eyes. I do not believe my ears. ALLAH has promised me, and ALLAH will guide me." This was a test from ALLAH. ALLAH split the sea with a stick. ALLAH saved him.

Another Hadees, when someone came to the Prophet (PBUH), told him that his brother was sick. The Prophet (PBUH) said, "Give him honey." That person later on came back and said he was not cured. The Prophet (PBUH) said, "Give him honey." On fourth time, the Prophet (PBUH) said, "ALLAH is telling me the truth, but the stomach of your brother is lying. ALLAH is telling the truth. What ALLAH says—that is the truth. ALLAH has described honey as cure, 'Shiffa.' The stomach of your brother is lying."

Ibn-e-Kheer explained that the man did not give his brother a sufficient dose of medicine. He did not give him enough. If you have trust in ALLAH, believe in what ALLAH has promised.

Abu Bakar Siddique was saying, "I am going to follow the way of the Prophet (PBUH)." We have to keep in mind that Abu Bakar Siddique was setting the ground rules of Khalifah. The Khalifah should follow the Prophet (PBUH). I am a follower, not an invader.

At that time, Ansaar came to Umar bin Khitab and said, "Abu Bakar Siddique is not going to keep the army in Madina. Therefore, ask him to appoint a leader of the army who is older than Osama. Osama bin Zaid is eighteen years old. We have difficult situation. We want a leader who is more mature and has more wisdom."

There had been already talks about the leaders. The Prophet (PBUH) had said, "If you are talking about the leadership of Osama, you have already said the same about his father before. His father was befitting for that position. I love his father, and also I love Osama. He is the son of Zaid."

Umar bin Khitab went to Abu Bakar Siddique and said, "Would you consider appointing someone older in age?"

Abu Bakar Siddique sprung up. He was angry and said, "Your mother be bereaved for you and be destitute for you. Oh, Umar bin Khitab, the messenger of ALLAH appointed him, and you ask me to dismiss him. The Prophet (PBUH) appointed him, and you want me to change him."

Abu Bakar Siddique refused to change him and refused to change any leader after that. Now the army was gathered in Al-Jurf and ready to set out. Abu Bakar Siddique was on his camel, and Abdul Rehman bin Qaf was leading the camel. They went out to a place called Sha-el-Jash, escorting the army. The Prophet (PBUH) used to walk with the army until it left and then would give his favor well. Abu Bakar Siddique was following the same Sunna.

Abu Bakar Siddique was walking, and Osama bin Zaid was eighteen years old, riding his camel. Out of respect, one comes down from the camel and allows the older person to ride the camel. The one who does not respect the older, he does not belong to us. Also, the one who has no mercy for children doesn't belong to us.

Therefore, Osama bin Zaid, wanted to come down from this camel, and he was asking Abu Bakar Siddique to ride the camel.

Abu Bakar Siddique said, "I want my feet to get dirty walking in the path of ALLAH."

The Prophet (PBUH) said, "The person whose feet are dirty by walking in the path of ALLAH will be safe from hellfire."

Abu Bakar Siddique wanted to walk on the ground to get his feet dirty by walking a few steps because he was not going to with the army.

Abu Bakar Siddique delivered a speech, Khutabah, to the Muslim army. This is a kind of Muslim constitution. There are rules and regulations of war in Islam.

He addressed the Muslim army: "Stop, I shall order you ten things. Learn these from me by heart. You shall not engage in treachery. You shall not steal from booty. You should act faithfully. You shall not engage in deception. You shall not engage in mutilations. You shall not kill children, old men, and do not kill women. You shall not chop down palm trees or burn them. You shall not cut down any fruit-bearing tree. You should not slaughter a sheep, cow, or a camel except for food. You will pass people who occupy mysterious—leave them alone. Leave them to do what they are doing. You will come to people who will bring vessels full with variety of food. If you eat anything form that, mention the name of ALLAH over them." These words of advice Abu Bakar Siddique gave to his army or armies.

Please note some statements Abu Bakar Siddique said: "You should not engage in treachery or deception." Well, we know the Hadees of the Prophet (PBUH). Well, first we note the contradictions, and we shall comment on those. Abu Bakar was saying, "Do not engage in deception," but the Prophet (PBUH) said war is deception. Abu Bakar Siddique said, "Do not kill children, old men or women." Well, people can say people can mention at least two cases where the Prophet (PBUH) ordered execution of women. We know the Prophet (PBUH) used to send survyias, attacking residence at night; and in those kind of attacks, there is collateral damage, and some innocent people get hurt.

Abu Bakar Siddique was saying, "You should not chop down palm trees and should not burn them." We know for a fact in Gazwa of Banu Nadier palm trees were cut down and were burned. Well, these issues are contradictory.

The first issue that you should not engage in deception, the Prophet (PBUH) said, "War is deception." During war, one can engage in deception, can trick the enemy, but should engage in deception when you have made an agreement with your enemy, if you have truce with the enemy, if you negotiate with the enemy, if negotiating ceasefire with the enemy. There should be no deception. Therefore, while the battle is raging, you can engage in deception; but when you sit down with the enemy and you are expected that your word should be respected, then there should be no deception. Well, the hope is that two are clear.

Next, do not kill a young child, an old woman nor an old man nor a woman. The prophet (PBUH) never killed any of them because they are noncombattant, but in a situation where a woman did not engage in one way or another in fighting the Muslims, the Prophet (PBUH) did approve their execution. The reason that old men and women are spared—because they are noncombatant. As soon as they turn combatant, then the same rules will apply to them.

The issue of Toheet—when the army would attack the enemy at night. Noncombatant should not be harmed, but in a situation where the Muslim community will be harmed, then it is a priority to protect the Muslim. The protection of the Muslims is paramount all the time. The protection of Muslims comes before anyone else. In this situation, where there is need for Toheet or like the Siege of Taif, where catapult was used—there is no idea where the missiles are going to land—but the general rule is that noncombatant should not be harmed. You should not chop off palm trees or burn them.

In Ghuzava Banu Nadier, Banu Nadier decided they will hide in their fortresses. They had these powerful fortresses. They had enough gunpowder and so much food in those fortresses, and therefore, they will be able to resist a long siege. Their farms and farmlands were outside the forts. Forts have resident people, and farmlands are outside.

After betraying the Prophet (PBUH), they fell since the prophet (PBUH) does not corrupt the land; therefore, their farms would be safe. To their amazement, they saw that Muslims were cutting their palm trees and burning them. Well, they knew they cannot survive a long siege now, and their forts fell one after another. They were going around, saying the Prophet (PBUH) says he does not cause corruption in the land, but here he is cutting down our palm trees. Question is is this corruption or not?

ALLAH revealed Ayyat clarifying the situations. ALLAH says,

> Whatever you have cut down, the palm trees, or left them standing in their trunks, it was by permission of ALLAH, so ALLAH will disgrace the disobedient. ALLAH approves what the Prophet (PBUH) did. Therefore, it cannot be called Fitna.

Corruption in the land—the enemy thought they could take advantage of the kindness of the Muslims and the tolerance of the Muslims and use that against the Muslims, but the Prophet (PBUH) was making it clear: "You will not take advantage of him."

It is true the Prophet (PBUH) does not like destroying the farmlands and cutting down the trees, but if the enemy will take advantage by doing that, we would not allow the enemy to do that. The rule is that Muslims are tolerant, but Muslims want peace and security. However, the tolerance of Muslims is not going to be used against them. The general rule is we should not chop off trees nor we should kill animals. Hence, Abu Bakar Siddique was saying, "Do not slaughter animals unless you are going to eat food." That is a general rule, but if this is going to be used against the community, then of course, deny the enemy that opportunity. Same will mutilations—do not mutilate.

The Prophet (PBUH) never mutilated dead bodies of his enemies, nor did he torment them, but in one situation, it was mentioned in Bukhari. The case stands out the Prophet (PBUH) did not do this before and did not do it after. The Prophet (PBUH) held these shepherds, and he had their eyes plucked out, their arms and legs amputated, and they were left in the desert to die out of bleeding and thirst. The narrator of the Hadees said,

> He saw them rolling and licking the sand out of thirst. Nobody would give them water. This is something the Prophet (PBUH) did before nor after.

But this happened because of the cruelty those shepherds were involved in. These people were not shepherds but men from Orana. Those men killed the shepherds of the Prophet (PBUH). The way they did that was by plucking out their eyes and leaving them in the desert to die out of thirst.

These men came to Madina saying they were Muslims and gave witness Sahaba. We have witness that there is no GOD but ALLAH, and Muhammad (PBUH) is his slave and his messenger. They became ill in Madina. They asked the Prophet (PBUH) for cure. The Prophet (PBUH) told them to "go out and drink milk and urine of camels." In this particular case, it was medicine for them. They went out with camels, and these camels were of Sadaqa belonging to the Prophet (PBUH). They killed the shepherds of the Prophet (PBUH). They took the camels and ran away. The Prophet (PBUH) immediately sent the army to bring them back because of the betrayal and cruelty. The Prophet (PBUH) wanted to teach them, nomads Badoos, a lesson. This was act to deterrent, failing them. You are not going to take advantage, and you are not going to come to me, stating you are a Muslim and then kill shepherds and take my camels away. This was a very strict punishment for them, but it proved to a determent for the tribes, and they never committed anything like that again.

The Ameer had to make the judgment—when to apply the general rule and when to apply an exception to the rule. Abu Bakar Siddique was stating the general rule here. For example, for the monks, Abu Bakar Siddique said, "You will find these Christian monks, who devote their lives as celibates, life of Zuid, that life in worship, those lifestyles. They would live in these mountains they would not get married as celibates. They would engage with some extreme measures. There was this saint in Indhless. She was a nun. She was very proud for what she had done. She said she had never ever had both with the exception of the tips of her fingers when she would perform mass. These monks are involved in strict worship, but ALLAH did not command them."

Abu Bakar Siddique said, "Leave them alone. Do not kill them. Do not harm them. They will fight. They are combatants. Therefore, do not harm them." Even though they were involved in doing wrong, Abu Bakar Siddique was saying, "Leave them alone."

The question is should that be applied to Templers. The Templers are priests, but they are fighting the order of the church. They are most severe, strict or tough out of all crusading armies. The most brutal and cruel were the Templers, and those were monks—fighting monks. If these rules apply, they are a very fanatic order. They have caused havoc in Muslim lands in Palestine. There must be a judgment where to apply the rule and where not apply. Many of the deeds were done by the Khulfas because of their passion.

Umer bin Abdul Aziz was considered one of the scholars of the Ummah. There was a lot of what he had done. He was more than a Mufti or a scholar because as an Ameer, he had to decide in the real world the need for that knowledge. That was the reason that one of the conditions for the Khalifa is knowledge. Khalifa needs to be knowledgeable; he should be able to decide in a situation they are faced with.

Questions: What was the result of sending the army of Osama by Abu Bakar? Was Madina ambushed or destroyed? Were Muslims killed? *Subhanallah*, look at the results. The army marched out, traveling all the way from Madina to Shaam, Syria. The army cut through northern Analia, a show of force in front of all the tribes who were planning to attack Madina. The law of the desert—if one is weak, that will be attacked. All the tribes wanted to take advantage of death of the Prophet (PBUH) to listing an end to the Islamic state. The army was marching in front of the tribes who were planning an attack. They were thinking that the Prophet (PBUH) passed away only a few days before and the Muslim army was going to fight with the Roman Empire. Fighting the Romans from Arab tribes was something unthinkable—that was the Roman Empire which put so much fear in their hearts that they would not even think about that.

Just like when the Prophet (PBUH) was seeking support from Banu Shaban for hardening Persians. They said, "We shall protect you from Arab side but not from Persian side. That is something beyond us." Arabs had so much respect for Romans and Persians they would not dare to wage a war against them. When the tribes saw that Abu Bakar Siddique was sending the army to wage war against Romans, they thought those people must be very strong. They changed their mind and would not think about attacking Madina. They reversed their plans. Therefore, the least fear of attack came from Northern Arabia. Those tribes saw the army of Osama—they never attacked Madina. That was the safe area even at the time of Ridha. Although there were many tribes in that area, there was no trouble, and the area was safe.

Heracle, a Roman commander of the Roman Empire, was so worried about this near phenomena of the Islam. He left his base and set up camp in Antakia. Antakia is in Syria. He wanted to be alone in this forgotten land of Arabia. Nothing was happening in there. Armies would cross back and forward, but they would not even look at that activity in the desert. There were no resources, hardly any people in that area. What would anybody want from that wasteland? The Persian Empire and the Roman Empire, at the height of their power, would attack because it was a wasteland. What would they do with it? Therefore, they never invaded Arabia, but now the Roman Empire. He left his base and went to Antakia just to monitor events in Madina. He was so worried now that he moved out of his capital. This is from ALLAH that he received the news about the army of Osama attacking him and also the news of the death of the Prophet (PBUH) on the same day.

Heracle thought and said, "What is going on? The Muslim Prophet and Muslim leader just passed away, and they are sending the Muslim army to fight the Romans." He changed his mind and allowed the army of Osama to make it into the death of the Roman Empire, to take booty and leave unharmed. Osama bin Zaid marched with horses over the land where his father was killed. He made deals and negotiated with the Arab tribes in the area. He signed agreements with them and took Jazia, also took booty of war and went back. Heracle is there but did not send out army to meet Muslims army. This was the result of deep faith of Abu Bakar Siddique. This is what happens when there is deep faith and trust.

If the mother of Moses (PBUH) did not have faith and trust in ALLAH and rather than throwing her child in the river, which looked like certain death for the child, ALLAH told her, "If you feel for the safety of the child, throw him in the river." Tell any mother to throw her newborn child in the river. This was if she felt fear from Pharaoh, but to throw the child in the river? The solution seems to be worse than the problem.

But ALLAH told her, "If you do that, do not be afraid or sorrowed. He will come back to you, and I shall make him a messenger. Do what is told, and it will happen."

She had trusted in ALLAH, and she threw Moses, a newborn child, in the river. If she had kept Moses in her arms and not believed in the promise of ALLAH, the soldier of Pharaoh, his intelligence would have discovered Moses and would have killed Moses because of the order of Pharaoh to kill all male children of Israel; but because she believed in the promise of ALLAH, he was picked up by a soldier of ALLAH, the wife of Pharaoh—she was a soldier of ALLAH. She loved Moses. She adopted him as her child.

Now Moses would not drink milk from the breast of any woman but his own mother. Moses would be carried to the house of his mother, surrounded by royal guards, and they were paying a salary to the mother of Moses so that she would breastfeed Moses, who was, in fact, her own child. All this happened because she had deep faith and trust in ALLAH.

ALLAH said, "The soldiers of Pharaoh picked up Moses, but he will be their enemy." They did not know this—that newborn child—he could barely see—would be the one who would bring the burning end to Pharaoh and his army and the end of his power rule. This was the result of trust in ALLAH.

The army of Osama came back, and there was a huge celebration and happiness. He was successful, and Osama and his army were received in Madina. This was a victory and the policy of Abu Bakar Siddique a success.

After that event, the Sahabas realized that and adopted the policy to follow Abu Bakar Siddique. He had favors of ALLAH, blessing of ALLAH, support of ALLAH.

Next, the wars of Ridha, What is Ridha? Nowie, a scholar, said the definition of *Ridha* is learning Islam, discontinuing Islam; if a person has intention of leaving Islam, he has left it. Some words or a statement can make a person apostate or an action allows to make a person apostate. Sometimes an action or statement was done or made out of mocking joking. For example, someone makes fun of the statement or out of belief, then he says, "If you make Halal what is Haram or vice versa." That is also Ridha—if a person has made the intention of leaving Islam and to become a non-Muslim. Even if he was debating whether to become an apostate, like he is not sure whether to remain in Islam or leave Islam, that is also Ridha.

Ridha comes in different forms; for example, not applying the order of ALLAH. If someone does not apply the rule of ALLAH, they are nonbelievers. Another common form of Ridha is "O you who believe, if you follow the way of disbelievers, they will make you retreat." *Ridha* means "retreat." They will make your retreat, and you will become losers.

The Prophet (PBUH) said, "Whoever follows the nonbelievers' ways becomes one of them." This is an Ayyat. The Prophet (PBUH) said, and this is Hadees, "That is if you love people, you are one of them." At the time of Abu Bakar Siddique, the categories of Ridha were three. First type of Ridha: there people went back to worshipping idols, reverted back to what they were doing before Islam. That is pagan worship. Second type of Ridha: the people who follow Muslimsa Kazab and Al Ansey—these two men who claimed to be prophets. This was the second type of Ridha. Third type of Ridha: these apostate; they remained Muslims but refused to pay Zakat. They said Zakat should only be paid to the Prophet (PBUH). They were like Muslims but refused to pay Zakat. Abu Bakar Siddique considered them as apostate who were Muslims but left Islam.

This Ridha, in fact, started at the time of the Prophet (PBUH) and not at the time of Abu Bakar.

In the first year of Hijra: this was the time when the Muslims were spreading all over. There were some weak-hearted people, who joined Islam because of the fear of the sword. Just because Islam was becoming stronger and was strong, these people accepted Islam; but in fact, that was out of fear, and they were not true Muslims; they did not really believe in Islam. They were just riding the wave. Prophethood was not really known among the Arabs before, but now when people saw the Prophet (PBUH) successful, they also accept Islam. In Arabia, no one had claimed prophethood before the Prophet Muhammad (PBUH); but when Arabs saw that Muhammad (PBUH) is the undisputed leader of Arabia, those people also joined Islam.

Muslimsa Kazab, Asad Ul Ansey, Talah ul Asdey, and Sujja—three men and one woman. The most dangerous were Muslimsa and Al Ansey Al Yamama. These two were rising quickly, and danger to Islam was also rising very fast. They were having huge armies and were becoming a real threat against the Muslims. Both Muslima and Al-Ansey claimed to be prophets during the life of the Prophet Muhammad (PBUH).

In the tenth year of Hijra, the Prophet (PBUH) saw a dream. The Prophet (PBUH) said in the dream he saw he was wearing two bracelets of gold. The Prophet (PBUH) in the dream disliked that and he blew at them and the bracelets flew away. The Prophet (PBUH) explained as two liars the liar of Yamama and the liar of Yeamon. The Prophet (PBUH) saw two bracelets—these two were the danger to the community—and there was a third Jaliaha, but the Prophet (PBUH) only saw two bracelets. These two were the most dangerous. They were gold, and the Prophet (PBUH) said he disliked them.

Gold stands for the Zena of this world, attachment to this world. Muslimsa and Al Ansey were doing this not for Al Akhara but for this world. In general, gold carries negative connotations in dreams even though these are very dangerous, but by bellowing at them, they flew away. Although covering both arms, very dangerous, meaning even though they will be very strong, at the end they will disappear, and nothing will remain. Even Muslimsa and Al Ansey were a great threat too, but nothing remained—they vanished and disappeared. The Prophet (PBUH) blew at them—meaning the religion of ALLAH will destroy them. That happened at the time of Abu Bakar Siddique. These are the three type of Ridha.

Quran says the Ayyat, "There is no compulsion in religion." It is a very strong, authentic mutwater Hadees in all books of Hadees. The Prophet (PBUH) said, "I am instructed to fight with the people until they say there is no GOD but ALLAH and Muhammad (PBUH) is his messenger and servant."

Answer: This tradition Hadees refers to fighting a specific group of idolaters who were waging a war of aggression against the Muslim community. It does not mean Muslims should force people to enter Islam or fight all people in general. We should bring together all the narrations and verses that mention the context in which the Prophet (PBUH) made this statement and interpret then comprehensively and consistently rather than taking a single narration out of context. Other narrations make it clear that "fighting the people" here refers to the Arab tribes who reveled against the authority of the Muslim community in Mecca after the city was liberated from the idolaters' aristocracy. The demand for them to accept Islam was not to compel individuals to practice Islam but, rather, to compel them to accept that the Holy City would no longer serve as a pilgrimage site for idols.

Jabir, reporter, the messenger of ALLAH (PBUH), said, "I have been commanded to fight the people until they say there is no GOD but the ALLAH, then their lives and wealth are protected from we except by night of justice and their reckoning is with ALLAH."

Then the Prophet (PBUH) recited verses:

> Verily, you are only a reminder you are not over them as a dictator. (88:22; source: Sahih Muslims 21, grade: Sahih)

In other narrations, the prophet (PBUH) said,

> I have been learnt commanded to fight the idolaters (Sunan Abu Dawod 2642, after declaring the command to fight these specific idolaters)

The Prophet (PBUH) recited verses affirming that his duty was only to deliver the message of Islam, which indicates that he was not sanctioning compulsion in religion?

Ibne Rajah commented on this tradition:

> Your duty is only to remind them about ALLAH and to preach to them. You do not have authority to enter faith into their hearts by force, and you are not responsible for that. (Jami Uloom wal-Hikam 8)

The Prophet (PBUH) was commanded by ALLAH to fight the idolaters in order to defend his community from their aggression, but if they stopped waging war against Islam, then there was no justification for fighting them.

ALLAH says,

> Fight them until there is no more persecution and worship is for ALLAH. But if they cease, then there is to be no aggression except against oppressors. (Surat Al-Baqarah 2:90)

And ALLAH says,

> So if they remove themselves from you and do not fight you and offer you peace, then ALLAH has not made for up a cause for fighting against them. (Surat Al-Nisa 4:90)

Hence, the people to be fought are only those who persist in aggression and hospitality against Islam. On the contrary, Islam requires Muslims to make peace with whoever offers them terms of peace.

Ibne Taymiyyah commented on this tradition:

> To fight those who are waging war, whom ALLLAH has called us to fight, and it does not mean to fight those who have made peace with whom ALLAH has commanded us to fulfill their peace. (Majmu Al-Fatwa 19/20)

It was not necessary for these idolaters to accept Islam in order to make peace with Muslims. If they discontinued their hospitality against Muslims and sought asylums, then the Muslims were required to grant them protection and safe passage even if they did not accept Islam.

ALLAH says,

If anyone of the idolaters seeks your protection then grant him protection. So that he may hear the words of ALLAH and then deliver him to his place of safety that is because they are people who do not know. (Surat Al- Tawlah 9.6)

Moreover, numerous verses of the "Quran" prohibit compulsion in religion and affirm the freedom of people to practice their own religion.

ALLAH says,

There shall be no compulsion in the religion the night course has become clear from the wrong. (Surat Al-Baqarah 2:256)

And ALLAH says,

Had your Lord willed, those on earth would have believed all of them entirely. Then would you compel the people in order that they become believers? (Surrat Yunus 10:99)

And ALLAH says,

The truth is from Lord, so whoever wills, let him disbelieve. (Surrat Al-Kahf 18:29)

The Prophet (PBUH) never forced anyone to become a Muslim, and he only fought to defend his community from aggression.

Ibne Al Qayyim wrote:

The Prophet (PBUH) did not force the religion upon anyone, but he only fought those who waged war against him and fought him. As for those who made peace with him or conducted a truce, then he never fought them and he never

239

compelled then to enter his religion. (HidAyyat Al-Hayara 237)

Therefore, the tradition under discussion refers to fighting a particular group of hostile idolaters who had been persecuting Muslims and waging in a war of aggression. It does not mean Muslims are allowed to force anyone into Islam or to fight people just because they have another religion.

Sources come from ALLAH, and ALLAH knows best.

The delegates of some Arab tribes came to Madina to negotiate with Khalifa of Muslims, Abu Bakar Siddique, ALLAH be pleased with him.

They said, "We did not leave Islam—never. We bore witness and testify that there is no GOD but ALLAH and Muhammad is a messenger of ALLAH. We pray to ALLAH, but under no circumstances we shall pay you Zakat."

There Arab tribes sent very high-level delegates, people with old connections with notables of Madina. They arrange in a way that friends of this leader will stay with him and friends of others will stay with their friends. They were not dealing with the Khalifa directly, but also they had with some notable Muslims speaking on their behalf. All these questions were mounting on the Khalifa. Also, from a religious standpoint, it was not clear to Sahaba yet. Even Umar bin Khitab was discussing this with the Khalifa Abu Bakar Siddique.

It should be clear in our minds that Umar bin Khitab was not doing this under any pressure from any sides. He was speaking from his own understanding and with evidence from Sharia.

Umar bin Khitab went to Khalifa and said, "This is in Bukhari. How can you fight them?"

When the Prophet (PBUH) said, "I was commanded by ALLAH to fight the people until they testify that there is no GOD but ALLAH. If they do, then they have protected themselves and their wealth."

This Hadees came in various forms, but the Hadees is authentic. This Hadees is of the highest level. The authentic "mutwater" Hadees is the one which comes through so many important narrations that it is difficult to refute, to prove wrong. It is the highest level

of authenticity. This Hadees was mentioned by so many important Sahaba. There are a few names mentioned here: Abu Huraira,
Anees bin Malik, Abbas, and many more; approximately twenty
Sahaba narrated this. In Bukhari Muslims, Abu Daud, many more
books, Tirmisey, Ibne Maja, nearly in all books of Hadees. Hukme,
Dharmay, Tabrani, Muslims, Imam Ahmed; the Hadees is very
strong. The Hadees is the Prophet (PBUH) said, "I was instructed to
fight with people until they say there is no GOD but ALLAH." Well,
when this Hadees is mentioned, people think that this contradicts
with the Ayyat of Quran. There is no competition in religion. The
Ayyat of Quran says, "There is no competition in religion, and the
Hadees is that the Prophet (PBUH) says, 'I was instructed to fight
with the people until they say, "There is no GOD but ALLAH and
Muhammad (PBUH) is his servant and his messenger."'" The other
narration is that they pray and pay Zakat.

Question is how do we combine these two texts? There are quite
a few interpretations by scholars referring to this Hadees. One of the
explanations is that the Prophet (PBUH) was instructed to fight the
people until they accept either Islam or Jazya. Therefore, by paying Jazya, they may have not accepted Islam but accepted the rule
of Islam. They accepted the order of ALLAH. Well, the whole earth
should be ruled by the law, or rule of ALLAH; but as individuals, Islam
cannot be forced upon them. Therefore, one cannot force a religion
on a person because this is an issue which causes back to convictions.
It is something that is in the heart of a person. One cannot force
a person to convince him. Therefore, there is no compulsion; but
in the law of ALLAH, people should fight until the law of ALLAH is
accepted.

Umar bin Khitab went to the Khalifa Abu Bakar Siddique and
said, "How can you fight these people when they bore witness there
is no GOD but ALLAH and Muhammad (PBUH) is his messenger and
servant and they are praying. How can you fight them?"

Neither Abu Bakar Siddique nor Umar bin Khitab heard any
different that they pray and pay Zakat. If they do, there should be
no argument.

The response of Abu Bakar Siddique: "In the name of ALLAH, I will fight with whoever differentiate between Salat and Zakat. If they prevent me, one camel, another relation, a rope, to tie the neck of a camel with if they prevent me, while they used to pay to the Prophet (PBUH). I shall fight them over it."

Umar bin Khitab said, "When I saw the conviction of Abu Bakar Siddique, I realized that this is the truth. There again Abu Bakar Siddique is setting the rules for the Khulfas after him." Umar bin Khitab was wondering, thinking whether a person after the Prophet (PBUH) has a right to fight against people who are claiming to be Muslims but not fulfilling all the duties of Islam, but Abu Bakar Siddique was saying that is the part of the Khalifa who takes over after the Prophet (PBUH). He was talking to the Khulfa after him—"That is your responsibility to enforce the law of Islam—even the people who break it are Muslims." Well, this is another case where Fiqa of Abu Bakar prevails. It is established as correct.

Umar bin Khitab said, "He realized that his opinion was the right opinion." All these issues are relating to Islamic politics. The authority which is given to the Muslim leader, Abu Bakar Siddique, was establishing a Sunnat. He made this clear to all the delegates, and they left without any agreement.

Umar bin Khitab went to Abu Bakar Siddque and said, "Ya Khalifa tul Rasool ALLAH, be lenient with them and bring them close." No matter the circumstances we are in, we have to be lenient with people, need to show the soft side. Well, one might think about the statements coming from Umar bin Khitab. The Umar we know was not like this, but Umar bin Khitab was keeping in mind the circumstances and the situations. Madina was in danger; the entire religion was in danger; the Muslim community was in danger. Umar bin Khitab was not saying to negotiate on the issue of religion, but he was saying to be a little more lenient with these tribes. They were claiming to be Muslims; therefore, try to reach a deal.

The response of Abu Bakar: Abu Bakar grabbed the head of Umar bin Khitab and said, "O son of Khitab, you were a tyrant before you became a Muslim, and now once you are a Muslim, you want to become lame, fragile, and weak," and then he said, "The religion has been left by the Prophet Muhammad (PBUH) complete. Do you think I shall allow it to be weak while I am still alive? I am not going to allow the religion of ALLAH to diminish. I am not going to allow going down while I am still alive. As long as I am alive, I shall fight for this religion."

Therefore, the other tribes who were calling him the father of the young camel were proved wrong—he was a different person than what they thought. When the delegates left, Abu Bakar Siddique went to the Sahaba and told them, "The land has sunk in disbelief and their delegation have seen that you are few. Therefore, you will be unaware when you are approached by day or by night. The nearest of them is a stage from you. The people were expecting that we shall reconcile with them, but we refused them and dissolved their treaty. Therefore, get ready."

Abu Bakar told the Sahaba, "Those delegates wanted to make a treaty with us, but we refused. They came to Madina. They have seen we have limited numbers." When they saw the army of Usama, they thought it is a huge army; but now they came to Madina, they saw the reality. There were not many people there. This was a kind of weakness of Muslims, and that was exposed. Muslims were limited number. Abu Bakar Siddique said, "Be ready. They could attack us any moment."

The plan of Abu Bakar Siddique was to defend Islam. First of all, the soldiers were sleeping in the Mosque. They could be ready at a moment's notice to defend. In case of an attack on Madina, people will be ready to defend. The force was ready, and they established the base in Masjid-e-Nabvi. Secondly, guards were placed on all the mountain passes; all the routes leading into Madina were guarded. These posts were manned to give early warning of any attack. Abu Bakar appointed supervisors over these guards. Ali bin Abu Talib, Zubair bin Awam, Talha bin Abdullah, Saad bin Abu Waqas, Abdul Rehman bin Auf, and Abdullah bin Masood—these were the heads of security guards. They were surrounding Madina from every direction. Thirdly, he tried to mobilize the tribes surrounding Madina. They were still Muslims. There were tribes like Faria, Johana, Islam, names of the tribes. These Badoo tribes did support, for exam-

243

ple, Johana tribe; they sent many camels into Madina, put them under the hand of Khalifa to use as he saw fit. They offered some help. Within three days, as was expected, the tribes who were just in Madina prepared an army to attack and made their moves. The Sahaba who faced them were fighting them on camel. The enemy found this invasive way of scaring the camels. They made balloons out of animal skin. They would throw these balloons and roll them in front of the camel. Camels were terrified and ran away. It was so bad that camels turned around and went back to Madina along with the Sahaba. Simply, camels were out of control, and Sahaba could not bring them back. The impression the enemy got—that Muslims are weak and they have ran away. This was the order of ALLAH—that they were dragged to Madina.

In the mean time, Abu Bakar Siddique was preparing a large army. He led the army himself, and they went out under the cover of the dark night to ambush the enemy, and the enemy did not know that Muslims were coming. The enemy did not expect that Muslims will come out.

Suddenly Muslims attacked the enemy from every direction just before Fajar. It was still dark. By the time the sun was arising, the enemy were turning back and running away. That was the first victory and is called the beginning of the opening. The news spread, and in that same night, Sahaba saw some people coming into Madina. They assumed that the enemy was attacking, but Abu Bakar Siddique told the Sahaba, "This is not enemy but a good news."

They found that these were the people bringing Zakat. Some of the tribes were coming to pay Zakat. One tribe came and delivered the Zakat in the night, second tribe midnight, and third tribe before the end of the night. Well, immediately within one day, things were turning around. Abu Bakar Siddique went to fight again.

Ali bin Abu Talib, with other Sahaba, went to Abu Bakar and said, "You should not go out and fight yourself. Appoint someone to lead the armies because if you are killed, it will be difficult for Muslims and victory for the enemies of ALLAH."

But Abu Bakar Siddique said, "No, but I am going to go myself to give an example."

The old man over the age of sixty was leading the war by himself, and he did that in three consecutive campaigns. Dahrara bin Aswar, to show how Abu Bakar was managing this, these events were happening so fast. The dead of the Prophet (PBUH), the appointment of Khalifa, Ridha, wars against apostates, the news coming from every corner of Arabia about armies messing and preparing to attack Muslims, and how Abu Bakar dealt with all this—this was the disaster news from every direction.

Dahrara bin Aswar was leading the campaign toward northeast against Talah Ul Asdey. He was one of three people who claimed to be prophet during the time of the Prophet (PBUH). The situation got worst after the death of the Prophet (PBUH). The invitation of Talah Ul Asdey was spreading like wildfire. His army power was growing day by day. Dahrara Biin Aswar, who was appointed to lead the army against him, came back to Madina and delivered news to Abu Bakar Siddique, ALLAH be pleased with him.

He said, "I have never seen anybody after the Prophet (PBUH) who was calm in the face of disaster like Abu Bakar Siddique. I delivered the news about Talah Ul Asdey. It looked like I was giving him good news."

Later on, they asked Abu Bakar Siddique, "You were carrying a heavy load on your shoulders. It was so heavy. If it was placed on the oscines, it would empty them. But we did not see that you were becoming weak."

Abu Bakar Siddique replied, "I never felt fear in my heart after that day in the cave with the Prophet (PBUH), but on that day, I was fearful. I told the Prophet (PBUH) if one of them looked down on his feet, they will see us."

The Prophet (PBUH) said, "What do you think about two and ALLAH is their third?"

ALLAH brought down his tranquility. Well, that tranquility came on them—both the Prophet (PBUH) and Abu Bakar Siddique. Abu Bakar Siddique would not fear anymore in his life after ALLAH brought tranquility on him with the Prophet (PBUH) in the cave.

Abu Bakar said he never felt fear after that. That was how calm and steadfast he remained in the face of all these storms. Abu Bakar

Siddique adopted many methods for fighting of apostates. He sent eleven armies to fight in different corners. He also employed the method of strengthening Muslims within the apostate tribe because apostasy was not a moment where everybody gave up Islam. In some cases, entire tribes would give up Islam, in some majority of the tribe and in others, minority of the tribe would give up Islam and some tribes were steadfast on Islam. Whenever Abu Bakar Siddique came to know that a tribe had gone apostate, he would try to established links within and would delegate the responsibility to bring back the tribe to Islam and to fight with them. By this method, Abu Bakar was trying to reduce the load on Ansar and Muhajareen because it was not possible to fight with each and every tribe at the same time. Abu Bakar tried to delegate, for example, Yuman; Abu Bakar Siddique did not send any army to deal with Asad Un Ansay but tried to establish links with Muslims who were there. Abu Bakar Siddique wanted to keep the strong forces to deal with other dangerous ene-mies—for example, Ridah of Muslimsa Qazab, Talah Ul Asdey at the time. With them there was Sajjah in the north and Asad Un Ansey in Yuman.

Abu Bakar also used letters. He would send out letters, giving invitations to apostates, and making it clear that "I shall accept nothing but Islam from you. If you don't come into the line religion, then you will have to face the sword." These terms were made very clear to them.

We start with Asad Ul Ansey. He was from Al Ansey, close to Sannah in Yaman. He claimed prophethood in the tenth year of Hijra during the life of the Prophet (PBUH). He used to receive information from devils. This man had connections with devils. He was possessed by demons. In the beginning, he started out his mission secretly, then he announced, and suddenly his invitation was spreading very fast. Initially, he engulfed all his people in Ansey. Then he started spreading out and advanced toward Sannah, in Yaman, and fought with the Badaan, the governor. When Yaman became Muslims, Sannah was ruled by a Persian family because Yaman was invaded for some time. Abbrah invaded Yaman Ashram, and then they sought help from Persia which caused Persia to send an army to

Yaman. That army fought with Akbarah and defeated him and took over. There were remnants of Persia in Yaman.

When the Prophet (PBUH) sent letters to them, inviting them to Islam, these Persians became Muslims, and Budhan was incharge, governing Sannah at that time he became a Muslim. The Prophet (PBUH) approved him in his position as governor of Sannah. The Prophet (PBUH) appointed him over Yaman. When he passed away, the Prophet (PBUH) split Yaman into different states, and his son, Sharb, continued his rule over Yaman.

Asad Ul Ansey was marching toward Sannah. He met with Sharb bin Baddan, in Shoub, next to Sannah, and defeated him. Now Asad ul Ansey was ruling over Sannah. He sent his army to take over Najran. He was able to reach in Tolodge. Ansey was expencing his control. The Prophet (PBUH) sent a message to his leader in Yaman to deal with the situation of Asad Ul Ansey either by deception (war is deception) or by brought force. The message was clear to meet him from inside or from outside with armies when Asad Ul Ansey killed Sharb bin Baddan, a Persian king of Yaman. He married his wife Azad. He tried a close relationship with Albeena, the Persian people. Among them was Feroz and others. The head of the army of Al Ansey was Al-cosh.

Now Feroz started to plan and made a plot to get rid of Asad Ul Ansey. The plan was to kill him from inside by assassinating him rather than facing him in battlefield. The idea was that the whole problem will be solved if this one person is eliminated. Feroz was able to gather around him some likeminded people who were Muslims and firm on Islam, willing to sacrifice for the sake of Islam. They went Kase, the head of the Asad Ul Ansey army. There were rumors that there was a dispute between the two.

They approached Kase and told him, "We are willing to work with you to get rid of Asad Ul Ansey." They agreed—not necessarily that Kase wanted to go back Islam, but he had a political dispute with Ansey about power. He was fearful that Asad Ul Ansey will get rid of him.

Feroz consulted with the wife of Al Ansey, Al-azad, a Persian woman, told her the plan.

"How can you help us?"

She responded that "Asad Ul Ansey is always surrounded by guards. They do not leave him unguarded until he gets into this particular room." She said, "There is no way you can reach him unless you came from this side," and she provided a layout of the place. That particular room was his bedroom where he used to sleep with his family. That was the only place free from the security guards. There was an access to that room from outside. She gave them the plan and layout and the way they can reach in that room. She also planned to leave some light late at night in that room and weapons. Feroz was the cousin of Azad, the wife of Al Ansey; therefore, he was allowed to go in that area. Therefore, Asad Ul Ansey would not suspect anything out of place.

The wife, Azad, decided to help, and they arranged for the night to attack. Feroz, along with two other men, broke into that room. As soon as they picked up the weapons and arrived in the room, Satan came to Asad Ul Ansey. The devil made him sit up at night and speak to Feroz.

Asad Ul Ansey was in his sleep, but this was Satan speaking on his tongue. The devil was saying, "Feroz, I know what you want to do."

Asad Ul Ansey was a huge, powerful, well-built man. Feroz was terrified. Asad Ul Ansey was speaking to him, but that was the devil speaking to him. Now Feroz had to decide either to retreat—a plan would fail. He did not have time to grab the weapon. He simply jumped on Asad Ul Ansey, got on top, got hold of his neck and broke the neck, and then he walked out. Azad, the wife, did not know that Ansey was killed, but she thought Feroz was running away.

She asked, "Where you are going?"

Feroz replied, "I am going to tell the other two companions."

He went and called them from the other room, and they came in and found that Asad Ul Ansey was not dead; he was tossing around in the room even though his neck was broken. GOD only knows whether there was a djinn inside him or what? He was tossing around in the room.

Feroz said, "I tried to grab him, but the man was strong."

He could not grab him, and other two came in and grabbed him for Feroz. Then Feroz got a knife and beheaded him. They waited in the room. Until morning they stayed there.

Feroz said when he cut his head off, Al Ansey made a very loud noise, a big roar. The guards came running and asked, "What is happening?" The wife of Al Ansey said, "Do not worry. The Prophet is receiving revelations." Anyway they waited in the room until morning. They made their way out an Azaan. Nothing was heard for a long time. Soldiers were amazed, and that was the sign for the soldier of Feroz to come and attack. They threw the head of Al Ansey in front of his supporters, and that was the end of Asad Ul Ansey. They stayed in the room and made Azaan that was not heard for a long time. This was the sign for the soldier of Al Feroz. They realized and came in and threw the head of Asad Ul Ansey.

The night this took place, Angel Jibrael came to the Prophet Muhammad (PBUH) and delivered the news. The Prophet (PBUH) in the morning was telling the Sahaba. Asad Ul Ansey had been killed, and he told the Sahaba that Ansey had been killed by a blessed man from a blessed family.

The companions asked, "Who is this man?"

The Prophet (PBUH) said, "Feroz."

Now we know Feroz was a blessed man, and his family is blessed. This plan was carried out by a Persian man and the Persian woman—at that time the wife of Asad Ul Ansey. He married her when he defeated her husband, the son of Baddan. He was governor, appointed by the Prophet (PBUH). Azad was the Persian woman. The Prophet (PBUH) called him a blessed family. Well, the story of Feroz was used as an evidence by Fiqa to support overthrowing a Murtad government through assassination because Yaman was ruled by Islam, and then Asad Ul Ansey, apostate, was ruling over Yaman. The Prophet (PBUH) sanctioned what they did. However, when the news of the death of the Prophet (PBUH) came in Yaman, the remnant of the army of Asad Ul Ansey got together and started to revolt again. This time, the Ridha was worse because it was happening in different places. It was happening in Sannah, in Najrom, Hazreenath, in Indha and Maraha, in Laudgh, and in Edden—just as it was happening in the Arabian Peninsula. Wherever there were new Muslims, they were weak; therefore, there was Ridha.

Kase was head of army of Al Ansey. He joined in a plot to kill Al Ansey. He joined with the forces of apostate. The reason was that Abu Bakar Siddique appointed Feroz as the leader over Sannah and Kase did not like that. Therefore, he broke ranks and joined with the forces of apostate. Now, Al Majhor bin Umia and Maaz bin Jabbal and other Sahaba who were in Yaman started fighting with apostates in different areas, and slowly they defeated all the forces of Ridha. They brought the whole county under the rule of Sharia again. That was the Ridha of Asad Ul Ansey, which started in the life of Prophet (PBUH). We have tried to brief but did not go in details. Because there are so many names and places, they will be confusing. Secondly, our purpose is to learn the lesson. Wherever there are strong lessons to be learned, we shall go through the incident and learn the lessons. Our topic is the life of Abu Bakar Siddique and his time. If we teach everything, it will take a very long time. We will go through some of the events which happened, then we shall move on to the Ridha of Talah Ul Asdey.

The example of a righteous woman and an evil woman. Azad is an example of a righteous woman. She sacrificed for a religion like Asia binte Mazain, the wife of Pharaoh. Asia was the wife of Pharaoh, the most powerful king on the face of the earth. She had everything that a lover of this world would want. She was living in a great palace. That palace is mentioned in Quran—that rivers are flowing beneath. Pharaoh said, "Rivers are flowing beneath me." She had so much wealth that she would want, but it did not satisfy her. She was praying to ALLAH, asking ALLAH to replace her with a palace in heaven rather than a palace on earth.

Azad was the wife of Asad Ul Ansey, the most powerful man in Yaman during his time. She was a Muslim, and she described her husband by saying, "ALLAH has not created any human being more disliked to me than Asad Ul Ansey. I never hated anybody in my life like I hated this man." She said, "He does not do any good, and all of his action are evil." She sacrificed, knowing well that if caught, she will pay dearly. If the plot was uncovered by Asad Ul Ansey, she would have been killed. Asad Ul Ansey was a very vicious person especially in his treatment of Muslims. He would cut them into pieces and let them die a slow death.

There are some evil women. ALLAH gave the example of Asia, a good woman in Quran and gave the example of bad women in Quran, the wife of Loat and the wife of Nooh (PBUH). Well, both examples happened in Yaman. Whenever the rules of Islam come to a place, there are people who are not happy with it. Everybody does not vote for Islam. There are always people who dislike the law of ALLAH. People believe the law of ALLAH restricts their freedom and liberty. These people tend to go with the part of aristocracy. People who do not want any limit on their enjoyment in this world, their pleasure and their sensations. There were people like this all over the place, every state which fell to Islam. In Hezaramouth, there was a movement called the movement of prostitutes. These were around twenty prostitutes from different villages from Hezaramouth. When the Prophet (PBUH) passed away, they covered their hands in Berah, and they celebrated the death of the Prophet (PBUH) by singing songs because these women were evil; they felt Islam restricted their lives. Well, they were like flies which can only survive on filth. When Islam came and removed their filth, they felt they were starving and dying—death. They felt they could not breathe, felt suffocating. When the Prophet (PBUH) passed away, they were happy and celebrated.

One of the men in Hezaramouth sent a poem to the Khalifa Abu Bakar Siddique describing the situation and asking for help. The Khalifa sent a letter to the governor of Hezaramouth, Al Muhajir bin Abu Umia. He instructed him: "I command you to take the army and amputate the arms of these women. If anybody stands in your way, tell them the law of ALLAH and invite them to Islam and fight them."

Abu Bakar Siddique knew that these women were not speaking on their own behalf. They were presenting certain segments of the society that society will rush to defend them. As he knew, evil always come together to support their cause. Whenever they were attacked by Al Haq, all those people who think Islam deprives them of their way of life came together to protect these women. They came forward to fight Al Majhor. Al Majhor spoke to them and invited them toward the truth or face the consequences. Many of them agreed, and Al Majhor fought with the rest. The women's arms were amputated and some of them died because of that and others left Hezaramouth and settled in other places. The point is that in all ages and all times, there will be people who will decide to fight the truth until the last woman.

There was the blessing that happened to one of the righteous men of the ALLAH, Abu Muslims Fulani. Abu Muslims Fulani, ALLAH be pleased with him, was one of Tobaheen. He did see the Prophet (PBUH) but met someone who had met the Prophet (PBUH).

Asad Ul Ansey captured him and asked him, "Do you testify that Al Ansey is the messenger of ALLAH?"

Abu Muslims Fulani said, "I cannot hear you."

Next question Al Ansey asked him: "Do you testify that Muhammad (PBUH) is the messenger of ALLAH?"

Abu Muslims Fulani said, "Yes."

Second time Al Ansey asked, "Do you testify I am the messenger of ALLAH?"

Abu Muslims Fulani said, "I cannot hear you."

Second time again: "Do you testify that Muhammad (PBUH) is the messenger of ALLAH?"

Abu Muslims Fulani said, "Yes."

Al Ansey repeated that three times, and the answer was the same. Al Ansey ordered that Abu Muslims Fulani should be burned alive. They threw him in the fire to burn him, but he came out walking unharmed. Only the rope got burned, the rope they had tied him with, but he came out unharmed, safe. The follower of Al Ansey advised to Al Ansey to force Abu Muslims Fulani to leave his land. Otherwise, he will be a Fitna for the peoples. This blessing was enough for some people to revert back to Islam. People near to him asked him to send Abu Muslims Fulani out of the land.

Abu Muslims Fulani went to Madina. He came into the mosque. He was praying.

Umar bin Khitab, ALLAH be pleased with him, asked, "Is this man from Yaman?"

Umar bin Khitab called him after he finished his Salat. Umar bin Khitab asked him to "tell me about the man who was burnt in the fire by Asad Al Ansey."

He replied, "That man is Abdullah bin Masood."

"His name is Abdullah bin Sauud or Masood?" Umar bin Khitab asked in the name of ALLAH. "Is that you?"

He said, "Yes, that is me."

Umar bin Khitab immediately hugged him and started crying and said, "Praise belong to ALLAH, who made me live until I see a man whom ALLAH saved from fire as he saved Ibrahim (PBUH)."

Umar bin Khitab said, "ALLAH be praised who made me see a man from the Ummah of the Prophet Muhammad (PBUH) who was saved from fire just like Ibrahim (PBUH) was saved from fire." This was a blessing that happened to the follower of the Prophet (PBUH). It is similar to a miracle that occurred, happened to a prophet of ALLAH.

Abu Muslims Fulani was one of the fascinating figures among the Tobaheen. There are so many stories about him, but we will just mention only one about his death. He was fighting alongside with Bushan bin Arter against the Romans. His leader was Bushan bin Arter. Abu Muslims Fulani was injured.

Before his death, he called his leader, Bushan bin Arter, and told him, "After my death, I want you to bury me far away further into the land of the enemy, and my grave should be a head of all other martyrs. Then I want you to appoint me the leader over the martyrs and give me a banner of war that you bury with me so that on the day of judgment, when we are reselected, I can carry that banner and lead the martyrs on the Day of Judgment." He did not want his Jihad to stop in this world. He wanted to come on the Day of Judgment, carrying the banner and leading the martyrs on the day of judgment. This was the blessing that happened to Abu Muslims Fulani, ALLAH be pleased him.

Abu Bakar Siddique was very harsh with some of the apostates and showed clemency, kindness to others, to some others depending on the situation—there were no fixed standards. Abu Bakar Siddique would make a judgment according to the situation. Whenever he would see people with potential to service land in the future, he would allow them to go. He gave clemency to Amar bin Mujakaram and to Kasar Muradi, the one who was the head of the army of Asad Ul Ansey. He was set free and also Al Asha bin Kafe, who fought against the Sahaba in Hezaramouth. This was the vision of Abu Bakar Siddique that he gave clemency to these three men because these three men played very important roles during the Jihad of Umar bin Khitab. During the time of Abu Bakar Siddique, he gave his instruction that no one who apostate should be allowed take part in victory when the wars of apostates were over, and now the armies were sent to fight with the Persian and the Roman Empires.

Abu Bakar Siddique ordered that none of the apostates should participate in these armies, but this was overruled at the time of Umar bin Khitab, and there were reasons for that. We shall talk about those reasons later on.

Next incident, Abu Bakar Siddique sent Akarma bin Abu Jahil. He became a Muslim when Mecca was opened or conquered. Abu Bakar sent him to lead an army of seven hundred horsemen to the land of Muslimsa Kazab. Akarama was in a hurry and got into a premature confrontation with Banu Hanifa. Akarama was defeated. The news reached to Abu Bakar Siddique. Abu Bakar sent him an urgent message, telling him, "I do not want to see you. Do not come back because that will weaken the moral of our forces. I want you to leave and go to Yaman immediately and support the Muslims who are there and to enter from Oman."

What was the wisdom behind that? Abu Bakar Siddique did not want the Muslims who had lost against the forces of Muslimsa Kazab and to meet with any army that was going to the same direction because they will share the news and speak about the forces of the enemy, and that will weaken the morale of the Muslim forces going in the same direction. Abu Bakar Siddique told Akarama bin Abu Jahil to leave immediately and do not come back to Madina because that will do not good for the morale of people in Madina. Go to Oman.

He came to Oman and joined forces with other Sahaba in Yaman. That shows the wisdom of the leadership of Abu Bakar Siddique when Maaz bin Jabbal came back to Madina. He was appointed by the Prophet (PBUH) to go to Yaman to teach people Islam when he came back. When a governor would come back, Abu Bakar Siddique used to sit down with them and go through all the records and would hold them accountable for everything that happened during the term of his governorship.

Maaz bin Jabbal said, "Do you want me to go through to reckoning—a reckoning with ALLAH and reckoning with you? I shall never assume the position of leadership with you anymore." He meant "I am already going to be held accountable by ALLAH, and now you want to hold me accountable." But that was the way of Abu Bakar Siddique, and Umar bin Khitab followed the same policy. We are finished with Ridha in Yaman.

Ridha of Talah Ul Asdey, this was among Ast-Gutafan and Abis and Bulian. These are four Arab tribes. Talah Ul Asdey was a Muslim himself, and a delegation from Ast came to the Prophet (PBUH).

They said, "He had come to pledge over allegiance to you. We are Muslims. You did not ask us to come. We come by ourselves. We became Muslims." They carried on bragging about this.

ALLAH revealed the Ayyat:

> They considered it a favor to you that they have accepted Islam. Tell them…say do not considered your Islam a favor to me rather ALLAH has conferred a favor upon you, that ALLAH has guided you to faith if you are truthful. This is in seventeenth Hijra. This is a favor of ALLAH on you, not that you are telling the Prophet (PBUH) that you are doing a favor to him. This is the favor from ALLAH that ALLAH allowed you to become Muslims. ALLAH has guided you to the straight path.

Talah Ul Asdey later on changed his mind, and he claimed prophethood. This was because when they were in the desert and had no water, someone riding on the camel of Talah Ul Asdey, sound of water, they considered that a blessed camel belonging to a blessed man. He took advantage of that incident and claimed that he was the Prophet of ALLAH. He would make some funny Surrahs just like Musilma Kazab.

Talah Ul Asdey was a very courageous man, strong fighter, a very skilled leader. Therefore, that claim was very dangerous to come from such a man. Talah Ul Asdey convinced his people from Ast. After that, they got into agreement with Gutafam. Gutafam joined in with him, and then they had reinforcement from Abis and Lubian. Now he had the backing of four large tribes and was a huge force. All this happened under the leadership of Talah. Well, these new prophets were springing up everywhere. It is not that Arabs are religious people nor they had any convictions in these prophets. The nature of the Badoo people is that they are not religious people, but people assumed that Quresh are religious people; and because of that, they were against Islam. This is nowhere near the truth. The Quresh people were not religious, but they were very tolerant toward religion. Well, this is something that people do not realize. Generally, Arabs were most tolerant people when it came to religious practice. In other parts of the world, it was expected that people follow the same religion. Homogenous societies in Persia Zeshoristic society. Among the Romans, they would persuade Jews. Jews were persuaded in the Holy Land. Therefore, it was expected that everybody follows the same religion. In Arabia, for example in Yaman, there were Jews, Christians, these prostitutes. The movement called "the movement of prostitutes" were Jews; her name Hira bin Yaman, Yedia. This prostitute set a record in prostitution, and she set an example. They would Ismanaheer. Whenever a woman was accused, people would say she was more of a prostitute than Hir in Yaman. There were Jews, Christian pagan worshippers, and had zorishian. Persians and their people were very tolerant. In Mecca, Veraka his Nofal was Christen said was Hanffi following the religion of the Abuahame (PBUH). There were people who did not follow religion at all. A speaker would go and talk about everything. Mecca was no different than present-day Hyde Park. It was a tolerant society when it came to religion.

Zaid bin Nofail would stand next to Al-Kaba and speak to the people of Quresh that "your religion is false" and would tell them, "You should not make sacrifices to these idols."

He would get away; nobody would harm him. It was only when the Prophet (PBUH) started his invitation to Islam that they became intolerant. A very tolerant society can become very intolerant when it comes to Islam. One should be careful for what they see. The people of Mecca turned upside down. One of the most tolerant societies in the world became most intolerant when it came to religion. The reason is that they are not dealing with a religion, but they are dealing with truth. They know when truth comes, it is either truth or falsehood. Two cannot coexist. Evil can get along with evil, but when there is truth, then either that is truth or a lie.

These tribes joined Talah Ul Asdey out of nationalism; they did not want to submit to men who were from Quresh. Before there was a Prophet of ALLAH, but now, after the Prophet became Abu Bakar Siddique, for them people, they were not ready to give biea to Abu Bakar Siddique; therefore, those tribes came under the banner of Talah Ul Asdey.

Abu Bakar Siddique, for this important mission, gave the banner to Khalid bin Waleed, ALLAH be pleased with him. These were the men about whom the Prophet (PBUH) said, "He is the sword of ALLAH, which is drowned against the enemies of ALLAH, non-Muslims."

Abu Bakar Siddique gave the banner of Islam to men who never, ever in a war had his banner fall down. Khalid bin Waleed never, ever either—in Islam or even before Islam—lost in a battle. Now Abu Bakar Siddique sent him to fight against Talah Ul Asdey.

Abu Bakar Siddique told Audey bin Hatim, "Go and save your people, else Talah Ul Asdey will mislead them."

The tribe of Thai was neighboring the territory of Talah Ul Asdey that did not join Talah Ul Asdey as of yet. Abu Bakar Siddique wanted Audey bin Hatim to go as soon as possible and save his people from hellfire.

Abu Bakar Siddique said, "Hasten towards your people before Talah Ul Asdey. If he is successful, that will be to your people, determinant. That will be bad for your people." For Abu Bakar, the issue was clear. Talah Ul Asdey will lose. Abu Bakar was telling Audey, "Go and save your people before they perish." For Abu Bakar, it was not a fifty-fifty chance, but it was clear that Khalid bin Waleed will be victorious, Inshallah. He knew the results. Anyone who joins Talah Ul Asdey, that will be the losing side in both worlds—in this world and the next world.

Audey bin Hatim was a Muslim. He came and pledged his allegiance to the Prophet (PBUH), and he was one of the Sahaba. He was the man who came in wearing the cross. Audey was a Christian; he was wearing a cross when he came to meet the Prophet Muhammad (PBUH). The Prophet (PBUH) saw the cross hanging on his chest.

The Prophet (PBUH) said, "They have taken their rabbis and priests as gods besides ALLAH."

Audey responded, "We do not consider our priests to be gods." Audey bin Hatim was trying to correct the information about Christianity. He said, "We do not consider our priests to be our gods."

The Prophet (PBUH) said, "Their priests made what was Halal and what was Haram as Halal what ALLAH made legal."

They said, "Yes."

The Prophet (PBUH) said, "That is worshipping them besides ALLAH."

When St. Paul said, "All the laws of the Bible are dissolved now. Do not have to follow the law of 'TORA'"—what is that? It is making Haram as Halal. When Eisa bin Mariam (PBUH) came to fulfill the law jat by jat and dat by dat and letter by letter, and then St. Paul came and overruled and said, "No, you do not have to follow the law," that is worshiping him beside ALLAH. Going back to the religion of the Arabs, northern tribes were Christians. Ali bin Abu Talib was asked about eating their meat because they did not know anything about Christians except drinking wine. That is what they know about the Christian religion. These people are not religious. They are not into religion.

Audey bin Hatim went to plead with his people. He asked Khalid bin Waleed, "Give me three days."

Khalid bin Waleed was ready to attack.

Audey said, "Wait." Audey had already sent some fighters to fight with Talah ul Asdey. They were already stuck—not all, but they had sent some of the people to fight alongside Talah Ul Asdey. Audey said, "Just give me three days." He also told Khalid bin Waleed, "Is it not better that I saved them from hellfire? Would you rather send them to hell or save them from hell and not fighting?"

Khalid bin Waleed gave him three days. Audey went to his people.

His people said, "We are never going to pledge allegiance to the father of young camel, Abu Al Faisal." *Bakar* means "young camel, full of vigor," but they called Abu Al Faisal. *Faisal* is a newly born camel, and that is weak. They nicknamed as Abu Bakar as the father of weak camel, considered him to be a weak man, and said, "We people of Thai—do you want us to pledge allegiance to the father of young camel?"

Audey bin Hatim told them that "His armies are coming to your land one after another. They will teach you the lesson that he is the father of stallion and not father of the young camel. You better listen to me and your Biea to him," but they refused.

He stayed there, trying to convince them for three days. That was one branch of Thai. The tribe of Thai had two branches. He convinced one branch, then went Khalid bin Waleed and asked him one more time. He saved one branch and wanted to save the other branch of Thai as well.

Khalid bin Waleed said, "You can try to convince the other branch as well."

Audey bin Hatim worked very hard and managed to pull them out from the alliance of Talah Ul Asdey. They the tribemen, said they had to call their fighters from the army of Talah Ul Asdey. The fear was that "If Talah Ul Asdey finds out our intention and finds out that we are Muslims, he will kill our men." But they managed to withdraw their men successfully.

Ibne Kaseer said,

> Audey bin Hatim is considered the most blessed person for his people. He saved them from hellfire.

Khalid bin Waleed sent two men on a reconnaissance mission to gather information about the army of Talah Ul Asdey. These companions were Akasha bin Mosin and Salit bin Kase. These two were very prominent sahaba. Talah Ul Asdey and his brother were out on a mission, spying on Muslims. Talah Ul Asdey was a very courageous man. He went out by himself with his brother. They were alone. They killed Akasha and Salit. When they did not come back, Khalid bin Waleed with his army went looking, and they found two bodies. In the book of history, that was a great setback for Muslims—two great companions of the Prophet (PBUH) were killed. It was a very difficult moment for Muslims, but Khalid bin Waleed made his move; the Muslim army attacked and defeated Talah Ul Asdey. Talah Ul Asdey had alliance with Aima bin Hussan. He was the one who came to the Prophet (PBUH) and gave their pledge but broke the pledge. These men would go back and forward, these Badoos in and out of Islam. Aima bin Hassan made alliance with Talah Ul Asdey while the fighting was going on in the battlefield.

Talah ul Asdey was sitting in his tent, waiting for revelations to come to him.

Aima went to him, asked him, "Have you received Angel Jibrael yet?"

He replied, "No, not yet."

Aima went away but came back and asked again: "Has Jibrael come?"

Answer was no.

Aima came a third time and asked, "Has Angel Jibrael come?"

Talah ul Asdey said, "Yes."

Aima asked, "What did the angel tell you?"

He replied, "I am giving you a millstone, a great new.

In fact, Aima was not waiting for any news; he was waiting for something else.

Aima asked, "Tell us what to do?"

Talha Ul Asdey said, "You are going to get a great news."

Aima left and told his fighters, "Just leave."

Well, that was the beginning of the end for Talha Ul Asdey. When Talha realized he was losing, he himself, his brother, and his wife, with some of his close friends, mounted on their camels and horses and ran away to Iraq and Syria, Sham. Well, that was the end of Talha Ul Asdey. This was a great victory for Islam and Muslims. The news came and reached to Abu Bakar Siddique. He sent a letter to Khalid bin Waleed:

> May that what ALLAH has granted you by way of following that increase for you. Fear ALLAH in your affairs, verily ALLAH is with those who are pious and who do good work. Take seriously the command of ALLAH and do not be lenient who fought the Muslims, punish them severely and make them an example to warn others. Kill those who show disrespect to ALLAH. Also who opposed ALLAH, if you think there will be some benefit in doing so.

These are the orders of Al-Khalifah Abu Bakar Siddique—to punish severely apostates to make an example out of them.

Khalid bin Waleed remained in that territory for the entire month, going up and down, right and left, capturing, arresting apostates, punishing them, burning them in fire, starving them to death, throwing them from mountaintops, throwing them into the wells, and piercing them with arrows—very harsh punishment. This was to set an example for Murtudeen. This was to show that Ridha will be punished.

Al-Fuja was one of those men who came to Abu Bakar Siddique, ALLAH be pleased with him. He said, "I shall fight the murtudeen. Give me an army."

Abu Bakar Siddique provided him with weapons and camels. Al-Fuja left and used these arms and camels given by the Khalifah to fight everyone who meets them, Muslims or non-Muslims, to raid their belongings—a bandit in the desert. When Khalifah heard this, Abu Bakar Siddique sent an army to follow him and pursue him. They captured Fuja, tied him up, and brought him back to Madina. The Khalifah ordered that they burn him to death in O'Bikia, in front of everyone. This was the punishment for his actions.

Tulla-ul-Asdi later on became a Muslim. He very much regretted what he had done. He also performed Ummrah during the time of Abu Bakar Siddique. Abu Bakar Siddique was informed about his whereabouts. Abu Bakar Siddique refused to take any action against him because he had already accepted Islam, but he was unharmed from taking part in the Muslim armies. Later on, he did join when Muslims conquered and were victorious. He did set some examples in courage and in bravery for the sake of ALLAH. ALLAH guides whoever and whenever he wants. This man claimed prophethood. Because of him, many hundreds of people were thrown into hellfire, but he himself became a Muslim with the guidance. It is Qadar—mercy of ALLAH. We know Abu Talib, the very dear uncle of the Prophet (PBUH) who assisted the Prophet (PBUH); all his life went to hellfire. And at the other hand, Abu Sufyan fought against the Prophet (PBUH) all his life and became a Momin. The guidance is in the hands of ALLAH.

Astan Gutfan regretted what they had done when Talha-ul-Asdi deserted them. They came to the Khalifah, Abu Bakar Siddique, and wanted to make Tabah. They came to Khalifah and said, "We want to make truce between you, the Khalifah, and us."

What did the Khalifah say? Abu Bakar Siddique, ALLAH be pleased with him, responded, "I give you two options—either a war of extermination or a humiliating plan."

They said, "We know the meaning of war of extermination—meaning you will finish all of us. But what is humiliating deal?"

Abu Bakar Siddique said, "First of all, you give up all your weapons, and you follow the tails of your camels." Well, for them, stripping off their weapons is dishonoring them. At present, this is not a problem, but with them, even in ignorance, living without weapons is dishonoring them.

But Abu Bakar Siddique said, "Without weapons, you and your camels are the same. Same without your arms—there is no difference between you and your camels. You give up your arms and follow the tails of your camels until ALLAH puts in the hearts of the Khalifah and in the hearts of the Momineen to accept your apology. You hand over your weapons, and whenever ALLAH puts in the hearts of the Khalifah and Momineen to accept your apology, we shall go ahead with this. I cannot promise you anything. Secondly, you disclose publicly that the ones who are killed amongst you are going to hell-fire and the ones who are killed amongst are going to paradise. I want to hear from you publicly in front of your people. Thirdly, you pay the blood money for the people you killed amongst us, and we will pay you nothing for the ones we killed amongst you."

Umar bin Khitab, ALLAH be pleased with him, said, "I disagree with this last point. He said they should not to pay us blood money because the ones who are killed amongst us are martyrs and they died in the path of ALLAH. Therefore, there is no less on our behalf. It is an honor for the martyrs but he liked all the rest." Umar bin Khitab—that was what he wanted. Great. Abu Bakar Siddique gave them the lesson that he was the father of a stallion and not the father of a young camel. They had no choice but to agree. They gave up their weapons and went following the tails of their camels. "Later on, Khalifah will decide when to accept your apology—apology for what you had done."

End.

Praise belongs to ALLAH, who helped me to write about the life of Abu Bakar Siddique and his works and time as Khalifah-tul-Rasool ALLAH.

www.ingramcontent.com/pod-product-compliance
Lightning Source LLC
Chambersburg PA
CBHW070915120626
46546CB00001B/276